G000080085

floating your COMPANY

Helping you float.

If you're planning a flotation, talk to Pinsent Masons first.

With extensive experience advising on both full and AIM listings,
we can support you through every stage of the process.

Once you're quoted, you can also rely on us to provide the service
and expertise that has made us a top ranked adviser to many companies
in the FTSE 100 and 250, as well as on AIM.

Ring us now. Call **Martin Shaw** on **0845 300 32 32**
or e-mail **martin.shaw@pinsentmasons.com**

Pinsent Masons

floating *your* COMPANY

The Essential Guide to Going Public

3rd Edition

Consultant Editor:
JONATHAN REUVID

Pinsent Masons

KOGAN
PAGE

London and Philadelphia

First published by Kogan Page Limited as *Going Public* in 2003
Second edition published as *Floating your Company* in 2006
Third edition 2007

120 Pentonville Road   525 South 4th Street, #241
London N1 9JN   Philadelphia PA 19147
United Kingdom   USA
www.kogan-page.co.uk

© Kogan Page and individual contributors, 2003, 2006, 2007

ISBN 978 0 7494 5056 4

British Library Cataloguing-in-Publication Data

A CIP record for this book is available from the British Library.

Library of Congress Cataloging-in-Publication Data

Floating your company : the essential guide to going public / [edited by] Jonathan Reuvid. -- 3rd ed.
    p. cm.
 ISBN 978-0-7494-5056-4
1. Going public (Securities). 2. Close corporations--Finance. I. Reuvid, Jonathan.
  HG4028.S7G65 2007
  658.159224--dc22   2007031953

Typeset by Saxon Graphics Ltd, Derby
Printed and Bound in Great Britain by Cambridge University Press

Contents

Part III   The flotation process

Part IV   Living with the listing

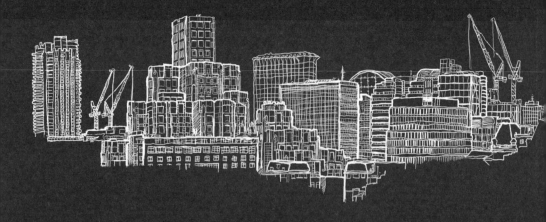

Contributors' notes

Bevan Brittan LLP

Bevan Brittan LLP is a dynamic and adaptive UK law firm, offering commercial legal services to clients across both the private and the public sector. The firm has 68 partners and over 500 staff in three main offices in London, Bristol and Birmingham, with an annual turnover of over £40 million. The firm focuses on providing in-depth, highly specialized expertise across a selected range of core practice areas and business sectors. The firm is structured around the four principal market sectors of: commerce, industry and services; built environment; health; and government.

Sarah Cartwright is a partner in Bevan Brittan's corporate team, with nine years' experience of mergers and acquisitions and corporate finance. Sarah has acted on a substantial number of initial public offerings (IPOs) and secondary fund-raisings (in each case Main Market and AIM) and for both companies and financial advisers. She has also delivered a number of high-profile presentations on the subject and the post-IPO environment.

Charles Stanley Securities

Charles Stanley Securities provides comprehensive financial advisory services, equity research, and sales and sales trading coverage of a growing range of smaller and mid-cap UK listed companies. It is a division of Charles Stanley & Co, one of the UK's leading wealth management groups.

Tim Davis joined Charles Stanley Securities in 2002 and is responsible for marketing and business development. Prior to this, he performed the same role at smaller-company stockbrokers Teather & Greenwood. His earlier career was spent in media and investor relations.

CMS Cameron McKenna LLP

CMS Cameron McKenna LLP is a full-service international law firm with offices in London and Central and Eastern Europe. It is a founding member of CMD, the alliance of major European law firms.

Peter Smith is a partner in CMS Cameron McKenna LLP's corporate department and specializes in corporate finance and merger and acquisition transactions. He has advised on numerous independent public offerings (IPOs), secondary fund-raisings and takeover offers involving companies joining or admitted to the London Stock Exchange's Main Market and AIM. He regularly acts for nomads, sponsors and issuers.

Corfin Communications

Corfin Communications specializes in media, corporate and financial public relations. The firm delivers a high level of contacts, an inside knowledge of how news organizations work and campaigns of sustained media coverage around the financial calendar, crisis management, merger and acquisition (M&A), independent public offering (IPO) and general reputation management, together with a long-term and direct experience of senior business and financial journalism.

William Cullum is a director of Corfin Communications and a very seasoned adviser. He joined the public relations (PR) industry in 1999 and over the last eight years has worked with businesses large and small and on a variety of issues ranging from conventional financial calendar work to multimillion-dollar mergers and acquisitions through to highly sensitive corporate change and restructuring activities. Prior to joining the PR industry, William was a top ten-rated investment analyst.

Ernst & Young

Ernst & Young is one of the largest professional services firms in the UK. About half of its 470 partners and 8,000 staff work in its London offices, which together form the largest Ernst & Young presence in any city in the world. In addition, Ernst & Young have offices in a further 19 cities around the UK.

David Wilkinson is the Northern Europe, Middle East, India and Africa independent public offering (IPO) leader at Ernst & Young.

Freeth Cartwright LLP

Freeth Cartwright LLP is an East Midlands-based leading regional law firm with offices in Nottingham, Derby, Leicester and Manchester. The firm acts for both private and public companies on a regional and national basis. Its policy is to give its clients straightforward and straight-talking advice, not just options.

Mike Copestake heads the Freeth Cartwright corporate finance department and is senior partner of the Derby office. The flotations in which he has been involved include Kingfisher Leisure, Crestchic and Inditherm, all on AIM. In respect of Inditherm, the firm has also been involved in two further placings. Mike is the author of the firm's handbook on AIM and has given several seminars in the Midlands.

Bethan Davies is a professional support lawyer in the corporate finance department of Freeth Cartwright and has 15 years' experience of corporate law.

Grant Thornton

Grant Thornton is one of the world's leading organizations of accounting and consulting firms, providing assurance, tax and specialist advice to owner-managed businesses and their owners and to fast-growing, entrepreneurial people and businesses. The strength of each local firm is reflected in the quality of the organization. Grant Thornton operates in over 100 countries, bringing together 20,000 personnel in 600 offices worldwide, where experienced professionals combine local market knowledge with technically advanced systems. All firms share a commitment to providing the same high-quality service to their clients wherever they choose to do business.

Colin Aaronson is a director of the capital market team of Grant Thornton Corporate Finance, the largest independent nominated adviser to AIM companies. Colin has been a member of the capital markets team since January 2000. A Chartered Accountant, he joined Grant Thornton in 1998 after more than 12 years' experience in the industry. He has since completed numerous AIM flotations and has advised on a number of takeovers and reverse takeovers. Colin works mainly with technology and life science businesses.

Mike Thornton is head of valuation services at Grant Thornton and has a wealth of corporate finance knowledge, having worked for a private equity firm as well as in corporate finance advisory services. He has extensive experience in the valuation of unquoted shares, business, goodwill and other intangible assets for a wide variety of purposes across a wide range of sectors.

Hazlewoods LLP

Hazlewoods LLP is a firm of chartered accountants based in Gloucestershire and was recently ranked 38th in size in the United Kingdom, with just over 200 staff. The firm has considerable expertise in assisting companies throughout the UK through the flotation process. The firm is a member of Praxity, an international alliance of independent accountancy firms.

David Main has been a partner with Hazlewoods LLP since 1992 and has been carrying out reporting accountant assignments since 1985. He is a former member of the Auditing Practices Board (1994–2002) and a former member of the Council of the Association of Chartered Certified Accountants.

Hoare Govett Limited

Hoare Govett Limited provides corporate finance and broking services supported by strong equity distribution and research capability. The firm has over 100 UK listed clients and acts as nomad and broker to a number of AIM-quoted companies, with widespread experience across the UK equity market.

Justin Jones is a managing director and leads the financial advisory team at Hoare Govett. He has specialized in advising smaller, faster-growing companies for many years, gaining considerable experience of initial public offerings (IPOs) and acting as nomad, together with cross-border M&A, public bids and secondary fund-raisings.

H W Fisher & Company

H W Fisher & Company is a long-established firm of chartered accountants consisting of 26 partners and some 260 staff. The wider Fisher Organization includes specialist consultancies in corporate finance, company recovery and recon-struction, property finance, wealth management, and financial services and infor-mation technology.

Gary Miller specializes in corporate finance both as a partner in H W Fisher & Company and as a director of the firm's sister company Fisher Corporate PLC. He has extensive experience of mergers and acquisitions, floating companies on AIM and PLUS markets, and has acted as a strategic adviser to many businesses, including corporate restructuring and long-term planning.

The Irish Enterprise Exchange

The Irish Enterprise Exchange (IEX) is the Irish Stock Exchange's market for small to mid-sized companies. IEX was first launched by the Exchange in 2005 with an initial base of eight companies. By mid-2007, 30 companies from a wide range of sectors were quoted on IEX. IEX provides its constituent companies with access to capital and a wide pool of investors, a means of valuing and trading their shares, enhanced liquidity and a higher public profile.

Daryl Byrne is Head of Corporate Listing and Policy at the Irish Stock Exchange. He joined the Exchange in 2000 and is responsible for the Exchange's Corporate Listing team that reviews prospectuses and circulars and monitors ongoing compliance by listed companies with the Listing Rules. He is also responsible for policy matters in respect of securities admitted to listing on the Exchange, and heads the development, technical support and promotion of IEX to companies, advisers and corporate finance houses.

KBC Peel Hunt

KBC Peel Hunt is an investment bank for companies in the small and mid-cap sector, and part of the KBC Group, one of Europe's largest banks. It provides a full range of investment banking services including sales, market making, corporate finance and broking, research and trading to over 120 UK listed companies.

Patrick Booth-Clibborn is a corporate finance director and head of business development at KBC Peel Hunt, with 15 years' experience in corporate finance. Patrick was involved in the admission of the first companies traded on AIM in June 1995 and works on business across the range of transactions undertaken by quoted companies, such as independent public offerings (IPOs), mergers and acquisitions, secondary fund-raisings, pre-IPO and private equity fund-raising.

David Davies started at Touche Ross & Co (now Deloittes) as a Chartered Accountant. He joined KBC Peel Hunt in 1996 and provides capital markets and mergers and acquisitions advice to full-list and AIM companies, primarily in the real estate, construction and support services sectors. He has been Head of Corporate Finance at KBC Peel Hunt since June 2006.

Lawrence Graham LLP

Lawrence Graham LLP is a leading law firm providing clients with legal and business solutions. The firm is based in London but its reach, like that of its clients, is global. The main sectors in which Lawrence Graham's clients operate are real estate, hospitality and leisure, wealth planning, banking, financial services and insurance and reinsurance. The firm has strong working relationships with law firms around the world – in particular in the United States, Europe, the Middle East, China and India.

Geoffrey Gouriet is a partner at Lawrence Graham, where he specializes in corporate finance, having previously worked in investment banking. He regularly advises entrepreneurs and growth companies from the UK and overseas, as well as nominated advisers and brokers, on independent public offerings (IPOs) and secondary issues on AIM.

The London Stock Exchange

The London Stock Exchange is the world's premier international equity exchange and a leading provider of services that facilitate the raising of capital and the trading of shares. The Exchange is the most international equities exchange by trading in the world and Europe's largest pool of liquidity. Over 500 new companies listed on the Exchange's markets in the financial year 2007, bringing the total number of companies on the Exchange to 3,245. £3.4 trillion worth of UK shares were traded on its markets in the financial year 2007.

Martin Graham is Director of Markets and Head of AIM at the London Stock Exchange. Martin is responsible for the market-facing functions within the Exchange, as well as the development of domestic and international markets services, including client relationships, market operations, market reputation and RNS, the Exchange's regulatory news service.

Pinsent Masons

Pinsent Masons is an international law firm with over 270 partners and 1,000 lawyers worldwide, providing a full range of corporate and commercial services. The firm ranks amongst the top 100 global law firms. With headquarters in the City of London, Pinsent Masons' operation spans the UK, continental Europe, the Middle East and Asia Pacific. In the UK, the firm also has offices in Birmingham, Leeds, Manchester, Edinburgh, Glasgow and Bristol. Internationally, Pinsent Masons is based in Shanghai, Beijing, Hong Kong, Dubai and Brussels. Through the Pinsent Masons Luther Group (PMLG), the firm is allied to independent law firms in Germany, France, Austria, Hungary and the Baltic States.

Andrew Black is a corporate partner at Pinsent Masons, specializing in public company work. He advises on flotations, placings, rights issues and takeovers, as well as acquisitions and disposals for both public and private companies.

Philip Goldsborough is a corporate partner at Pinsent Masons, specializing in corporate finance work. He advises on a wide range of corporate finance transactions including flotations, placings, rights issues and takeovers, with a particular emphasis on advising both public and private companies on acquisitions and disposals.

Rob Hutchings is a corporate partner at Pinsent Masons with wide experience in both domestic and international corporate work. He has particular expertise in public and private mergers and acquisitions, stock exchange matters, venture capital investments and joint ventures.

Robert Moir is a corporate partner at Pinsent Masons, with considerable experience in a broad range of corporate transactions, including mergers and acquisitions, initial public offerings (IPOs), fund-raisings, joint ventures and reorganizations. He acts for a wide variety of public and private companies in a number of sectors, with a particular focus on manufacturing and engineering, energy and real estate.

Martin Shaw is a partner in Pinsent Masons and is Head of Corporate Europe, with a wealth of corporate finance experience. He is a nationally rated expert, advising extensively on stock exchange-related matters, including full listings, AIM and OFEX admissions, takeovers governed by the City Code, and fund-raising secondary issues. He also advises on a broad range of mergers, acquisitions and company reorganizations. He acts for a number of major UK clients and has wide experience of transactions in Europe and the United States.

PLUS Markets Group

PLUS Markets Group, the provider of primary and secondary equity market services, is the independent UK market dedicated to small entrepreneurial companies. Since its launch as Ofex, PLUS Markets has assisted over 850 small and mid-cap companies with a combined market capitalization in excess of £150 billion. It is a cost-effective market with a broadening appeal to investors, companies, advisers and market makers.

Nemone Wynn-Evans joined PLUS Markets Group plc in November 2004 as a member of the new management team that took over the company. She has played a pivotal role in developing the company's equity market offering over the last two years, enhancing its appeal to investors, companies and professional intermediaries. Previously at the London Stock Exchange and with a City background in equity capital markets and corporate finance lead advisory work, she holds a number of professional qualifications in investment banking and in marketing, including a Cranfield MBA.

PricewaterhouseCoopers LLP

PricewaterhouseCoopers LLP (PwC) has a network of member firms that provides industry-focused assurance, tax and advisory services to build public trust and enhance value for its clients and their stakeholders. More than 140,000 people in 149 countries across the network work collaboratively using connected thinking to develop fresh perspectives and practical advice.

Simon Boadle is a partner in PricewaterhouseCoopers' corporate finance business, with over 20 years' merger and acquisition (M&A) and equity capital markets experience in investment banking and at PwC. He currently leads PwC's national M&A team across the UK and its public company advisory team, focusing on mid-market transactions.

Steve Gilder has been a tax partner at PricewaterhouseCoopers for 14 years, advising fast-growth companies and their shareholders. He acts for several smaller listed clients, mainly on AIM but also on foreign exchanges, and a number of companies aspiring to list. He advises regularly on corporate and international tax, employee reward structuring and personal tax, and lectures on tax issues on listing at the London Stock Exchange.

Helen M Jeffery is a member of the corporate finance team at PricewaterhouseCoopers, specializing in public company transactions including public to privates.

Kate Wolstenholme is a director in PricewaterhouseCoopers' mid-tier assurance practice. She works with a broad range of clients from listed companies to equity-backed and owner-managed growth businesses, focusing on the entertainments/media professional services, and renewable energy/clean technology sectors. Kate provides audit services and transaction support to her clients, including independent public offering (IPO) work.

Punter Southall Transaction Services

Punter Southall Transaction Services (PSTS) is the specialist transactions consulting division within the leading actuarial firm Punter Southall. PSTS advises private equity houses, investment companies and other corporate entities on the acquisition and disposal of defined benefit pension schemes, as well as the ongoing management of pension liabilities.

Richard Jones is a qualified actuary with more than 10 years of experience advising corporate entities on pension and investment issues. He is the lead consultant for an investment company, with several pension schemes with over $3 billion in assets. Richard has also worked for a variety of corporate clients and been involved in a number of international mergers and acquisitions.

ShareMark

ShareMark is a share-trading platform for infrequently traded shares or loan stock. It provides shareholders with an exit route and valuation, and can be used to introduce new investors. Unlike other markets, ShareMark executes trades at a single price, overcoming the wide bid–offer spreads suffered by infrequently traded stock. It is simple, lightly regulated, cost-effective and flexible.

Emma Vigus is head of ShareMark. Emma joined ShareMark in February 2002 from AngelBourse Group, where she was sales and marketing manager. Prior to that, she had several years' experience in marketing within the investment management industry. Emma holds a BSc Honours degree in business management and the environment from Cranfield University.

Foreword

Martin Graham, Director of Markets and Head of AIM, London Stock Exchange

According to the old adage there is more than one way to skin a cat. There is certainly more than one way to finance your company.

After remortgaging the home, borrowing money from friends or getting a business development loan from the bank, people then turn their minds to the possibility of a stock market listing.

However, just as there are many forms of finance, there is no single route to access a public market. In fact, there are many things to consider before choosing the market that is right for you. There are some key questions to ask.

First: does this market enable the company to raise capital effectively at launch and on an ongoing basis? One of the key reasons for floating a company is access to capital. If the market is not widely supported by investors then it may well be that there is no appetite for your company and it may not get the valuation it deserves.

Second: does it create a market for your company's shares? The market should supply a mixture of retail and institutional investors to provide you with a broader shareholder base and give existing shareholders a value for their investment.

Third: is the market able to create a heightened public profile, stemming from increased press coverage and analysts' reports, helping to maintain liquidity in the company's shares? This increased visibility will help to enhance status with customers and suppliers, who are reassured by the regulatory processes and disclosure involved in the company's quotation.

AIM, the London Stock Exchange market for smaller, growing companies is now the world's premier growth companies market. Its 12-year-old recipe, to combine access to equity capital with appropriate standards for smaller companies, has been hugely successful. AIM is now a market of over 1,600 companies, with 462 additions last year. Its strengths are undeniable.

AIM is a proven venue for capital raising on admission. Last year a total of almost £10 billion was raised in new money to grow and develop a number of high-growth businesses. For further issues too, the market continues to provide ongoing capital for growth. Last year almost £6 billion was raised for further growth.

AIM last year raised as much capital as NASDAQ and substantially more than major exchanges in Frankfurt, Tokyo, Toronto and Sydney.

For liquidity and visibility AIM is also unrivalled. The value of shares traded on AIM increased to £58 billion last year – demonstrating how AIM has become a mainstream asset class. Today, almost 57 per cent of AIM stocks are held by London's host of professional institutional investors.

So, when looking for a growth market that meets all your needs there is no market like AIM. It is unrivalled in its provision of capital, liquidity and visibility combined with an appropriate regulatory regime for growth companies.

This publication will provide useful advice for all companies seeking a flotation. It will help to shed more light on market requirements and offer expert advice on the listing process. I hope to see many companies coming to AIM as a result in the months and years ahead.

Introduction

The directors and owners of an established or growing business will need to examine thoroughly whether or not flotation offers the most appropriate financial strategy at the current stage of their company's development and is likely to provide optimum long-term benefits for shareholders.

In the UK, with its sophisticated hierarchy of stock markets under the jurisdiction of the London Stock Exchange, dynamic start-up businesses may apply for early admission to the lower-tier markets of PLUS or AIM. Even admission to the Main Market requires a minimum financial track record of no more than three years.

Of course, the first step for directors and shareholders is to decide whether or not flotation is the best way forward, and Part I of *Floating Your Company: The Essential Guide to Going Public* focuses on this basic decision-making process. Alternative financial strategies and sources of finance are examined, as well as the necessary and sufficient conditions for flotation against the present equity investment environment of 2007.

All directors and shareholders engaging in the debate will find the detailed information they need to participate intelligently. If the outcome of the debate is to delay flotation or to pursue this strategy in parallel with alternatives, then the ingredients for revisiting the issue will remain the same and are all contained in this book.

This third edition of *Floating Your Company* has been extended to five parts instead of the previous four. As before, Part II of this new edition provides further briefing for directors where flotation is an option in the form of an overview of the regulatory framework and a review of the alternative markets. Chapters for this section are contributed by the London Stock Exchange on AIM, PLUS Market, ShareMark and the Irish Enterprise Exchange.

Part III of the book examines the flotation process in detail, including the roles of each of the key professional advisers and practitioners that a company will need to engage for an application to list and a successful flotation. Key issues for the nomad, the broker and the company are discussed, and the complex techniques of company share valuation are explained. Although these matters will be of most interest to financial directors, all directors of the company are involved in the flotation process in varying degrees and share collectively in responsibility for the accuracy of the prospectus, accounting and other documents. The amount of time and degree of involvement required in the process, in a period when the executive directors will be striving to deliver company best performance, may seem daunting.

Part IV dwells on life after the listing. The company's status as a public listed company brings with it new obligations in terms of financial reporting, auditing, corporate governance and communication as well as the benefits and perils of a higher public profile. There will be additional administrative costs and demands on directors' time and increased pressures to deliver ever-improving financial performance. It is important for directors to understand what they and the company will be 'in for' once the company is floated and to make the most of the company's listed status.

The new Part V of this edition includes two chapters on topics of key interest to shareholders and directors: taxation issues and pension arrangements. Two further chapters are included on the opportunities for non-UK companies on AIM, and the alternatives for returning the company to private ownership in the event that listed public company status becomes inappropriate or that the disadvantages outweigh the advantages.

Each chapter of the book has been written by an experienced professional practitioner from a leading firm in the relevant field. We are particularly grateful to the book's three sponsors, Pinsent Masons, KBC Peel Hunt and Punter Southall, and to other eminent contributors who have supported the book by advertising. Martin Shaw and his colleagues at Pinsent Masons have again authored many of the chapters of Parts II, III and IV relating to regulatory and legal matters and the obligations of directors. The chapters relating to financial, accountancy and taxation matters have been written this time by a combination of Ernst & Young, Hazlewoods, PricewaterhouseCoopers and Grant Thornton. As before, I am personally indebted to Colin Aaronson and Mike Thornton of Grant Thornton for updating three of the chapters in the first three parts of the book from the previous edition. Similarly, my appreciation goes to the authors at CMS Cameron McKenna, Hoare Govett, Charles Stanley Securities, HW Fisher, Corfin Communications, Freeth Cartwright, Bevan Brittan and Lawrence Graham, each of whom has written instructively on their areas of expertise.

Finally, our appreciation is again due to Martin Graham, Director of Markets and Head of AIM, London Stock Exchange, for his Foreword and to him and Nemone Wynne-Evans of PLUS Markets Group, Emma Vigus of ShareMark and Ann Clarke of the Irish Stock Exchange for authoring their chapters in Part II.

We hope that directors of both UK and non-UK companies, their shareholders and those who advise them will find this new edition of *Floating Your Company* a useful addition to their business bookshelves.

Jonathan Reuvid

To float or not to float – planning your company's future

The equity environment

Colin Aaronson, Grant Thornton Corporate Finance

Summary

- Benign conditions led to an 18-year bull market from 1982 to 2000, as inflation fell from 8.5 to 2.1 per cent.[1]
- Those conditions were also extremely favourable for raising money through flotations, particularly from 1998 to 2000.
- The period following the collapse of the technology bubble, from the summer of 2000 through to early 2003, was one of retrenchment – IPO activity was markedly lower than it had been between 1998 and 2000 but by the end of 2002 advisers were beginning to predict an active 2003.
- Overall, markets have been particularly buoyant since 2003. AIM, in particular, has recovered well, attracting companies operating in a wide range of sectors and from many different countries.
- Increasing raw material prices have driven an active natural resource sector, particularly since 2002. AIM has also benefited by attracting investment vehicles targeting sectors such as property, green technologies and private equity.
- Money for ideas is more difficult than in the years leading up to the millennium, when the dotcom boom was at its peak. AIM investors are increasingly looking for profitable businesses, with good visibility of earnings at a price that represents good value.
- Pre-revenue businesses such as natural resource or biotechnology companies can still raise money, although investors are looking to de-risk through investing in mining production rather than exploration and later-stage drug development.

For such companies, the business and the people behind it must be of particularly high quality.

■ The outlook going forward is uncertain. Unless conditions remain benign, as they did overall throughout the 1980s and 1990s and since 2002, we cannot expect to see the same level of capital growth as took place in that period. Where capital growth is less certain, investors will place an increased emphasis on yield.

Introduction

Companies do raise money in both bull and bear markets, although investor interest will be greater when confidence is high and share prices are increasing. The period from 1982 to 2000, and the 1990s in particular, were especially favourable for raising money in the City and in other financial markets. It was not an entirely smooth ride for investors, with the overall trend line punctuated by blips in individual market sectors and the market as a whole. At the height of the boom in 1999 and 2000, brokers were so busy raising money that the problem was not finding the money but getting an appointment. Between 2000 and 2002, those same brokers became rather more available for lunch, and some even for interview.

As merger and acquisition (M&A) and initial public offering (IPO) activity abated, investment banks and brokers and other professional firms laid off or redeployed staff. While activity was at a lower level in 2002 than in 2000, deals were still taking place, and from early in 2002 a number of large private companies were signalling that they intended to come to the market. Even in recession flotations continued to take place.

When the first edition of this book was drafted in the summer of 2002, the outlook was uncertain and the long-term effect of corporate failures such as Enron

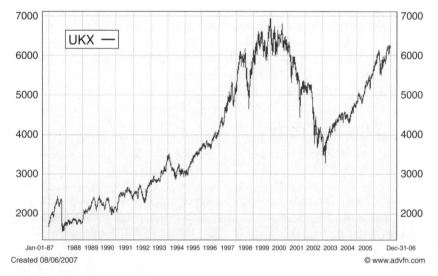

Figure 1.1 The FTSE-100 1987–2006

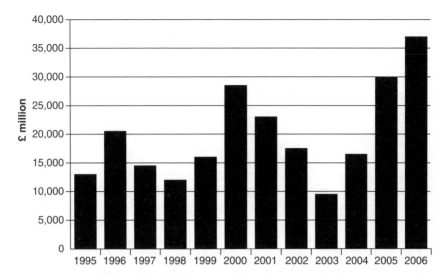

Figure 1.2   Equity raised by UK companies listed on the LSE or quoted on AIM or the USM

and Marconi unclear. Looking back from the middle of 2007, markets seem to have coped remarkably well with these events. In 2007, as in 2002, inflation and interest rates are at levels such that there is some scope to fall, although rising natural resource prices and other factors may well support them at or above their current levels. Now, as then, political events worldwide are capable of dealing a blow to even the most robust recovery.

Investors never really had it so good as they did in the years 1988 to 2000. An investor who put money into an index fund at the start of 1988 would have seen £1,000 reach over £4,000 by the millennium,[2] whilst average house buyers would have seen the value of their home increase by 69 per cent. Companies found it easier to raise equity capital than ever before. In 1988, £3,790 million was raised through flotation in London; by 2000, that figure had become £11,399 million.[3] Yet things would have looked very different in October 1987.

The exuberant 1980s

The 1980s saw a vigorous recovery following the severe recession of 1980–82. The liberalization of financial markets had led to a rapid growth in consumer spending fuelled by growing confidence and funded by easy credit. Share prices rose on the back of improved company performance and the confidence that came from the sense that things really were different under Conservative governments on both sides of the Atlantic. It really did feel like morning in the United States and the UK, open for business. Share prices both in London and on Wall Street rose by approximately 250 per cent between January 1982 and September 1987.

In the 'can do' economy that Britain was becoming, wealth creation became fashionable again and, spurred by privatization windfalls, equity investment became an activity practised by ever-larger numbers of people. Greed apparently became a virtue and even the leader of the Labour Party, in a distracted moment, wondered if 'yuppies' might be a suitable role model. Investment banking became more global, and overseas financial institutions moved into London to take advantage of the new opportunities. This inflow of institutions and people enlarged the skill base and deepened the pool of capital available in London. The old order finally gave way to the new in 1986 as 'Big Bang' did away with independent jobbers, brokers and merchant banks and combined them (or at least most of them) into large multi-function investment houses. These houses played an important role in the events that were to follow, thanks in large part to their computerized dealing systems.

Five years of growth in equity prices came to an abrupt end on 19 October 1987 as share prices suffered the sharpest one-day fall since 1929. By the time prices had stabilized on 9 November, the FTSE 100 had fallen by 36 per cent from its high on 16 July 1987. There were widespread fears that the reverse 'wealth effect' of falling stock prices would cause such a contraction in consumer spending that the crash of 1987 would be followed by a depression that mirrored the great depression of the 1930s. Like his counterpart in Washington, the Chancellor of the Exchequer lowered interest rates in an attempt to support demand. House prices continued rising for a while, but by 1988 they had also begun to fall, and the phrase 'negative equity' entered our vocabulary.

We now know that the crash of 1987 did not reflect a fundamental reappraisal of our economic prospects but was a stock market 'correction', amplified and accel-erated by programme trading. Share prices had indeed reached a level at which a correction was in order, but the scale of the adjustment was both unprecedented and unforeseen in terms of its speed and magnitude; an adjustment that would previously have taken two years took place in the space of less than four weeks. As investors clambered out from among the wreckage of the previous week's hurricanes to survey their battered investments, they would have been justified in fearing the worst; things simply would never be the same. As it happened, they got even better – so much so that 1987 represented one of the greatest investment opportunities in history.

With hindsight, we can see that between 1987 and 2000 there existed a set of conditions that would support the relentless increase in share prices. During these years, the FTSE 100 index rose by almost 300 per cent,[4] GDP increased by 36 per cent,[5] corporate profitability improved and the average P/E ratio doubled. Dividend yields fell from 3.73 per cent to 2.80 per cent.[6]

The benign environment

Crucial to the steady increase in share prices was the fall in inflation. The sharp recession in 1980–82, exacerbated by tight monetary policy, had dampened demand for goods and labour and put pressure on the price of both. When the recovery did take place, there was a new approach to industrial relations as a result of the recession and the Thatcher government's confrontation with the unions, which meant that wage demands were more moderate than they had been in the 1970s.

The period was also marked by a reduction in raw material prices, notably crude oil prices, which fell from approximately $45 per barrel in 1982 to *circa* $20 per barrel in 1987. By 1998, the price of oil had fallen to approximately $13 per barrel, a figure that seems scarcely credible looking back from the middle of 2007 with crude prices in excess of $60 a barrel.[7] Falling commodity prices during that period increased corporate profitability and reduced inflation. As inflation fell, interest rates followed suit and share prices rose to let dividend yields follow interest rates.

Advances in information technology were dramatic and had profound consequences for the service sector and the people who worked in it. The increased power and availability of information technology did lead to the elimination of certain types of clerical work, but they also made possible the dramatic growth of financial services and led to the creation of whole new industries, based around personal computers and call centres. These industries created more jobs than were lost. Employment in manufacturing industry was still in long-term decline, but demand for services was rising, creating jobs in tourism, design, childcare, catering and domestic service. Computer technology could be applied to consumer goods, which became more exciting and desirable, generating profits for companies that could design, create and distribute these products, and jobs for those who worked in them. Spending on leisure increased by 64 per cent between 1982 and 1987, and by 184 per cent between 1987 and 2000.[8]

Share prices and property prices were not only driven by positive fundamentals: they were buoyed by the need for money to find a home. Pension funds enjoyed huge tax advantages and grew in size from £84 billion in 1982 to £228 billion in 1987. By 2000 the equivalent value was £699 billion.[9] The only investments that could realistically provide the levels of growth that these funds sought were equities and property. Other money was also looking for a place to go. Fortunes made in the Klondike that was Russia after the collapse of communism found their way to Europe and the United States, accompanied by wealth that was leaving Hong Kong prior to its return to China in 1997.

The privatization of British Telecom and other nationally owned utilities and businesses in the 1980s had introduced the British public to share ownership. The introduction of personal equity plans (PEPs) gave even greater incentive to individuals to invest in shares. We were becoming a share-owning democracy. Some of this money found its way into the stock market, where it supported share prices and, aided and abetted by City executives anxious to generate fees, funded new issues.

The end of the bull market

The bull market had begun to run out of steam in 1998 as the market reacted to the shocks of the Long-Term Capital Management collapse and the Russian economic crisis, which had been foreshadowed by the Far Eastern economic crisis and stock market crash of 1987. Prices of a number of 'old economy' stocks had fallen in the

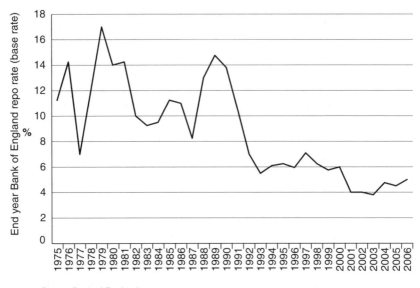

Source: Bank of England

Figure 1.3   Interest rates

two years to March 2000, but the market as a whole was to increase dramatically thanks to a phenomenon that became known variously as the 'dotcom boom' and the 'TMT bubble' (technology, media and telecoms). Underlying this phenomenon was the rise and then fall in value of major technology and telecoms companies such as Vodafone (see Figure 1.4).

The high-profile element of the TMT bubble was the dotcom phenomenon. The internet represented for many the great new 'virtual' frontier and, as internet access became cheaper and more widespread, people left highly paid jobs in the City and elsewhere to go prospecting in the ether. Driven by greed and the fear of missing out on an opportunity that no one really understood, people poured millions into businesses that had no history, had no immediate or even foreseeable prospect of making a profit, and in some cases were run by people with no relevant experience. Some people believed that the world had changed and that it was now appropriate to talk of a new paradigm. Some of the companies coming to market in this brave new world had no revenue and no clear idea where that revenue was going to come from. As new measures were developed for valuing these businesses, marketing companies became 'technology' stocks, aerospace companies became 'old economy', and a loss-making (virtual) bookshop became more valuable than the world's largest aircraft manufacturer. Private investors were among the keenest to subscribe to new issues, and brokers were reporting an almost insatiable investor appetite for new issues. It was intoxicating and hugely enjoyable while it lasted, but it could not go on for ever. Eventually people began to realize and then acknowledge that the emperor was indeed wearing no clothes; when that happened investors lost confidence and share price graphs took on a precipice-like appearance, as stocks went into free fall, losing 90 per cent or more of their value. To be sure, the huge

VOD

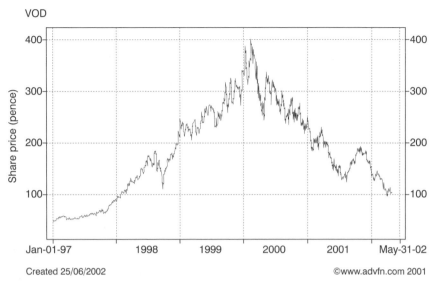

Created 25/06/2002   ©www.advfn.com 2001

Figure 1.4 Vodafone

amounts invested in 'technology' stocks, particularly infrastructure companies such as Global Crossing, have transformed the world of business, creating the flat world articulated so memorably by Thomas Friedman.[10] The people who did not benefit were the people who invested in them.

To a small extent the collapse of technology stocks was the elimination of froth, but behind the collapse lay something more fundamental. The large telecommunications companies had assumed near crippling levels of debt as they attempted to outbid each other in acquiring 3G licences, and in many cases had no cash left to fund the roll-out of new networks, so were forced to delay investment. Barriers to entry have been lowered, and telecoms operators face intense competition both from other operators and, increasingly, from internet-based operations such as Skype. Inevitably, the price of telecoms stocks fell, as did the share prices of equipment manufacturers and software companies. AIM company share prices fell along with those of the larger telecoms companies and with it came a fall in IPO activity.

A period of retrenchment was inevitable and lasted from 2000 to 2002. From 2003, financial markets have thrived and fortunes have been made in a way that dwarfs those made in the 1980s. There have been a number of elements to this recent boom. Globalization and the opening up of China in particular and to a lesser extent India and the former Soviet bloc have contributed to a global expansion that has benefited many companies in the world's developed economies. Industrial expansion, particularly in China, has driven raw material prices and raised investor demand for natural resource companies. Increased funds have been made available for private equity investors looking to acquire underperforming companies, which has had a major knock-on effect on asset prices and equity markets.

AIM

AIM opened its doors for business on 19 June 1995, its primary function to address what had become an apparent funding gap for UK businesses. The Main Market had long been an excellent source of fund-raising for large, well-known companies, but increasingly new, innovative, mid-market businesses were finding it difficult to attract the money they needed to start and build their activities. These were the kinds of companies that were typically too large to rely on traditional sources of equity finance such as that provided by business angels, from friends and family, and yet too small to access the major capital markets and not appropriate for traditional venture capital or private equity.

AIM was designed to attract these smaller growing businesses by providing companies with the opportunity for market-based intermediation but with a more flexible regulatory environment and a much lower fee structure than the London Stock Exchange's Main Market. Coupled with these already powerful incentives, tax benefits were created for both companies and investors in an attempt to make the market more attractive.

The start-up dotcoms were exactly the sort of business that AIM was designed for: young, smaller and riskier than companies on the Main Market, but with the potential for spectacular growth. All that remained to be seen was whether private and institutional investors would support such businesses.

AIM turned out to be a success from its inception, admitting an average of around 100 companies a year until 1999, with 2000 the busiest year thus far by a considerable margin (with a total of 277 admissions). The height of the dotcom boom coincided with AIM's busiest period of activity to date, something that fell dramatically after 2000. However, on an annualized basis, admissions in 2002 were actually running at a level similar to that of the late 1990s.

To some extent, this represented a return to a more normal state of affairs. It also demonstrated the continuing enthusiasm for the market, which admitted more companies in 2001 than the Main Market, NASDAQ and Neuermarkt (which later closed) combined.

From 2003 to 2006

After two years of retrenchment, confidence began to return towards the end of 2002 and, with it, IPO activity. The busiest year since AIM was established was 2004, and it was only to be eclipsed by 2005 and 2006. Both the number and the size of IPOs had increased and activity was spread over a range of sectors. Nonetheless, there were a number of notable trends relating to both the type of company and the sectors represented as well as to the nature of AIM investors.

Until the collapse of the technology bubble in 2000, private investors were among the most enthusiastic investors in AIM companies. AIM, however, was never meant to appeal to private investors. While there are still many private investors who will invest in AIM companies, it is primarily an institutional market. AIM's institutional investors have a longer time horizon than private investors, and many expect to provide their companies with follow-on investment.

As a source of development capital (rather than an exit) and with a comparatively narrow spread of shareholders and limited liquidity, AIM has a number of the characteristics of private equity. It may, in fact, be best described as private equity in a quoted environment. Private investors still buy AIM stocks but without the irrational exuberance of the years leading up to the millennium and now with more substantial companies to invest in.

The changing nature of admissions

AIM was originally seen by many as a stepping stone to other markets, particularly the Main Market and, for technology businesses, NASDAQ. However, over time AIM has become a market to which officially listed companies have chosen to transfer. Forty companies transferred during 2005, compared with 21 in 2004 and 50 in 2003. While AIM will continue to attract Main Market companies, the number of net transfers is likely to reduce simply by virtue of the smaller number of companies listed on the Main Market. AIM has also been admitting an increasingly large number of companies quoted on one of a number of overseas 'AIM designated markets' and availing themselves of the recently introduced fast-track rules. In 2006, 124 international companies were admitted compared with 120 in 2005 and 61 in 2004. There have been a number of international resource-related companies; investor interest in such issues is largely a reaction to the rise in oil prices to over $60 per barrel and gold prices to over $600 per ounce. However, there is an increasing level of interest in international companies in other sectors.

AIM has also been admitting an increasing number of investment companies covering sectors ranging from Vietnamese opportunities to Eastern European property.

By the end of 1995 AIM had 118 UK and three international companies trading with a market value of just £82 million. The picture appeared very different 10 years down the line. At the end of December 2005, the market counted 1,179 UK and 220 international companies trading with a combined market value of over £56 billion. Over this 10-year period, AIM grew over 11 times in terms of numbers and over 23 times in market capitalization. From AIM's inception in 1995 until the end of 2006, 2,664 companies had been admitted to trading on AIM, though some more transiently than others. At the end of 2006, there were 1,634 companies trading on AIM, with a total capitalization of £91 billion.

AIM has become the pre-eminent international market for small-cap companies. Other than a few special classes of investor that are not permitted to invest other than on the Main Market (eg ISAs), there are practically no investors not prepared to invest in AIM companies, or financial advisers, investment banks and brokers not prepared to advise them.

The success of any market will be measured, principally, by reference to the amount of funds raised on that market; AIM's fund-raising record is set out in Figure 1.5. Fund-raising patterns reflect the changing economic conditions over the past 10 years.

Table 1.1 Number of AIM companies

	Number of Companies			Market Value (£m)	Number of Admissions			Money Raised (£m)		
	UK	International	Total		UK	International	Total	New	Further	Total
19/06/1995	10	0	10	82.2						
1995	118	3	121	2,382.4	120	3	123	69.5	25.3	94.8
1996	235	17	252	5,298.5	131	14	145	514.1	302.3	816.4
1997	286	22	308	5,655.1	100	7	107	344.1	350.2	694.3
1998	291	21	312	4,437.9	68	7	75	267.5	290.1	557.6
1999	325	22	347	13,468.5	96	6	102	333.7	599.8	933.5
2000	493	31	524	14,935.2	265	12	277	1,754.1	1,319.7	3,073.8
2001	587	42	629	11,607.2	162	15	177	593.1	535.3	1,128.4
2002	654	50	704	10,252.3	147	13	160	490.1	485.8	975.8
2003	694	60	754	18,358.5	146	16	162	1,095.4	999.7	2,095.2
2004	905	116	1021	31,753.4	294	61	355	2,775.9	1,880.2	4,656.1
2005	1,179	220	1,399	56,618.5	399	120	519	6,461.2	2,481.2	8,942.4
2006	1,328	306	1,634	90,666.4	338	124	462	9,943.8	5,734.3	15,678.1

Source: London Stock Exchange.

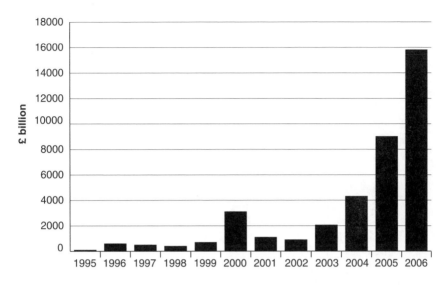

Source: AIM stats

Figure 1.5 Funds raised on AIM

During 2006, £15.7 billion was raised on AIM, of which £9.9 billion was at IPO rather than a secondary fund-raising (2005: £8.9 billion in total). The amount of money raised on admission averaged over £20 million per company, although most AIM companies still raise less than £10 million on admission. The overall average is distorted by a small number of very large fund-raisings. In 1995, by contrast, the average was £0.5 million. The reason for the growth in the size of fund-raising is that AIM has become the primary source of equity finance for quoted companies, including some very large businesses. Overwhelmingly, the main instrument used to raise money on AIM is straight equity. This is in contrast to the Main Market, which in terms of size is dominated by Eurobonds. This has much to do with the changing role of the Main Market and its increasing focus on servicing the further fund-raising needs of larger companies already listed on it rather than on initial public offerings, the majority of which now take place on AIM.

Larger, more established quoted companies can access bond markets, which generally offer lower-cost methods of further fund-raising. Smaller companies seeking a quotation for the first time (and many even after a period of being quoted) would find these markets closed to them. For many larger companies, the main reason for listing on the Main Market is actually to access the corporate bond market.

AIM companies are getting larger – fund managers need larger investee companies if they are to manage their portfolios efficiently. Such companies are, by definition, better established and more profitable than the type of company seeking admission in 1995.

Looking forward

So where are we now?

Overall conditions

■ The success of AIM as a market must not be confused with the ability of small companies to raise funds. Much of the recent AIM investment has been risk-averse, investing into fund structures.

■ Interest rates are relatively low, being 5.0 per cent at the end of 2006 (5.5 per cent in May 2007), having risen from a 40-year low of 3.5 per cent in 2003. At 5.5 per cent, there is some scope for improvement (as well as for further increase). At the end of December 2006, three-month Euribor interest rates were 3.725 per cent, and in a yield-driven market a reduction to such a level will have a significant effect. If the UK does join the euro, it will benefit from European-style interest rates. This looks unlikely to happen for the foreseeable future.

■ Conversely, there are forces that may lead to increased interest rates. There appears to be a consensus that the combination of a growing population and restrictions on house building caused by planning regulations will continue to drive UK house prices upwards. House prices have been rising steadily, despite a brief, short-term reduction in 2005. Whatever interest rates do, the main effect on quoted companies and prospective quoted companies is on valuation.

Shares being offered at IPO are priced to attract potential investors, typically at a discount of 10 per cent to quoted comparatives, with the result that they generally go to a premium. Traditionally, those favoured clients of stockbrokers lucky enough to get shares in an IPO expected to make an instant profit, either paper or cash (if they are 'stags').

A feature of the dotcom boom was the large number of private individuals buying shares in dotcoms and other high-risk companies at IPO; many lost considerable amounts of money in the process. As a result, private investors are investing only limited amounts in IPOs at the present time. So, it is back to the professionals, who are still prepared to invest in companies provided that the investment proposition is sound. Although there are exceptions – such as mineral exploration or biotech-nology – the businesses in which investors will invest are generally the same types of business that they have traditionally looked for: well-managed, *already* profitable companies with significant growth prospects, at a price that does not take account of the full value of the business. A really good business will still find investors, but the owner may have to reassess his or her estimation of value.

Sector focus

■ Sectors come in and out of fashion: 2001 was a good year for oil stocks, for example, and retail stocks performed well early in 2002, with companies posting strong sets of figures driven by buoyant consumer spending. There remains considerable investor interest in natural resource companies, although a number of problems with smaller natural resource companies have led the London Stock Exchange to monitor the sector more carefully. Demand continues for quality businesses providing outsourcing and other support services, particularly when underpinned by long-term contracts.

■ Identifying the sector likeliest to do well is never easy. Possible candidates are sectors where companies are well placed to benefit from expenditure by an ageing and increasingly wealthy population, and are able to offer environmentally sustainable solutions to energy, manufacturing and distribution problems. As well as companies with interesting new technologies, there will always be individual companies, even in unfashionable sectors, that can buck the trend and create exceptional value for their shareholders.

■ If there is one sector, however, that seems to have particularly interesting medium- to long-term prospects, it is the green technology sector. As governments and the public increasingly accept the urgent need to reduce carbon dioxide and other greenhouse gas emissions to avoid a global environmental catastrophe, companies manufacturing fuel cells, providing renewable energy technology and carbon-neutral building, all look promising.

■ Other companies likely to do well are those that are able to exploit the new flat world, using lower-waged, highly skilled staff in less developed and industrializing countries. Companies that supply luxury goods or that provide goods and services to the expanding middle classes in India, China and the countries of the former Soviet Union and Eastern Europe have done well recently and are also likely to continue to thrive.

Size matters

■ Most IPOs on AIM have raised less than £5 million, although the statistical average is distorted by a few very large fund-raisings. Nonetheless, the trend is towards larger fund-raisings as investors look to fund business with greater critical mass and advisers look to maximize their fees in a buoyant market.

■ The market for shares is polarizing. While AIM has become increasingly acceptable as a market for fund managers to invest in – indeed there are specialist funds, such as VCTs, that will invest predominantly or exclusively in AIM companies – those fund managers are looking to increase the size of company in which they invest. Europe is likely to follow the United States, where there are a diminishing number of funds that will consider investing in 'smaller' quoted companies, by which they mean companies with a market capitalization of less than $1,000 million. Already, many consider that a UK company with a market capitalization of less than £100 million (or even more) should be quoted on AIM rather than the Main Market. Except for the very largest companies, businesses seeking to float will increasingly look at AIM.

■ Consolidation has been taking place in most sectors, creating giant companies that dominate their sector. Fund managers looking to achieve a spread of investments in a particular sector are increasingly obliged to think in pan-European or even global terms. Exchanges themselves are becoming increasingly integrated, and the likely outcome is that institutional investor interest will focus mainly on giant pan-European companies quoted on pan-European exchanges. Nevertheless, there are still institutional investors interested in investing in exciting smaller companies.

■ Small, early-stage companies cannot generally consider a flotation on the Main Market. However, the size of business that floats on AIM is likely to continue to increase, as larger companies, no longer big enough for the Main Market, apply for admission. Some businesses will also prefer to float on AIM because of tax advantages and the lower cost of admission. Smaller companies already on the Main Market are considering transferring across to AIM to take advantage of better coverage in investment publications and by brokers and analysts, different rules for announcing and approving transactions and lower ongoing costs.

Conclusion

A company looking to float in 2007 has a realistic chance of success, provided that it has profits and/or growth prospects and represents good value to investors. Those investors will probably not expect to see the sort of capital growth enjoyed during the long bull market, and will place greater emphasis on yield. The quality of the company's earnings stream will therefore be particularly important. Lower overall capital growth will also emphasize the importance of stock-picking as opposed to an overall market or sectoral approach. The search for above-average growth in a comparatively stable market has also led to the proliferation of hedge funds and other special-situation investment vehicles.

There are sectors, for example in biotech or natural resources, where investors will fund a pre-profit business or even an idea. For this to happen, both the idea and the people behind it must be exceptionally good. For most businesses, however, the traditional virtues remain paramount – strong management, control of a market or a niche, and a unique selling proposition. And such a company, seeking to benefit from the funding and the advantages that a quotation offers, is most likely to consider floating on AIM.

Notes

1. All items excluding mortgage interest payments. *Source:* Office of National Statistics website.
2. Based on the FTSE 100.
3. New companies raising money on the Main Market. *Source:* London Stock Exchange.
4. From January 1988 to December 1999.
5. GDP seasonally adjusted, constant 1995 prices. *Source:* Office of National Statistics.
6. Based on the FTSE 30. *Source:* Office of National Statistics.

7. *Source:* WTRG Economics, www.wtrg.com.

8. Spending on recreation and culture. *Source:* Office of National Statistics.

9. Market value of pension funds. *Source:* Office of National Statistics.

10. Thomas L Friedman (2005) *The World Is Flat*, Farrar, Straus & Giroux, New York.

2

Necessary and sufficient conditions for flotation

Peter Smith, CMS Cameron McKenna LLP

Summary

- Requirements for admission to the Official List are set out in the Prospectus and Listing Rules.
- Requirements for admission to AIM are set out in AIM Rules for Companies.
- Admission to the Official List is subject to approval by the UK Listing Authority and will require production of a prospectus approved by the UK Listing Authority.
- Admission to AIM does not require production of a prospectus approved by the UK Listing Authority unless the company offers its securities to the public in the UK. Most AIM flotations do not involve this.
- For admission to AIM the company's nominated adviser must satisfy itself that the company is appropriate to join AIM and provide declarations to the London Stock Exchange.
- For admission to the Official List or Main Market the company will require a sponsor, who will owe certain duties to the UK Listing Authority in relation to the process.

Introduction

In the UK there are two principal public markets for companies' securities. They are the Main Market – intended for established companies – and the Alternative Investments Market (AIM) of the London Stock Exchange ('the Stock Exchange'), designed primarily for emerging or smaller companies.

The Main Market is regulated by the Financial Services Authority (FSA), which in this capacity is sometimes referred to as the UK Listing Authority (UKLA). The Official List is a regulated market for the purposes of EU legislation, and listed shares are traded in the Stock Exchange.

AIM is operated and regulated by the Stock Exchange and is not a regulated market for the purposes of EU legislation. One consequence of AIM not being an EU regulated market is that, provided that shares are not offered to the public, the company does not have to prepare a detailed prospectus approved by the FSA in accordance with the Prospectus Directive. Usually AIM flotations (or IPOs) are effected by means of a placing to institutional investors, so that no approved prospectus drawn up in accordance with the Prospectus Directive is required. Instead, the issuer must publish an AIM admission document, which has to contain some, but not all, of the information that would be required for a prospectus. An admission document does not need to be approved by the FSA. Instead the issuer's nominated adviser (nomad) must satisfy itself that the admission document complies with relevant requirements.

Both markets provide companies with access to capital for development and growth. However, through AIM, such access to capital has been extended to smaller companies that, perhaps because of their stage of development, size, age or type, are unable to join the Main Market. Consequently, the conditions that must be satisfied to list in AIM are much less onerous than the conditions for the Main Market.

Types of company whose shares can be admitted

First and foremost, in order for a UK company to be admitted to either the Main Market or AIM, the company must be a public limited company (plc). For a foreign company to be admitted to either market, it must have been duly incorporated in its place of incorporation or establishment and permitted under such law to have its securities admitted.

For a UK incorporated private company, this means having to consider the best way of restructuring itself to meet this requirement – it could either convert itself into a plc or set up a plc as a holding company. The company will need to adopt articles of association (or equivalent constitutional documents) suitable for a publicly traded company. A company's share capital may also need to be restructured.

If the company has different classes of shares it may be necessary to convert the various classes into one type of ordinary share. The company will also need to consider outstanding warrants or options to subscribe for or convert into shares. Finally, the company must make sure that the shares are capable of being traded electronically in preparation for admission to AIM or the Main Market.

Minimum assets, equity and/or working capital

For the Main Market, there is no minimum net assets value for most types of issuer; but property investment companies must have net assets of at least £30 million (44.5 million) (including funds raised on listing). Scientific research-based companies must raise at least £10 million (14.7 million) pursuant to a marketing at the time of IPO.

In AIM, a company whose primary business is investing funds in the securities of other companies, or a special purpose vehicle formed to acquire a particular business, must raise at least £3 million (4.4 million) in cash via an equity fund-raising on admission. Otherwise there are no minimum requirements, although LSE may impose special conditions where it sees fit.

Having said this, the decision to float must be based on an honest and realistic assessment of the company, in terms not only of its capitalization, but also of its prospects, management resources and stage of development. In order for a company successfully to float and attract investors, the market must perceive it as financially sound and stable, with a viable and realistic business plan and good prospects of generating returns.

Management quality and continuity

When floating in a public market, the company must also show that it has a strong senior management team in place with appropriate public company experience and expertise to run all areas of the business in the public spotlight, and be free of conflicts of interest that might hamper its ability to do this. Potential investors will be focusing their attention on the range and depth of its management experience. They will want to see that the board and senior management are composed of members who have had sufficient years of experience in running a publicly listed company.

Potential investors will also want to see a company with a management team that is united behind the company's plans, with a vision for its future. People at every level of the business must be ready to take on the inherent responsibilities and disciplines in having shares traded publicly and in being accountable to outside shareholders. Commitment to the business from key staff at and below board level could be reinforced through contractual arrangements or share option schemes.

Corporate governance

Although compliance with the corporate governance requirements set out in the Combined Code is not a legal requirement, early on in the IPO process changes will be appropriate in relation to the company's corporate and management structures. UK companies joining the Main Market are required to comply with or explain variations from the requirements of the Combined Code. Non-UK companies and companies joining AIM are generally expected to comply with the Combined Code or equivalent procedures suitable to their size and nature. The company should consider which systems need to be put in place in light of the flotation.

Relevant steps may include splitting the roles of chairman and chief executive, the appointment of independent board members (ie non-executive directors) and appointing a qualified finance director. Another suggestion is to create new board committees such as an audit committee, which oversees compliance with various regulations and laws, a remuneration committee, which is in charge of salaries and benefits to senior management, and a nomination committee, to create a system for nominating and managing directors that is open to scrutiny. It is also important for the directors of the company to obtain adequate directors' and officers' liability insurance, as the chances of directors being sued increases significantly once the company becomes listed. In addition, it is worth considering aiming for best practice as standard instead of settling for the minimum requirements.

Minimum public float

Consistent with the EU Consolidated Admission and Reporting Directive (CARD), the Main Market requires that at least 25 per cent of the shares being admitted to the Official List must normally end up in the hands of the public, ie persons who are not connected to the issuer or its directors, by the time of admission.

The AIM Rules do not specify a minimum proportion of shares that must be in public hands, but the LSE has discretion to impose a minimum if (for example) it is considered necessary to protect the orderly operation or reputation of AIM.

Track record

Usually the issuer in the Main Market must be able to show that:

1. at least 75 per cent of its business has earned revenue for at least the last three years;
2. it has controlled the majority of its assets for at least the last three years; and
3. its main activity will be carrying on an independent business.

Special modified or additional requirements apply to companies principally involved in mining, scientific research, real estate and investment in other companies and assets.

To be able to list in AIM, companies involved in exploration, development or production of mining, oil and gas resources must include in their admission document a report by an independent expert on the quality and existence of the company's material assets. The company's nomad is also expected to carry out full due diligence on the company and its assets prior to admission.

Financial information

In accordance with CARD and the Prospectus Directive (PD), the issuer in the Main Market must have published annual accounts in accordance with national law for at least three years prior to admission, and these accounts must be included in the prospectus. The accounts must have been reported on by independent auditors without modification.

Three years' audited accounts and at least 12 months' working capital (as if CARD and PD applied) are required to list in AIM.

More important is the fact that investors will want to see evidence that the company has a transparent and high standard of accounting systems and financial controls.

Restrictions on shareholdings

According to CARD, shares admitted to the Official List must be freely transferable. The only time when restrictions can normally be imposed is when a shareholder refuses to tell the company who is interested in its shares.

Shares in AIM must be freely transferable except that a company may limit the number of shareholders domiciled in a particular country in order to ensure that it does not become subject to a particular statute or regulation.

Independence from controlling shareholders

In the Main Market, the issuer's main activity must be an independent business. Apart from that, there are no specific requirements. Major shareholders and their influence will have to be disclosed in the prospectus.

In AIM, major shareholders and their influence will also have to be disclosed in the admission document or (if the IPO involves an offer to the public) the prospectus.

This is important, as potential investors could be put off by the presence of a controlling shareholder, because of the belief that their influence on the business's direction would be greater if no single dominant shareholder was in place.

Lock-in requirements

There are no lock-in requirements in the Listing Rules that apply to the Main Market, but in practice sponsors or underwriters to the issue normally require contractual lock-ins from management and major shareholders in order to secure an orderly market.

On the other hand, in AIM, where the issuer's main business has not been independent and earning revenue for at least two years, all directors, shareholders with 10 per cent or more of the issuer's equity, employers with 0.5 per cent or more, and certain other persons connected to the issuer must agree not to sell their shares for at least a year from admission. The nomad or broker will usually require lock-ins from management and/or major shareholders in other circumstances.

Sponsor or other financial adviser

Issuers in the Main Market must appoint one of the FSA's approved sponsors to guide it through the listing process and confirm to the FSA that certain requirements have been met. A sponsor is also needed every time the issuer subsequently publishes a prospectus, or a circular for a major transaction, and in certain other circumstances. Companies therefore tend to retain a sponsor at all times while their shares are listed.

Issuers in AIM must appoint and retain a qualified nomad at all times. The nomad guides the issuer through the admission process and confirms to the LSE that all the relevant requirements have been met. Where the issuer is not making an offer to the public, it must publish an admission document that is vetted by its nomad on behalf of the LSE. Nomads effectively act as intermediaries between an issuer and the LSE, and police the AIM Rules on the LSE's behalf. In 2007, the LSE issued a new rule book for nomads, *The AIM Rules for Nominated Advisers*. This was introduced in addition to the existing AIM Rules for Companies and codifies the role and responsibilities of nomads based on existing market best practice. The new rule book provides examples of the types of activities the LSE expects nomads to undertake in order to confirm to the LSE that a company is suitable for flotation on AIM and to ensure that it is able to comply with the AIM Rules on an ongoing basis.

Market maker or broker

No market maker is required in the Main Market, but an issuer must appoint a corporate broker (which may be the same firm as its sponsor).

No market maker is required either in AIM, but the issuer must retain a broker at all times (which may be the same firm as its nomad). If there is no registered market maker in the issuer's shares, the broker must use its best endeavours to find matching business.

3

Is flotation the right financial strategy?

Kate Wolstenholme, PricewaterhouseCoopers LLP

Introduction

The decision to float a company is a significant one, which should be based on careful assessment of a company's prospects, its stage of development, management's aspirations, and consideration of alternative sources of funding.

In this chapter we discuss some of the issues to consider when contemplating a flotation, and highlight the positives alongside the potential downsides. Amongst other benefits, taking a company public offers access to capital at a relatively low cost, an opportunity to realize value for shareholders and employees, and an enhanced corporate profile. However, these attractions are not without cost – in terms of ongoing compliance requirements, dilution of control, and the pressure of life in the public eye. Recognizing that flotation may not always be the optimal strategy at any given time in a company's development cycle, we offer an overview of other sources of equity and debt funding that, individually or in combination, might provide a viable alternative to flotation. We also consider the options (eg trade sale or management buy-out) where a complete exit is the preferred route.

Issues to consider

Access to capital

One of the primary reasons for flotation is as a means to raise capital. A flotation provides the company with access to a wider investment base from which capital can be raised. As well as the initial equity raised at IPO, it is common for further capital to be raised thereafter by way of rights issue or placing, and the market is usually open to this provided that IPO milestones have been met and there are sensible reasons for an additional finance requirement.

Once listed, a company not only has the capital raised on flotation at its disposal but it can also use its tradable paper as currency, for example to buy other businesses. This of course will entail dilution of existing shareholdings but can be an effective means of financing growth by acquisition.

State of the market

The success of an IPO will be highly dependent on the state of the market, and also the current market perception of specific sectors. If the IPO market is liquid and sector valuations currently attractive, existing shareholders will realize value on the IPO. However, an IPO typically takes about four months, and it is only at the end of the process that a company really knows what price it will get or indeed whether the shares can be sold. The market, particularly the Alternative Investment Market (AIM), can be fickle, with windows of opportunity opening and closing relatively quickly, such that an adverse and potentially unforeseeable change in the market may result in the IPO having to be scaled back or even postponed.

Once listed, price and liquidity of shares may well be influenced by market conditions beyond the company's control. Market rumour, economic developments and sector trends are all factors that can play a part in the valuation and liquidity of listed shares.

It is also worth noting that a valuation at IPO will not reflect any premium for control that may be payable by a trade purchaser.

Flotation as an exit route

Flotation provides existing shareholders with a publicly traded security, enabling them to trade their interest in securities at a 'market value'. As a minimum, there is a requirement on EU regulated markets for there to be 25 per cent of shares in public hands, so selling shareholders are forced to make this amount available (although for AIM, which is not an EU regulated market, there is no minimum requirement). A flotation provides shareholders with the opportunity to manage their exit over a prolonged period; after the initial IPO there is the option to sell further tranches of shares in the future, although lock-ups are nearly always put in place both on shares retained by the selling shareholder and on management's holdings, typically for six months to a year.

However, a flotation should not be viewed as an opportunity for shareholders to exit their investment completely: investors are usually unwilling to put in cash if management is looking to sell out, and we would typically expect management to retain a meaningful stake in the business on IPO.

It can also be the case that liquidity in the shares – particularly on AIM – may be limited, making it difficult to sell large holdings and increasing volatility in the share price. Smaller stocks are often little researched, and can be overlooked by the investment community. Therefore, some of the perceived advantages of having a public quote may not always be realized.

Of course, even a partial exit involves ceding some degree of management control to outside shareholders, carrying with it the risk of an unwelcome takeover in future.

Enhanced corporate profile

Flotation brings with it all the pros and cons of being in the public eye. A listing provides greater visibility of the company and can certainly enhance its public image, the benefits of which may flow through in a number of ways. The company may improve its prospects in competing for contracts, since listed companies will often be perceived by customers and suppliers as being more financially secure and reliable; this in turn may accelerate sales growth and enhance profitability by heightening public awareness of the company and its products. A listed company is better able to publicize its strategy and intentions, and may consequently gain access to corporate transactions that previously would not have hit its radar. There may even be the prospect of a potential takeover at a premium.

However, the pressures that come with life in the public domain are not to be underestimated. Management may feel constrained by short-term performance demands rather than long-term goals, to satisfy new shareholders' demand for a quick return on their investment. The City can be particularly unforgiving of unforeseen fluctuations in profit trends, resulting in sharp share price movements and unwelcome press coverage, with all the adverse implications that brings for the business. At best, this can result in loss of management flexibility; at worst, it may lead to management compromising the long-term success of the company through short-term decision making.

A public company is expected to behave as such, and therefore any previously blurred boundaries between company and personal affairs must be clearly drawn. Directors will also have to grapple with the potential conflict between protecting commercial interests and fulfilling their obligation to keep the market informed of price-sensitive information.

Key people incentivization

The effective incentivization of staff is critical to the success of a growing business, and flotation provides an opportunity to put in place plans that will attract and retain talented personnel. The liquidity of listed shares enhances the attractiveness of share option plans, such that employees have a transparent view of their company's value and can share in its success.

Companies need to take great care with the design of their share plans to manage the level of charge against profits under International Financial Reporting Standard (IFRS) 2. Typically, fast-growing companies will deliver more value to their employees using a leveraged share plan, such as options or share appreciation rights (SARs), rather than an unleveraged plan that awards free shares to employees. Conversely, a company with modest growth expectations will deliver more value with an unleveraged plan.

Companies also need to be mindful of dilution. The Association of British Insurers (ABI), which represents insurance companies as investors, recommends dilution of no more than 10 per cent of share capital over 10 years. Whilst options can be very dilutive, SARs deliver exactly the same economic value for much lower dilution.

Costs of listing and ongoing compliance

A company will incur significant expense in pursuing a flotation, including brokers' commissions (a percentage of funds raised) and professional fees. The latter will be higher for a Main Market listing than for admission to AIM. The overall cost of capital typically falls in the range of 7–12 per cent of funds raised, although it will rise for complex IPOs (eg carve-outs from existing businesses, or overseas businesses) and (in relative terms) where the amount of capital raised is low. As well as external costs, there is a price to be paid in terms of the considerable management time and effort that will necessarily be expended in discussions with professional advisers, drafting and verification of prospectus/admission documents and presentations to investors.

Once listed, a company and its directors are subject to ongoing obligations, reflecting the new responsibilities they have as the stewards of outside investors' money. Requirements will vary by country and by exchange, and further details are provided in Part IV of this book, but in summary a listed company may need to retain the services of brokers, investor relations advisers, non-executive directors, registrars and so on. Compliance with listed company reporting requirements also comes at a cost – in terms of internal time spent on such areas as interim reporting, corporate governance and enhanced disclosure requirements, as well as higher external audit fees.

Of course, whilst it is true that the process of listing and the ongoing responsibilities of a listed company can be expensive, the benefits of a successful flotation to a company, its employees and shareholders should outweigh the cost.

Personal considerations

The process of successfully completing a flotation is intense, and running a listed company may well entail a significant lifestyle change. Board-level departures in the public eye can have an impact on investor confidence, with a knock-on effect on share price, so anyone taking a business public ought to be thinking in terms of several years of commitment.

Table 3.1 Summary of advantages and disadvantages of flotation

	Advantages	Disadvantages
Access to long-term capital	✓ Provides the company with access to a wider investor base from which capital can be raised (eg for acquisitions).	✗ Dilution of existing shareholdings. ✗ Valuation will not reflect any premium for control that may be payable by a trade purchaser.
State of the market	✓ Opportunity to realize a premium in a buoyant, liquid market.	✗ Price and volume of placing is uncertain and subject to changing market conditions.
Exit route	✓ Provides existing shareholders with a publicly traded security.	✗ Only represents a partial exit for shareholders; management expected to retain a meaningful stake. ✗ Continuing shareholders (including management) will be subject to a 'lock-up'.
Enhanced corporate profile	✓ Provides greater visibility and enhances the company's corporate image. ✓ Prospect of potential takeover at a premium.	✗ Pressure on short-term performance at expense of long-term success. ✗ Directors' responsibilities increased.
Key people incentivization	✓ Liquidity of shares enhances attractiveness of stock option plans (often with tax advantages), enabling the company to attract and retain talented personnel. Employees can visibly share in the company's success.	✗ Options/long-term incentive plans (LTIPs) limited to 10 per cent of share capital (ABI guidelines) and subject to performance criteria. ✗ Potential profit and loss charge under IFRS 2.
Costs of listing/ ongoing compliance	✓ Net cost may be lower than private equity funding.	✗ Company is likely to incur expense in pursuing an IPO. ✗ Considerable management time and effort. ✗ Compliance with listed company reporting requirements, including interim reporting, corporate governance and the EU Transparency Directive.
Tax (see Chapter 26)	✓ Share values eligible for business asset taper relief. ✓ Tax-efficient share option schemes.	✗ LTIPs and share options treated as taxable income. ✗ AIM company shares retain exemption from inheritance tax, but not Main Market shares.

Alternative sources of finance

In considering whether a flotation is right for your company, regard needs to be given to alternative sources of finance. There are many other sources of corporate funding, and we consider below only those more common types, together with their relative advantages and disadvantages.

Private placing

It is possible to raise finance from private investors without an IPO, although this will usually be an initial funding round, to be followed up with a subsequent IPO to provide an eventual exit route. The company may be required to produce an investment memorandum, the content of which is to some extent dictated by the number and type of potential investors.

Compared to an IPO, a private placing has the advantage of being a relatively quick process, since it tends to involve a small circle of investors who can make fast decisions; furthermore, there is no extensive disclosure, due diligence or regulatory requirements.

However, companies looking to take this route are reliant on the contacts of their broker or banks to find relevant investors. Given that only a limited number of investors are likely to be approached (compared with an IPO), the level of funds raised is likely to be lower and at a less competitive price, and investors are also likely to require a discount for the illiquidity of their investment.

A company raising funds through private placing can expect much more direct contact with its investor base than a listed company, with some investors seeking a 'hands-on' involvement in the running of the company.

Private equity and venture capital

Private equity (PE) firms and venture capitalists (VCs) both provide medium- to long-term equity financing to unquoted companies with a view to realizing growth potential through sale or flotation. Whilst there is some overlap, the key difference between the two is that venture capitalists tend to provide a lower amount of capital to provide early support from seed to expansion capital, whilst private equity financing can occur at any stage in a company's development life cycle, including management buy-outs (MBOs) or buy-ins (MBIs).

The advantages of private equity/venture capital funding include:

- *Enlargement of the capital base.* This may enhance a company's standing with its bankers, customers and suppliers, and may enable the company to take on additional debt finance.
- *Availability of further finance.* The investor may be happy to contribute towards the financing of future projects, which may include significant internal projects or acquisitions.

■ *Provision of management expertise.* The investor is likely to adopt a 'hands-on' approach, bringing management skills and experience often in the form of a non-executive director.

These should be weighed against the following disadvantages:

■ *Dilution of control.* The entrepreneur will inevitably have to accept a reduced share of the business equity and with that some loss of control and possibly a degree of change in business culture.
■ *Greater accountability.* Investors will require regular management information to monitor their investment (although the discipline of producing prompt, reliable data is in many ways an advantage!).
■ *Demand for an 'exit route'.* The investor may exert pressure for an exit route at a date or using a mechanism that does not necessarily accord with management's long-term plans (although some investors are taking increasingly long-term views themselves).
■ *Cost.* Fees associated with the capital-raising process will include pre-acquisition due diligence, and the appointment of financial, legal and tax advisers. Additionally, investors will often require a high proportion of equity to achieve their required rate of return (typically 30 per cent IRR).

A management team seeking private equity or venture capital should consider the reputation of the PE house or VC fund, the degree of involvement sought, the flexibility of funding offered including capability to provide second-round finance if required, desired exit route and time line, and chemistry between the two parties.

The usual route to locating a source of funds suitable to the specific needs of the business is through an accountant or other adviser, although a company can also identify potential investors by contacting the British Venture Capital Association (BVCA).

In contrast to a listing, PE provides a more flexible form of financing. As the investors are often intimately involved with the business, the required levels of reporting and controls are less onerous than for public companies. In addition, investors will provide support over more difficult periods to ensure a high valuation is achieved on exit. To this extent, PE is often used to bridge a company from the private to the listed markets, typically enabling middle-market businesses to expand and to develop the appropriate controls and more predictable income streams that make them more suited to the public environment.

Corporate venturing

Corporate venturing typically occurs where a larger company invests cash and management resources in a smaller company. Whilst a venture capitalist is primarily concerned with return on investment, a corporate venturer may perceive additional value in such non-financial factors as:

- access to developing technologies in complementary areas;
- low-cost innovation and diversification into new products and markets;
- intelligence surrounding competitive activity;
- a future long-term partner or potential acquisition target.

The investee company may be able to take advantage of the investor's existing marketing and distribution networks, get access to more competitive suppliers and pricing, and even gain an introduction to the investor company's customer base. However, it is important that the investee considers the longer-term implications of the association. Assuming the venture is profitable, the investor may well wish to acquire the balance of the investee's shares, and this eventual option should be discussed by both parties at the outset.

Owing to the specific demands of a joint venture, finding a partner can often be difficult. Organizations most suited to partnering may already be operating in similar areas, so clear agreements to protect commercially sensitive data need to be put in place at an early stage.

Bank loans/overdrafts

Bank loans and overdrafts are the most common source of secured finance. The cost of such finance will reflect prevailing rates of interest as well as the lender's perception of the risks involved – an immature company can expect to pay a higher rate than a business with a proven track record, although a lender may reduce the risk by obtaining a security over the company's assets. Taking on further debt finance can be risky in times of rising interest rates or market uncertainty.

Overdrafts are relatively simple to arrange and are widely used to fund short-term working capital needs, with interest accruing only on the debt outstanding at any point in time. A disadvantage of overdrafts is that they are repayable upon demand, which can result in uncertainty for the business regarding the availability of funds for the medium or long term.

Leasing

Leasing offers a flexible source of finance, enabling management to alleviate the cash flow impact of capital expenditure. Leases fall into two categories: finance leases and operating leases. The former occurs when the lessee assumes substantially all the risks and rewards of ownership, whilst an operating lease is akin to renting an asset for a period of its life. A company can also release funds tied up in its own fixed asset base by establishing a 'sale and leaseback' arrangement whereby the asset is sold to a lessor and then leased back by the vendor, resulting in a one-off cash benefit followed by a stream of lease rental payments.

Invoice discounting and factoring

Debtor-based finance allows companies to borrow against the value of their sales ledger; it is often used as a means of financing in rapid growth situations, since it reduces the working capital requirements that arise from timing differences between incurring cost of sales and actually receiving cash from debtors.

Exiting the business

We have considered the advantages and disadvantages of flotation, and the alternative sources of finance available. These options all assume that, for the medium term at least, the owner wishes to retain some degree of ownership of the company. Where a complete exit is sought, a trade sale is the simplest option. Corporate finance advisers will be able to help identify a purchaser who might look to benefit through, for example, improved market share, expansion of the target market, synergistic benefits, economies of scale or acquisition of key personnel. The price paid is likely to be a fixed sum, with a possible earn-out where the vendor is likely to remain involved for a period post-sale; it may be higher than that earned on flotation or through private equity injection, to reflect the synergies available.

Other options to consider are MBOs or MBIs. An MBO may allow the owner a means of rewarding employees by offering the option to buy into the company at a lower price than would be available to a trade purchaser, or provides an alternative exit route where there is no trade interest. An MBI involves a new management team coming in to buy and run the business. Whilst the original owners will have achieved their required exit and realized their investment, the MBO or MBI teams will themselves have to raise the necessary capital required to take the business forward.

Conclusion

A wide range of strategic and funding options is available to a growing company. The external sources of finance discussed in this chapter range from conventional bank borrowing, through unsecured finance from private equity/venture capital, to public flotation, with trade sale or MBO/MBI as a further option where a complete exit is sought. Amongst other things, management must weigh up the degree of control they wish to retain, the extent of outside influence sought, their appetite and readiness for life in the public domain, their long-term ambitions, availability of capital, and cost and pricing issues. The decision to float a company should not be taken lightly – it is worth taking the time to understand all the implications and consider the alternatives, to ensure that you arrive at the approach which best matches your corporate and personal objectives.

4

Alternative sources of finance

David Wilkinson, Ernst & Young

Introduction

For many businesses, a float is the end goal: their marker for success. This idea is often reinforced by the team of investors who look at a flotation as a convenient exit.

This is understandable. After all, the London Stock Exchange markets give UK and international companies access to one of the world's deepest pools of investment capital. The markets contain every kind of company, from start-ups to the world's largest and most successful businesses.

They come because they're attracted by the diversity, the location, the stability and the opportunities of the London market. They're also attracted by the choice. The London Stock Exchange offers two markets – AIM and the Main Market. Which one a company joins depends on its size and what it wants to achieve from the flotation; each has different costs, different routes to entry and different reporting requirements.

Whichever market a company joins, the directors and shareholders must get used to being in the public eye. This is not always an easy adjustment to make. There are stringent reporting requirements that must be met, and companies need to plan in far greater detail than previously what they want to say and when. There will also be additions made to the board such as non-executive directors, and the need to observe the requirements of the Combined Code.

A float takes significant time and money and a real commitment to a process that can take anything up to 18 months to complete successfully. Can a would-be plc afford this? Is the management team prepared to follow this through?

Little wonder that the implications of going, and then staying, public prevent some organizations from listing. What, then, are the alternative means to raise funds?

Alternative routes to raising cash

Trade sale

If you are looking to get out of the business or at least to realize some of your holdings, then a trade sale can be an attractive alternative to an IPO – especially if there is a buyer prepared to pay a premium. It is currently a seller's market, with a host of buyers looking for investment opportunities. There is a lot of M&A activity, and debt multiples are now as high as five or six.

Debt funding

Another possible alternative is debt. Debt today is a relatively cheap and low-risk way to raise cash. The number of suppliers is outstripping demand, which means that it is possible to negotiate a good covenant, although this will still depend on the company's finances, credit rating, product and history.

Under debt financing, loans are secured by way of fixed and floating charges. A clear advantage of debt financing is that management retains ownership of the company (on repayment of the loan). However, the danger is that the company is too highly geared: that debt is not balanced by equity. The company then becomes acutely vulnerable to outside factors, thus affecting its ability to repay the debt. Defaulting on payments would of course negatively impact the company's reputation and credit rating, as well as incur penalties.

MBOs

A management buy-out (MBO) is another option, where the existing managers of the company take ownership of the business. This can be funded by debt financing or private equity (PE) and can ensure that ownership of the firm is not diluted. In addition, the due diligence process is likely to be limited, as the buyers obviously already know and understand the company.

An MBO may raise corporate governance issues (as would be the case whenever existing management benefited personally from the sale of their company or its assets). Moreover, a successful MBO is predicated on the new owners' ability to develop a strong second-tier management team.

PE is another possible alternative. PE is a medium-term source (typically up to five years) of financing by investors, in return for an equity stake. The PE market is bigger now than it ever has been, and PE houses are always looking for more opportunities. Indeed, the British PE market is second only to the US one in terms of size and the pool of cash available for investment.

PE houses are traditionally adept at increasing value and lowering costs in high-growth businesses, thanks to their previous experience. What they look for in return is businesses with good support, solid financial forecasts and a strong management team. One of the common misconceptions about PE is that these investors will take over the business entirely. That is not necessarily the case. Rather, they are looking for the same positive growth that the owners would be seeking. Therefore, the best PE partnerships are ones where the owner and investors work in tandem, agreeing their mutual aims and ambitions. Still, there is no overlooking the fact that the equity of the original owners will be diluted.

Private placings

Then there are private placings. Under this arrangement, new shares are issued to groups such as established institutions or high-net-worth private investors. There are also rights issues, where a company offers existing shareholders the right to buy, in proportion to the shares they already own.

Both of these routes can be complicated, and the amount of available funds will be smaller than if the company had chosen to go to the public market. However, it does give the company control over its shareholder base.

These are some of the alternatives to floating. However, that is not the end of the story.

The multi-track process

Many businesses are now choosing a triple-track process – simultaneously preparing themselves for an IPO, a trade sale and a venture capital/private equity round, depending on the balance of advantage. It is rare for a company today not to start with a plan A, a plan B *and* a plan C, and then eventually make a decision at the cut-off point and choose which route it is going to pursue once it knows which is the most attractive option.

This is due in part to confidence in the economy and the strength of the market, which are fuelling (and being fuelled by) PE activity, outbidding public markets for companies or buying up fledgling companies and taking them to IPO themselves. It is also due to an appreciation of the importance of risk management.

All fund-raising options have different benefits and pitfalls, so if a business is looking to raise funds for the next stage of its growth it is worth keeping options open with a multi-track process. Moreover, as there is considerable overlap in the due diligence required for the various routes, a double or triple track can be executed without doubling or tripling costs. Yes, a multi-track option requires preparation and planning, but it is this planning and preparation that will also ensure maximum flexibility.

Case study: Land of Leather

Land of Leather explains why it ultimately chose the IPO route, having considered the other options available to it.

Land of Leather's experience

The UK's second-largest leather sofa retailer, Land of Leather, floated in July 2005 in a tough retail climate. Fundamental to the float's success was establishing the business's suitability for float and the investor appetite. Another significant challenge was convincing analysts that Land of Leather had a strong growth proposition despite the numerous retail failures dominating the media. Finance Director Clive Hatchard explains.

Why we floated

We took the decision to float to provide an exit for our venture capitalist (VC). Our VC had invested in Land of Leather as part of a grand plan to consolidate the furniture sector. They already had Furniture Land, they had 50 per cent of us and they wanted to bring together £500–600 million of turnover into one group because the furniture sector is quite fragmented, and then they were going to float the whole thing. It became quite evident to us that they weren't going to go through with their strategy, as they were missing out on big groups that were in play. So we went to them and suggested the float.

Testing the waters

Once we'd decided to float we spent a day with Ernst & Young at one of their bespoke Float Rooms™. Five partners and our management team tested our suitability for IPO. They tested the business in terms of the market competition and future trends. They questioned our management team on both the business reasons and our personal reasons for floating. They talked about the shareholder objectives and how we were going to align those and helped to pressure-test whether flotation was the right exit or whether we should be taking a different route.

It is important to only kick off the float process if you know that you are going to get to the end game. When you start the process you open a can of worms in terms of people's emotions. Everybody suddenly wants to take that next step and leave their private environment to become a public company. And that is probably half of the pressure pot that you put yourself in. You don't want to go back having failed and try to reassemble a jigsaw from a pile of pieces with very different objectives.

Testing the investment appetite

We went for a pilot fishing trip because the retail environment was so bad. We did a mini-roadshow – eight presentations – and we got seven out of eight saying they would play at the right price. The most disinterested, stony-faced investors can often be your best investors, and those who appear to love you, are really engaged and ask all the questions often don't invest.

Timing it right

We had a strong growth story to take to market. Over the prior three years our financials showed £80 million, £100 million and £156 million in turnover. Profits had quadrupled. The trends looked good.

Making money is all about timing. Our figures were perfect for float. I didn't want to risk waiting another year that might be stagnant or show a contraction in growth – and then your record looks horrible so it takes another three years to get into a position to float again.

Timing it right also requires a decent future of growth – don't leave it too late, until after the business is exhausted or near the end of your growth trajectory. We had very obvious medium-term growth prospects. The market was growing, leather was still a popular product and we had a very simple store roll-out plan. You can't go to market having already exhausted all the obvious gains.

Challenges

The short period between buy-out and float was an initial concern for investors. We found the market was very cynical about venture capital-owned companies. They think venture capitalists know exactly when to get in and when to get out, so there is always concern that the market will be left with the baby.

We had the additional challenge of trying to float in a tough retail climate, with newspapers splashed cover to cover with stories about retail doom and gloom.

The first thing we had to do in each presentation was explain why we were coming to market one year after an MBO and in a depressed retail environment. We had to show that our value proposition had potential and we had to educate the market that buying patterns had changed and sofas are now more disposable products.

Benefits for management

Beyond the obvious prospect of capital gain, float represented an opportunity to retain control rather than selling the business. Some of the team had been there since we'd had three stores, and had grown it to 72. The business was their baby and they wanted to see it through and to be able to look back and say 'I created that'. And for some of us, including me, it was the next challenge. We'd done private, we'd done venture capital, and the next step was to play in the public arena.

What we learnt

- The right broker/analyst is vital.
- Get to know the sales team.
- Get a good company secretary.
- Invest in a good chairman.
- Pick non-execs with a name in the City.
- Appoint a project director to run company involvement.
- Use experienced advisers.
- Do what you can up front:
  - recruitment;
  - tax planning;
  - share option schemes;
  - committees/governance rules;
  - alignment of shareholder expectations;
  - due diligence;
  - property/pensions/legal due diligence.

Land of Leather is the UK's second-largest retailer of leather sofas. The group currently trades from 85 retail outlets in the UK and the Republic of Ireland. In July 2005, the company floated on the Main Market of the London Stock Exchange as Land of Leather Holdings plc with a market capitalization of £77.5 million. Since flotation, the company has rolled out 18 additional store locations.

II

Alternative markets

5

The regulatory framework

Martin Shaw and Robert Moir, Pinsent Masons

Introduction – basic choices

A company that is seeking to float and have its shares publicly traded has the choice of a variety of markets. The choice of market will be influenced by a range of factors, including the following:

- the level of regulation and/or the degree of disclosure required by a particular market;
- the entry requirements of a particular market;
- the profile of the companies listed on that market;
- access to potential investors; and
- the relevance of the market to the company's business.

The potential markets include the London Stock Exchange (LSE)'s Main Market for listed securities (coupled with a listing on the UK Listing Authority's Official List), AIM (also operated by the London Stock Exchange) and Easdaq (aimed at high-growth companies with total assets of €3.5 million and €2.0 million of capital and reserves). Overseas choices include Easdaq's US cousin, NASDAQ, and the markets operated by continental exchanges such as EURO.NM. Each has its own rule book and pool of typical investors.

For a significant UK company that falls outside the fairly limited scope of Easdaq, the primary choice is likely to be between a listing on the Official List coupled with admission to trading on the London Stock Exchange's Main Market (referred to as 'full listing'), and a listing on AIM.

The London markets have many advantages for companies over the alternative European markets – in particular, a higher profile (particularly in the United States), a proven track record of attracting companies and investors, critical mass, a concentrated pool of investors in the Square Mile, and investor confidence engendered by a well-regulated market.

London Stock Exchange plc

The London Stock Exchange plc ('the Exchange') is one of the world's oldest and largest stock exchanges. The Main Market comprises those securities admitted to the Official List by the Financial Services Authority (FSA) acting through its division the UK Listing Authority (UKLA). The listing of such securities is subject to the FSA Listing Rules (and related admission and disclosure standards), the Prospectus Rules, the Disclosure Rules and the Transparency Rules.

The Exchange has introduced 'sub'-markets within the Main Market: techMark, extraMark and AIM.

techMark

In November 1999, the LSE introduced techMark, to bring together both listed and new innovative technology companies, cutting across industrial sectors and size bands. techMark acts as a market within a market, rather than as a separate trading platform – grouping together companies from a wide range of FTSE industrial sectors into a market with its own identity and its own FTSE indices.

The introduction of techMark involved the creation of a new market segment for the techMark companies, the development of new indices that include only techMark companies and the introduction of Listing Rules for certain categories of companies that do not have a three-year track record.

The introduction of techMark was intended to have the following effects:

■ investors to be able to target technology stocks more easily, without having to pick through individual sectors;
■ the pricing of technology stocks to be more uniform; and
■ new (and smaller) applicants to be seen alongside their more established and larger technology counterparts.

Application for listing under the Listing Rules and application for inclusion in techMark are two separate processes. The UKLA will make its own decision as to whether a particular company should be listed under the Listing Rules. The decision as to whether to include a particular company in the techMark index will be a decision made by the LSE in consultation with a body of individuals within City institutions known as the Technology Advisory Group.

extraMark

In 2000, the Stock Exchange created a new market called extraMark for innovative investment companies and products to provide investors with special investment opportunities.

AIM

AIM is the Exchange's Alternative Investment Market and was launched in 1995. AIM is a separate and alternative London market for new or small companies.

AIM was developed to meet the needs of the smaller, growing companies that might not meet the full criteria for a listing on the Main Market or for which a more flexible regulatory environment is more appropriate. The entry criteria for AIM make it possible to gain admission without a trading record, an established management team or any minimum market capitalization.

AIM is not bound by the Listing Rules and, since October 2004, has not been an EU 'regulated market' to which more onerous rules attach. AIM has a bespoke (and shorter) set of rules and AIM companies benefit from a more flexible regulatory environment. This can act as a stepping stone for those companies that ultimately aspire to the Main Market.

The AIM Rules cover admission requirements, such as the free transferability of shares, public company status and use of recognized accountancy standards. Unlike the position under the Listing Rules, there is no minimum trading record or percentage of shares required to be in public hands. The AIM Rules also cover continuing obligations, general disclosure obligations, changes in broad structure, and transactions outside the ordinary course of business that are entered into by AIM companies. Unlike companies subject to the Listing Rules, AIM companies do not need to obtain shareholder approval for transactions other than reverse takeovers or fundamental disposals.

However, because AIM companies are young companies, the AIM Rules provide that the companies must at all times have a nominated adviser and a nominated broker who also owe duties to the Exchange, and detailed histories of the directors are to be set out in the company's admission document and on any appointment of a director.

The choice between the Main Market and AIM is largely a question of the company's size and the stage of its cycle. Assuming the decision is taken to launch the IPO on the LSE, the company's advisers can advise whether the company is more suitable for listing on the Main Market or on AIM.

Legal framework

The legal and regulatory issues in relation to the marketing of securities (principally a company's ordinary shares) in the UK are detailed and complex. Therefore, the chapters of this book are restricted to considering regulatory issues relating to a full listing and a quotation on AIM. They do not deal with the offer of securities by a private or foreign company, by a public company prior to its obtaining a listing (for example, to effect venture capital investment) or by a listed company where such securities are not themselves to be listed. The regulatory framework regarding the trading and transfer of already-issued listed and unlisted securities is also outside the scope of this work.

The marketing of securities in the UK is regulated by the Financial Service and Markets Act 2000 (FSMA), which replaced the Financial Services Act 1986. The FSMA has been implemented by a significant amount of secondary legislation introduced during 2001 and 2005. In very broad terms, shares may only be offered to the public in the UK (which has a much wider definition than might be expected) where a prospectus has been prepared and approved by the FSA under the Prospectus Regulations 2005 and related Prospectus Rules (with which the AIM Rules comply).

Furthermore, all listed companies are subject to the FSMA 'market abuse' provisions, which prevent the creation of a false or misleading impression in the market relating to the securities of the company or the manipulation of that market, and the misuse of unpublished price-sensitive information. The latter is also caught by the Criminal Justice Act 1993 'insider dealing' offences. A detailed commentary of this legislation is also outside the scope of this work.

UKLA and the Listing Rules

FSMA confers powers on the Financial Services Authority to make and administer rules for the granting of 'listed' status to securities by admission to listing pursuant to Part VI of the Act and by their inclusion on the 'Official List'. The FSA, which is the super-regulator for the financial services industry in the UK, operates through its division known as the United Kingdom Listing Authority in relation to listed securities; its rules are known as the 'Listing Rules'.

A two-stage admission process applies to companies that want to have their securities admitted to the London Stock Exchange's market for listed securities. Application first needs to be made to the FSA, through the UKLA, for the relevant securities to be admitted to the Official List in compliance with the Listing Rules. Second, application needs to be made to the LSE for the relevant listed securities to be admitted to trading on its market for listed securities.

It is only once both of these processes have been completed, and admission to the listing and to trading has become effective, that the securities are officially listed on the LSE. It is a condition of the Listing Rules that, to be listed, securities must be admitted to trading on the LSE.

AIM

The rules of AIM in relation to admission are based in large part on the Prospectus Rules drawn up under the Prospectus Regulations 2005, even though a formal prospectus is no longer required for admission to AIM unless a public offer of securities is made. Once admitted to AIM, companies are required to comply with the continuing obligation requirements under the AIM Rules.

Role of the London Stock Exchange

London Stock Exchange plc has responsibility for admitting companies and their listed securities to trading on the market for listed securities operated by the LSE. The LSE also operates and regulates AIM.

The Stock Exchange is currently the only operator of a market in listed securities in the UK, but the segregation of its role as 'competent authority' and 'market operator' recognizes that other markets for listed securities in the UK, such as NASDAQ Europe, could be created in competition.

Status of the Listing Rules and AIM Rules

It is worth noting that neither the Listing Rules nor the AIM Rules constitute 'laws' as such, and breach of them does not of itself constitute a criminal offence. A breach of these Rules can, however, still have serious commercial and legal consequences for a company and its directors involved, and these are examined in greater detail in Chapter 21.

Admission criteria

Main Market

The main regulatory requirements a company must meet to obtain a Main Market listing are as follows:

■ *Incorporation.* There must have been a formal incorporation as a distinct legal entity under the laws of the appropriate jurisdiction – in the case of a UK company, this means that plc status must have been obtained.
■ *Accounts and trading.* The company must have three years' published or filed consolidated accounts, audited to a period ending no more than six months before the float, which demonstrate trading and revenue earning during that period.
■ *Directors.* The company's directors and senior management must be able to demonstrate the right level of skills and experience to run the business and must be free of any conflict of interest that could interfere with this.
■ *Working capital.* The company must demonstrate, backed up by an accountants' report, that it has sufficient working capital for current needs and for the next 12 months.
■ *Public holding of shares.* At least 25 per cent of the company's shares must generally be held by the public (which excludes, for example, the directors, related pension funds or employee share schemes).

■ *Market capitalization.* The minimum acceptable market capitalization for shares is £700,000 (although, in practice, it will have to be substantially higher for the float to be economically viable).
■ *Free transferability.* The company's shares must be freely transferable without restriction.

The requirements for a three-year track record are relaxed to allow 'scientific research based companies' to obtain a full listing if at least £10 million is being raised where it can be demonstrated that funds can be obtained from 'sophisticated investors'. Certain other criteria must also be met in terms of market capitalization and information to be included in the prospectus and regarding continuing obligations (including quarterly financial reporting).

A company seeking a Main Market listing must engage a sponsor/listing agent whose identity is acceptable to the FSA, which must supervise the application process and confirm suitability of the applicant to the FSA.

Assuming these conditions are in place, the company can then proceed to prepare a prospectus or listing particulars required for the listing to take effect, providing the very detailed information specified in the Listing Rules and Prospectus Rules about the company, its business, management, capital structure and ownership, and the shares being listed.

AIM

AIM is marketed as the Stock Exchange's public market for smaller, younger and growing companies and, as such, its application criteria and continuing obligations are more relaxed than for the Main Market (making it potentially much less attractive for certain kinds of investor).

The principal admission requirements are:

■ incorporation as a plc (for a UK company);
■ the appointment of a nominated adviser and nominated broker (equivalent in many respects to a sponsor on the Main Market);
■ the prior publication of at least one set of audited accounts; and
■ shares that are freely transferable.

Where a company has been generating revenue for less than two years, substantial shareholders (holding 10 per cent or more), directors and their associates, and all employees who hold an interest of 0.5 per cent or more in the company's shares, must agree not to sell any interests they may have in those shares for at least one year after joining AIM.

Having fulfilled these requirements, a company may proceed to prepare its admission document in accordance with the AIM Rules, with more limited information to be included than for a full listing unless an offer to the public is made.

Having 'floated' and achieved a listing on the Main Market or AIM, a company will then have to ensure that it complies with the 'continuing obligations' under the AIM Rules; these are examined in Part IV.

6

Alternative stock exchanges

Colin Aaronson, Grant Thornton Corporate Finance

Summary

As one of the most important capital markets in the world, the London Stock Exchange finds practically no company or fund-raising too large for it.

For smaller companies wanting a quotation, but that are neither ready nor willing to bear the cost of a flotation, there are alternatives.

In most cases, it is hard to find a reason for a UK company to go elsewhere; indeed, costs of compliance and information requirements on NASDAQ illustrate why increasing numbers of US companies are considering listing in London.

Introduction

London has one of the largest and most sophisticated capital markets in the world, and provides a stock market for some of its largest companies. Given the substantial funds available and the convenience of a local market, it is not common for a UK company to list anywhere other than London.

However, during the second half of the 1990s, and particularly during the few years before the collapse of the TMT sector, 'technology' companies from around the world sought to float on NASDAQ, including ambitious UK technology companies that saw AIM as a stepping stone to that market. The decline in technology stocks after spring 2000, on NASDAQ and elsewhere, made it more difficult to raise money for young technology businesses. Combined with the success of

AIM, this has meant that considerably fewer UK companies see NASDAQ as a viable alternative to London. This realization may have contributed to NASDAQ's decision to acquire Easdaq, a Belgium-based pan-European exchange, in 2001.

As discussed elsewhere in this book, institutional investors are increasingly thinking in pan-European terms, and national markets are combining to reflect this trend. Euronext was the result of the mergers of the French, Dutch and Belgian markets, and the London Stock Exchange has been seen by some as a potential merger partner for a number of overseas exchanges. These markets will be competing for business and, for larger companies operating across Europe, a flotation overseas may be attractive.

There are also alternatives for smaller companies wanting a quotation. The Main Market or even AIM may not be appropriate, or the costs of listing may simply be judged unacceptable or unnecessary. For such companies, the main UK-based alternative market is the PLUS market.

The success of AIM

At the end of April 2007, AIM was home to 1,639 companies, of which 304 were registered overseas. Part of the recent growth – there were only 524 companies at the end of 2000 – has come from mining and exploration companies that have been established to capitalize on the recent rise in the price of natural resources and the growth in demand forecast to come from China and elsewhere. Another part of the recent growth has come from companies transferring from the Main Market or opting for AIM in preference to the Main Market. There are a number of reasons for this, including the comparative ease with which AIM companies can undertake corporate transactions and the favourable tax treatment given to AIM companies as compared to those on the Main Market. AIM companies are regarded as being 'unquoted' for UK tax purposes, enabling them to source funding from tax-favoured investors such as venture capital trusts. AIM has also become home to a wider range of funds investing in assets ranging from overseas property to green technology.

Overseas companies from several different jurisdictions have been joining AIM in increasing numbers. AIM has also admitted to trading a number of overseas companies that have been attracted specifically by the fast-track admission process for which companies listed on certain overseas AIM designated markets, such as NASDAQ and the Australian Stock Exchange, are eligible. It is widely believed that AIM is now unlikely to be surpassed as the international market of choice for smaller growing companies. However, there can be no assurance that AIM companies will continue to receive favourable tax treatment; should that situation change, other UK markets such as PLUS (assuming that PLUS companies continue to receive favourable tax treatment) may become attractive to smaller UK companies. But, for the time being, PLUS is seen by many as a stepping stone on the way to AIM.

PLUS is discussed in more detail in Chapter 8 and a third market, ShareMark, is discussed in Chapter 9.

AIM or PLUS?

Floating on AIM is more expensive than joining PLUS, and the ongoing costs are generally higher. However, considerably fewer institutional investors have previously invested in PLUS companies, which means that there are significantly larger funds available to companies on AIM.

The market for AIM shares would appear to be more liquid than for PLUS shares, but this is more a reflection of the size of companies that are attracted to it and the number of shares available for public trading. PLUS may therefore be appropriate when a company wants to list on a public market specifically designed for smaller companies, at a lower cost than on AIM, or perhaps as its first venture into the public arena.

PLUS and AIM have not traditionally seen each other as rivals. They were designed to satisfy different needs and see themselves as being appropriate for different stages of a public company's life. PLUS is regarded by many as a good training ground for a small company starting life as a publicly quoted company, with lower costs than AIM but with a view to graduating to AIM.

Overseas alternatives

A UK company whose business is predominantly overseas or that is of particular interest to overseas investors might consider listing overseas, either as a dual listing or even alone. For example, a number of AIM listed natural resource companies are quoted overseas as well as in London.

There are a number of reasons why a company might consider listing on a foreign market:

- to achieve a higher valuation;
- to provide easier access for local investors and achieve greater liquidity;
- to improve visibility within a particular market; and
- in certain circumstances, to access funds that might not be available in the UK.

Given the size of the domestic capital market – and the clear attractions of London and AIM in particular to overseas companies – UK companies seeking a listing overseas will almost certainly have investors question their motives, particularly if fund-raising is involved. The only circumstances in which the company will normally be able to justify its decision to float overseas are if it has foreign investors, customers or suppliers.

A dual listing has all the advantages listed above, but it also has a number of disadvantages. These include:

- the extra time taken to travel overseas to meetings with analysts and investors;
- higher costs arising from the different listing requirements of both markets and the greater amount of compliance work that is required;

■ announcements having to be timed with care to ensure that a piece of price-sensitive information that has been released to one market has also been released to the other. This problem is most likely to occur when the two markets are in significantly distant time zones, such as Sydney and London.

For a company that is prepared to bear the additional cost of floating overseas and can benefit from the advantages such a listing offers, there are a number of overseas markets to choose from. There are over 30 new markets around the world, half of which are in Europe, with most of the rest being in the Asia Pacific region. The largest new market in the world is NASDAQ, which is significantly larger than AIM in terms of both total market capitalization (over 20 times larger) and average capitalization per company. Even though comparisons are distorted by the presence on NASDAQ of companies such as Microsoft and Google, it is clear that NASDAQ is generally better suited to larger companies (say, with market capitalizations in excess of £500 million), where the higher valuations accorded to such companies may outweigh the costs of Sarbanes–Oxley compliance. Instead, AIM continues to plug the funding gap for companies too small to be properly catered for on other markets.

Admission requirements

Most new markets cater for local companies. The four main growth markets that a UK company might consider are AIM, NASDAQ, Alternext, which is part of Euronext (which itself has merged with the New York Stock Exchange), and PLUS. AIM, Alternext and PLUS do all have one significant advantage over NASDAQ and that is the lower cost of joining and increasingly the cost of ongoing membership and compliance.

In the past, UK companies might have considered the German Neuer Markt, which emerged as the European brand leader for technology stocks. However, with its reputation tarnished by reported failings of market regulation, the decision was taken to close it in 2002. AIM remains the leading European market for growth companies, although its companies are on average considerably smaller than on NASDAQ. The admission requirements for these markets are set out in Table 6.1.

Alternext was created with a view to replicating the growth market characteristics of AIM and has a number of features in common with it. In the two years since Alternext was founded in May 2005 it has attracted over 90 companies (including its first from North America) and has a market capitalization of approximately 5 billion. It is also seeking to attract the sort of international companies, particularly from China, that have been listing on AIM. However, whether it can genuinely compete with AIM as the leading growth market, even with the benefit of the NYSE brand, remains to be seen.

Table 6.1 The four main growth markets for UK companies

	AIM	NASDAQ	Alternext	PLUS
Total number of shares offered to the public	No minimum requirement	Minimum of 400 shareholders with a minimum of 1.1 million shares publicly held with a minimum market value of US$8 million to US$20 million, depending on listing route	2.5 million in public hands	No minimum requirement
Initial equity	No minimum requirement	US$0–30 million, depending on listing route	No minimum requirement	No minimum requirement
Market capitalization	No minimum requirement	US$0–75 million, depending on listing route	No minimum requirement	No minimum requirement
Trading history	No minimum requirement	0–2 years depending on listing route	2 years	No minimum requirement
Profitability	No minimum requirement	No minimum requirement	No minimum requirement	No minimum requirement

7

AIM

Martin Graham, London Stock Exchange

Introduction

For ambitious small companies in search of funds to fuel growth, a stock market flotation is an important – and potentially life-altering – consideration. Going public is one of the most critical choices in any company's development and much thought should be given to this key step. At the London Stock Exchange, we have a wealth of experience working with smaller growing companies that want to secure new investment via a quotation on AIM. Since AIM was launched 12 years ago, we have helped over 2,800 firms take their place on the public stage, raising a total of over £49 billion in the process. As at the end of June 2007, a total of 1,656 companies are quoted on AIM, including 304 international firms, with a total market value of over £109 billion. The number of firms choosing AIM is growing all the time. During 2006, a total of 462 companies joined AIM, and a total of £9.9 billion was raised in new issues with an additional £5.7 billion raised through further issues. AIM's continued ability to attract investors is reflected in the fact that almost as much money was raised on AIM in 2006, a record £15.7 billion, as in the previous three years combined – two of which were already record years for AIM fund-raising. Access to investors is a crucial factor in AIM's appeal, but not the only one. The ability to diversify the investor base, improve public profile, increase brand awareness and stimulate opportunities for growth are significant attractions.

In this chapter we explore the regulatory and other characteristics that have enabled AIM to establish itself as the world's leading market for smaller growing companies and look at the benefits and obligations of a quotation for a growing company, with particular reference to AIM.

Why a public flotation?

As an integral part of the portfolio of markets offered by the London Stock Exchange, AIM provides quoted companies with access to London's substantial and diverse investor base, which represents one of the largest pools of capital available anywhere worldwide. Notwithstanding London's access to investors and capital, a firm must first decide whether going public is the most appropriate funding source. If it is merely looking for funding, there are a number of potentially appropriate routes. The following are common reasons for choosing a stock market flotation above other funding options:

- *access to capital for growth* – the opportunity to raise finance both at the time of flotation and later, through further capital raisings;
- *creating a market for the company's shares* – broadening the shareholder base as well as giving existing shareholders an objective market valuation;
- *encouraging long-term employee commitment* – by making share schemes more attractive;
- *increasing M&A opportunities* – using quoted shares as currency;
- *heightening profile and status with customers and suppliers* – through both press coverage and a recognition of the obligations of a public market flotation.

Being a quoted company means change. Therefore firms should consider carefully the issues involved in joining a public market. There are responsibilities as well as benefits. People at every level of the business, from board members to employees, must be ready to accept the disciplines inherent in having shares traded publicly and in having outside shareholders whose interests must be taken into account. In particular, companies should be aware that flotation on a public market brings with it an exposure to the uncertainty of market conditions. A company's share price may be affected by a number of factors beyond its control, including market sentiment, economic conditions or developments in the same sector.

Flotation will inevitably lead to closer scrutiny of the company, its performance and its directors. In general, the board must be prepared for greater exposure and openness, both in terms of the company's finances and business strategy and in having to make prompt announcements about new developments, whether positive or negative. Investor relations activities can help increase demand for the company's shares and ensure that its flotation is as successful as possible.

AIM's regulatory regime and reporting obligations are designed to balance the needs of growing companies with those of the investors who support those companies. This approach remains at the core of evolutionary regulatory changes AIM announced in February 2007, designed to maintain the right regulatory balance as the market continues to grow and thrive internationally.

So what types of firms join AIM? Quoted firms include a diverse spectrum of businesses, with 38 sectors currently represented, ranging from young, venture capital-backed companies to more established businesses looking to expand further. AIM companies' backgrounds are also increasingly diverse: 319 international companies are quoted at present.

In principle, any company can seek a public market quotation, but what AIM quoted firms have in common is a sense that the investor base and regulatory environment suit their stage of development, size or type of business. For a small or young firm, simpler regulations are a clear attraction. Easier acquisition rules make growth through acquisition quicker and less costly, and AIM's unquoted status for tax purposes could be an advantage for some companies. The main differences between AIM and the London Stock Exchange's Main Market are as shown in Table 7.1.

Table 7.1 Differences between the Main Market and AIM

Main Market	AIM
Minimum 25 per cent shares in public hands.	No prescribed minimum shares to be in public hands.
Normally three-year trading record required.	No formal trading record requirement.
Prior shareholder approval required for substantial acquisitions and disposals.	No prior shareholder approval for most transactions.*
Pre-vetting of admission documents by the UKLA.	Admission documents not pre-vetted by the Exchange nor by the UKLA in most circumstances. The UKLA will only vet an AIM admission document where it is also a prospectus under the Prospectus Directive.
Sponsors needed for certain transactions.	Nominated adviser required at all times.
Minimum market capitalization.	No minimum market capitalization.

* Not applicable to reverse takeovers or disposal resulting in a fundamental change of business.

AIM: an international market

AIM's approach has always been led by the principle that smaller firms need a market tailored to their needs. Since 2000, we have exported this vision in the belief that new international issuers and investors will further stimulate the market as a whole. Our convictions have been borne out by growth in recent years; 750 firms were quoted on AIM in 2003, compared with 1,656 in June 2007. In 2006, a total of 334 new companies were admitted and a total of £9.9 billion was raised in new issues. It was also a record year in terms of money raised in further issues: £5.7 billion; total money raised: £15.7 billion; and the total value of shares traded: £58 billion. These figures were all record figures by a significant margin.

Foreign firms – and investors – have been attracted by the fact that AIM caters specifically for smaller companies: there were 124 new international joiners in 2006, taking the total to 304 overseas companies from some 27 countries. Firms from English-speaking countries have always been attracted but now AIM includes many Chinese, Russian and Eastern European firms, as well as 110 companies from the Western European area, with a combined market value of over £1.1 billion.

AIM has always had a healthy proportion of retail investors, but its ability to attract institutional investors has been integral to recent growth. Large institutional investors invest in a diverse range of industry sectors, with their exposure to growth stocks having grown year on year since 2003. In recent years, the continued growth in trading of AIM securities has been supported by the introduction of a number of new indices designed to attract additional investment into AIM, and thereby improve liquidity, by improving investors' ability to benchmark AIM securities.

In 2005, a new FTSE AIM Index Series was launched, composed of the FTSE AIM UK 50 Index, FTSE AIM 100 Index and FTSE AIM All-Share Index. In May 2006 these were joined by the FTSE AIM All-Share Supersector Indices, which are derived from the FTSE AIM All-Share Index and are based on the Industry Classification Benchmark (ICB). The new Supersector Indices provide investors with 18 new sector indices for AIM, helping them to identify macroeconomic opportunities for investment and trading decisions and to differentiate between the performance of Main Market and AIM companies in a given supersector. At the same time, the fact that the constituents of the FTSE AIM UK 50 can be traded on SETSmm, the Exchange's hybrid order book/market maker trading system, brings even greater liquidity to an already thriving market.

These innovations in AIM's index coverage and trading are helping to boost institutional interest and investment in AIM, with the result that almost every institutional investor now has exposure to the market. In 2003 a survey by *Growth Company Investor* found that 35 per cent of AIM shares were in the hands of institutions. The same survey in 2006 found that figure to be 56.7 per cent, confirming AIM's transformation from a retail-dominated market to a professional market in the space of a few years.

AIM's regulatory approach and joining AIM

While AIM's regulation is targeted at balancing the needs of smaller companies with those of the investors that support them, seeking a quotation brings a number of requirements. Generally, a company seeking admission to AIM will be required to produce an admission document, which will contain disclosures about areas such as background on the company's directors, the company's strategy, its financial position and its working capital. The admission document is designed to enable prospective investors to make an informed decision, and directors are responsible for its accuracy and for ensuring there are no material omissions. The contents required for an AIM admission document are based on a standard known as 'AIM-PD', which is itself based on the Prospectus Directive, the standard applied to companies seeking admission of their securities to an EU regulated market, and to any company carrying out a public offer above certain thresholds. AIM-PD was introduced by the Exchange in July 2005 and is based on the contents of the Prospectus Directive with certain sections 'carved out' as they were deemed inappropriate for smaller companies.

In addition, via the AIM Rules the Exchange has stipulated additional requirements to provide extra information to the market to ensure sufficient visibility for investors and ensure that there is orderly trading in a company's shares. Companies must ensure they comply with disclosure obligations on an ongoing basis after joining AIM. In response to ongoing changes in the global marketplace, the London Stock Exchange has continued to make targeted amendments to the AIM Rules to ensure all the objectives outlined above continue to be met.

With this in mind, following a consultation process launched in 2006, the Exchange introduced a number of changes to the AIM Rules in February 2007. These changes clarified nominated advisers' duties in relation to their AIM companies, and included a new requirement that every AIM company must have a website containing basic information about its business. At this time the Exchange introduced a new rule book, *The AIM Rules for Nominated Advisers*, which updated and enhanced the eligibility criteria for Nomads and set out the core responsibilities that the Exchange expects a nomad to satisfy. Also introduced were refinements to the *AIM Disciplinary Procedures and Appeals Handbook*, providing clearer guidance on the Exchange's approach to dealing with breaches of the AIM Rules.

In line with the AIM Rules, companies must take the following steps before they can be admitted to trading on the market:

- Appoint an approved nominated adviser ('Nomad').
- Appoint a broker.
- Have no restrictions on the free transferability of its shares.
- Be registered as a plc (public limited company) or equivalent – and be legally established under the laws of its country of origin.
- Prepare an admission document.
- Pay a fee according to the current tariff to the Exchange.

Ultimately, the key entry criterion is that a firm is considered appropriate for the market by its Nomad, a firm of experienced corporate finance professionals approved by the Exchange. The first step for a firm that has decided it wants to join AIM is to appoint a Nomad to support its application and to help it meet the AIM requirements on a continuing basis. The nomad will explain the AIM Rules to the company's board and ensure that the directors are aware of their responsibilities and obligations. Directors are ultimately responsible for their company's compliance with AIM's regulations, including the accuracy of the information in the admission document. Once the company has been admitted to AIM, the Nomad will continue to give ongoing advice and guidance on the AIM Rules. Should the AIM company cease to have a Nomad, trading in its securities will be suspended until a new Nomad has been appointed.

An AIM applicant will also need a broker, a securities house that is a member of the London Stock Exchange, which may be the same firm as the Nomad (if the company so chooses and the firm is an approved Nomad). The broker will play an important role in bringing together buyers and sellers of the company's shares and in making a success of both the flotation and the aftermarket trading. Other professional services required by an AIM quoted firm include a legal adviser (to oversee due diligence on behalf of the Nomad, changes to directors' contracts and verification of the statements in the admission document, etc), reporting accountants (to conduct an independent review of the company's financial record and prepare financial information) and investor relations advisers to manage the flow of information during the flotation.

Non-UK companies can join AIM via a streamlined process once their securities have traded on one of 10 AIM 'designated markets' without having to publish an admission document. Companies using the fast-track route to AIM need to make a detailed pre-admission announcement (assuming there is no public offer of securities also taking place) – making the admission process simpler.

Current AIM designated markets are:

- Australian Stock Exchange;
- Deutsche Börse;
- Euronext;
- Johannesburg Stock Exchange;
- NASDAQ;
- New York Stock Exchange;
- Stockholmsbörsen;
- Swiss Exchange;
- Toronto Stock Exchange;
- UK Official List (as issued by the UK Listing Authority).

The pre-admission announcement should include:

- confirmation that the company has adhered to the legal and regulatory requirements of the relevant AIM designated market;
- details of the business of the company and its intended strategy following admission;
- a description of significant changes in the financial or trading position of the company since the date to which the last audited accounts were prepared;
- a statement that the directors have no reason to believe that the company's working capital will be insufficient for at least 12 months from the date of its admission to AIM;
- the rights attaching to, and the arrangements for settling transactions in, the shares being admitted;
- any other information that has not been made public that would otherwise be required of an AIM applicant; and
- the address of a website containing the company's latest published annual report and accounts, which must have a financial year end not more than nine months prior to admission.

Day one of trading – and beyond

Once a firm has decided to join AIM, chosen its advisers and met the regulatory requirements, the admission process can begin. Under the timetable for joining AIM, an announcement of the company's intention to float on the market must be made, via the Exchange, at least 10 business days before the start of trading in the shares (or 20 business days if joining from a designated market). The application form signed by the applicant company and admission document together with a form of declaration signed by the Nomad must then be submitted at least three business days before admission to trading.

Once a company has joined AIM, it becomes subject to new and distinct disciplines, designed to keep shareholders fully informed of the company's development. The company's close involvement with the investment community during the admission process must continue after its shares have been admitted to AIM. The guiding principle is that the company must communicate with the market on a continuing basis, to ensure that the market is aware of its financial position and prospects, so as to enable investors to make an informed decision on the value of its shares.

Once the business is traded on AIM, there are also a number of continuing obligations that the company must fulfil in order to ensure an orderly market in its shares. Foremost among these is a requirement to notify the market immediately of any developments that could have an impact on the company's share price – such as corporate transactions, the progress of the company's business, and changes in directorships.

A business quoted on AIM must also ensure its published accounts conform to International Accounting Standards or US, Canadian or Japanese GAAP, and must be published within the required deadlines – which are within six months of the financial year end for audited annual accounts, and within three months of the end of the half-year for unaudited interim accounts. The company's directors and employees must also comply with certain restrictions on their freedom to trade in the company's shares while in possession of unpublished information.

By definition, the most dynamic growth stocks will not remain AIM quoted in perpetuity. Many firms will eventually consider whether AIM will continue to support the next steps in their business plans or whether graduation to the Main Market will help realize their future ambitions. More than 100 companies have graduated to the Main Market to date. There are no hard-and-fast rules about when companies should consider this step, and many firms continue to flourish on AIM long after their initial offering. In the first three months of 2007 alone, there were 791 further issues conducted by existing quoted firms on AIM, raising a total of almost £1.7 billion.

The outlook for AIM

In its first 12 years AIM has built a sound platform from which it can continue to offer smaller and growing companies from around the world all the benefits of a public quote, alongside the combination of lower costs and appropriate regulation. The London Stock Exchange is committed to maintaining and extending AIM's attractiveness to issuers in the UK and worldwide.

Whatever your business, wherever it is based and whatever its sphere of activity, if you are a young and growing or smaller company, AIM represents a viable route to a quote on one of the world's most prestigious markets. We believe you should take a closer look – as have the many companies that are continuing to join every year.

8

PLUS Markets Group

Nemone Wynn-Evans, PLUS Markets Group

Overview

PLUS Markets Group plc owns and operates the PLUS market, an independent equity market based in the City of London. It is regulated by the UK Financial Services Authority and is applying for recognized investment exchange status.

By the end of 2006, PLUS traded over 850 small- and mid-cap company shares, including around 200 quoted companies, representing a combined market capitalization of over £150 billion. During 2006 over half a million trades, worth a total of nearly £3 billion, representing over 5.75 billion shares, took place on PLUS.

The secondary market trading platform is based on a quote-driven model, the most efficient and effective system for trading shares in small- and mid-cap companies. Market markers commit their own capital to the market, playing a key role in providing both price formation and liquidity. Nearly 50 brokers and seven market makers are active on PLUS. Transaction data and current bid–offer information are shown electronically and distributed to the market via 10 data vendors.

PLUS is committed to providing investors with a market dedicated to offering quality investment opportunities. Investors are assured that PLUS is a select listing destination offering the best investment value, owing to stringent regulatory control and a particular focus on investor protection that has played a strong role in the company's business model.

PLUS competes directly with traditional exchanges with its offering of both listing and trading market services. Companies can access PLUS by having their

WELCOME

PLUS is the place to be for small and midcap companies.

Join the swell of support for the UK's only independent equity market.
Our unique regulatory framework and trading platform gives
exceptional ability to help growing companies prosper and flourish.

Want to know more?
Visit our website www.plusmarketsgroup.com

PLUS

Liquidity, choice, momentum

shares traded on the PLUS quote-driven trading platform, while listed or quoted elsewhere, or by being quoted on the PLUS primary market.

Reasons for floating your company

The most frequently named benefit of coming to a public market is the ability to raise equity finance, and PLUS has proven to be a successful source of equity finance for small and medium companies. Most importantly, the success of a public market is measured on the ability for existing issuers to be able to tap into the pool of capital and raise further funds to finance their growth.

A quotation on PLUS can achieve the following:

■ Enhance a company's profile, in particular with potential new customers who may become aware of your company for the first time. PLUS offers profile in a dedicated smaller companies marketplace.
■ Provide the wider market with the confidence that a company has gone through a rigorous scrutiny process. The disclosure requirements imposed on a PLUS quoted company show that it has appropriate systems and controls in place, has financial standing and has appropriate levels of management. This in turn could potentially allow a company to conduct business on more favourable terms with new partners or customers.
■ Provide an independent valuation for the business, allowing traded companies to use shares as an acquisition currency. This can be used for buying both private and quoted companies. It can also facilitate exit strategies; for example, a trade sale can be accelerated by the independent valuation achieved by the constant two-way pricing of traded stock.
■ Help existing shareholders – whether they are family members, founders or venture capitalists – to realize the value of their investment by providing a trading facility in the company's shares.
■ Support employee share schemes and share option schemes to incentivize, retain and motivate employees and to attract new employees. Having a visible and independent value for the company's shares may stimulate employee participation and engender long-term commitment to the business. For small entrepreneurial and family businesses, this can be a significant part of the benefits package to help to attract and retain highly skilled and motivated directors and senior employees.

Reasons for choosing PLUS

PLUS offers profile, liquidity, an audience receptive to growth and an environment where management can devote as much energy as possible to doing what their shareholders want them to do – to run the business. More importantly, the PLUS team are experts in understanding the needs of companies, their advisers and their investors.

Key benefits

- Access to raising funds from a deep capital pool of institutional and private investors.
- Greater access to UK retail investors who drive liquidity.
- Robust but less onerous due diligence process.
- Clear and straightforward admissions process where the PLUS regulation team works with the company's advisers during flotation.
- The PLUS regulation team applying the rules focused on investor protection through meticulous regulation with an uncomplicated, straightforward approach.
- Cost-effective access to the public markets, offering better value to companies and investors.

There are a number of tax benefits associated with holding PLUS quoted securities, including capital gains tax and inheritance tax reliefs, and eligibility for venture capital trusts and enterprise investment schemes. As a result of the Chancellor's increasing restriction on qualifying criteria for these schemes, many investors, including VCT funds, are investing in the kind of companies that would typically come to PLUS. PLUS quoted securities are also eligible for inclusion in self-invested pension plans (SIPPs).

When a company is ready for PLUS

The decision to be admitted to trading on any public market should be based on whether or not the objectives of a flotation will help in achieving the company's business goals. In making such a decision, a company should consider whether or not the business goals can be better achieved using alternative routes. A cost–benefit analysis might be undertaken and, in addition, the directors must also make an objective assessment of the company. This might include a review of its business plan and growth prospects, its stage of development, the management team and its internal procedures.

Objectives

Surveys illustrate that the main reason for companies to apply to be admitted to trading on a public market is to raise equity-based finance. There are alternative sources of finance provided by venture capitalists or banks or through private equity. Companies that choose to raise funds on a public market will have the additional responsibility of having to comply with the continuing obligations of that market. This means that a company is open to public scrutiny.

Business plan/track record

Companies that join the PLUS market typically have a proven business plan, are revenue generating and have a clear path to profitability. Investors will consider the financial track record of the company before making an investment decision and will want a detailed analysis of the growth prospects. In the case of new enterprises, a business plan will be required by PLUS.

Management team (including non-executive directors)

Investors will also consider the range and depth of a company's management team before making an investment decision. They will want to check that the board and senior management have the relevant experience to develop the company and will be looking for extensive industry expertise.

In addition, changes to the board may be necessary so that the company is managed appropriately and it can demonstrate suitable levels of corporate governance. Investors will want to fill in gaps that may appear in the management team of a company. For example, it is common practice to split the role of chairman and chief executive officer, to appoint a finance director and to add non-executive directors to the board.

The Institute of Directors (www.iod.co.uk) provides useful advice on corporate governance in the UK. Essentially, the role of the non-executive director 'is to provide a creative contribution to the Board by providing objective criticism'. The functions of non-executive directors are to bring independence, impartiality, wide experience, specialist knowledge and personal qualities. They are expected to focus on board matters, providing an independent view of the company that is removed from day-to-day running. They also determine the level of remuneration of executive directors.

Your internal control procedures

The flotation process and the continuing obligations mean that a publicly traded company has to have strong disclosure and reporting procedures. This will mean that appropriate management information systems as well as compliance controls need to be in place. In particular, companies are required under the PLUS Rules for Issuers to produce at least annual audited financial statements and semi-annuals.

Seeking admission to PLUS

PLUS is a disclosure-based market that is dedicated to the needs of small and medium-sized companies, especially when it comes to regulation. There is a clear and straightforward admission process, which means that there are no specific eligibility criteria but companies are required to satisfy certain standards.

Admission criteria

Companies seeking to become PLUS quoted companies need to fulfil the PLUS admission criteria and adhere to the PLUS Rules for Issuers before being admitted to the market. A company will need to accomplish the following:

- Appoint and retain at all times a PLUS corporate adviser. There is no requirement to retain a broker, but a company committed to investor relations and that is likely to use the market for further fund-raising is encouraged to do so.
- Demonstrate appropriate levels of corporate governance. In practice, this means that a company should have at least one independent non-executive director.
- Have published audited reports and accounts no more than nine months prior to the date of admission to trading.
- Have adequate working capital.
- Have no restrictions on the transferability of shares.
- Have shares that are eligible for electronic settlement.

The PLUS corporate adviser will act as the sponsor to the issue. PLUS corporate advisers are typically corporate finance boutiques, investment banks or accountancy practices. A number of other advisers will also need to be appointed to ensure the relevant documentation is produced, including solicitors, accountants, financial PR (if appropriate) and a registrar.

Process

Depending on the flotation objectives, a company can access the market via a number of different routes:

- *Introduction.* Companies that do not need to raise any funds but are simply looking to raise their profile or obtain an independent valuation of their business for employee share schemes, for example, can join by way of introduction. The PLUS corporate adviser files an admission announcement, together with completed application forms and supporting documentation to PLUS. This is the most straightforward way of joining the market.
- *Private placement.* This is for companies looking to raise funds from a select number of potential investors without requiring a full prospectus. Following the introduction of the Prospective Directive in July 2005, this can be to a maximum of 100 people. The PLUS corporate adviser files a private placement memo-randum for the shares to be admitted to trading. As the placing memorandum is not for public release, it does not have to go into as much detail as a full prospectus; therefore the cost of coming to market will be less than for an IPO.
- *Initial public offering (IPO).* A company wishing to raise money from the widest pool of investors available will need to produce a prospectus (unless the offering is less than 2.5 million). For an IPO of less than 2.5 million, a PLUS

admission document is required. This is the most expensive and time-consuming way of joining a public market, owing to the detail and the verification work that goes into producing a prospectus.

Joining PLUS can be more cost-effective than joining other markets, particularly for those companies looking to raise funds on debut of up to £5 million. Total admission costs by any of the routes described depend on the readiness of your company for a public market, eg whether restructuring is necessary, additional board members are required, the status needs to be changed from limited company to plc, etc. Companies considering joining the PLUS market should speak to a number of PLUS corporate advisers to obtain an accurate cost estimate.

The PLUS advisory team

The PLUS corporate adviser

The PLUS corporate adviser is a regulated member of PLUS and is authorized to bring companies to the market and provide advice on continuing obligations. The PLUS corporate adviser has an obligation to ensure that a company is suitable for the market and provide advice on the eligibility and disclosure obligations of the PLUS Rules for Issuers.

There are two categories of advisers – those with fund-raising capabilities and those without. If a company is seeking to raise funds when joining the market, it may want to choose an adviser with a broking facility in order to minimize flotation costs. The costs involved in the admission process vary from company to company, but usually amount to 5–10 per cent of funds raised.

When choosing a PLUS corporate adviser, it is recommended that a company meets with a number of advisers to discuss their approach to flotation, fee structures and what access they have to investors. As a great deal of time will be spent working closely together, both before the float and after, it is important that individuals at the company working on the float develop a good working relationship with their adviser. The adviser will also organize the roadshow to potential investors where a company will be required to present itself to people who may be interested in investing.

Once the PLUS corporate adviser has been chosen and instructed, an engagement letter is signed and an upfront deposit/instruction fee relating to the costs of flotation will be required. A further fee will be charged on a successful completion of the flotation process. Thereafter, a company is charged an annual retainer fee by the PLUS corporate adviser for continuing advice on complying with the Rules for Issuers.

The solicitor

The role of the solicitor is key through all stages of the float process. The solicitor's advice includes preparing the terms of engagement for the advisory team and advising on the preparation of the prospectus, admission document or private placement memorandum. The solicitor may also advise on any necessary constitutional changes such as limited company to plc status, review of the articles of association, etc, and on any changes that need to be made to the board.

The solicitor will carry out any necessary legal due diligence into the company and will oversee the verification process of any public document. It is this due diligence, in conjunction with the work carried out by a company's auditors, that will give the PLUS corporate adviser comfort that a company is suitable for trading on a public market.

In a flotation, the solicitor often fulfils two roles, acting both on behalf of the company and on behalf of the PLUS corporate adviser, for example preparing the placing agreement between the adviser and the company that governs any fundraising process.

The reporting accountant

The reporting accountant is responsible to both the company and the PLUS corporate adviser and will carry out the financial due diligence on the company. The principal documents that the reporting accountant will prepare are the working capital report, long-form report and possibly a pro forma statement of net assets.

Working capital report

This is a private document and is a review of the financial projections that are prepared by the company for the period following admission to trading. It supports the directors' statement made in the prospectus on the sufficiency of working capital for at least a 12-month period from the date of admission to PLUS.

Long-form report

This is a review of the historical activities of the company. The extent of the investigation and the level of detail required will be determined by the PLUS corporate adviser on the basis of his or her knowledge of the company, although it may include the following:

- corporate history and commercial activities;
- organizational structure and employees;
- trading results;
- assets and liabilities;
- cash flows;
- taxation;
- accounting policies and audit issues; and
- management information and control systems.

Pro forma statement of net assets

This might be necessary if there is an acquisition or restructuring at the same time as the admission, in order to provide meaningful information for investors. It illustrates the effect of the acquisition or restructuring on the assets and liabilities of the new group.

In addition to the above, the reporting accountant provides advice and assistance in respect of other matters, such as taxation and corporate structuring, and will liaise with the other professional advisers involved in the transaction to ensure its smooth progress.

The registrar

The registrar will have input into the application section of the prospectus and establishes the share register. During the fund-raising, the registrar will also receive applications and monies submitted. Once a company joins the market, the registrar maintains a record of the share register on an ongoing basis.

The financial PR/IR firm

Effective communications are indispensable to any company's success in achieving operational gains, raising profile and winning recognition for effective corporate strategies. Good company-to-investor communications have become a reliable benchmark for current investment audiences to judge how a business performs overall and for how future investors, employees and competitors will view the business.

In the past it was typical for larger listed companies to retain the services of a financial public relations (FPR) and investor relations (IR) consultancy. FPR advisers accurately communicate the benefits of the business and its stock to investment audiences through the media; IR advisers focus on developing company-to-shareholder relationships.

In recent times, however, as competition in the growth company arena has become more prevalent and opportunity for coverage and recognition has tightened, the need for small companies to use the advice and help of a communications consultancy has become an absolute necessity.

The best FPR/IR consultancies should have an excellent understanding of the growth company arena and your business model and ambitions, as well as having key media and City contacts UK-wide. Above all else, a good communications consultancy should have a myriad of case studies highlighting successes to date.

Life as a public company: continuing obligations

Companies quoted on PLUS must comply with the PLUS Rules for Issuers and ensure that the market is kept informed of any developments or any information that may have an impact on the financial situation of the company. All information must be disseminated via Newstrack PLUS, the in-house regulatory news service. The company's directors, in conjunction with the PLUS corporate adviser, are responsible for ensuring that the company complies with its continuing obligations.

Once admitted to the market, a company's shares are traded on PLUS and are visible to the market through leading data vendors, allowing investors to access a consolidated view of all UK trading activity.

Conclusion

PLUS is a market designed for small- and mid-cap companies. It offers a gateway to the London-based investment community, a pool of liquidity in which a rapidly growing number of shares are traded, and a regulatory environment suited to the needs of smaller quoted companies.

9

ShareMark

Emma Vigus, ShareMark

ShareMark was developed to be a simple, low-cost and flexible stock market. It aims to work together with companies and their shareholders to provide a stock market that works for everyone.

ShareMark is suited to companies with over 50 shareholders that want to:

- provide an exit route for existing shareholders, including employees;
- provide an internal market;
- value the company for taxation or estate valuation purposes;
- raise their profile and gain experience of being on a trading facility before moving to a more senior market.

Examples are:

- EIS companies with private investors;
- family businesses where shares are owned by several generations;
- companies with employee share plans;
- sports clubs;
- ex-mutuals;
- mutuals and cooperatives.

For these companies, the cost and work involved in joining and meeting the ongoing obligations of a more senior market may seem prohibitive, especially if fund-raising is not an immediate requirement. Furthermore, a more senior market may not be able to fulfil their requirements, particularly if companies wish to restrict trading to a defined audience.

ShareMark provides companies that need a trading facility for their shares, but do not require immediate access to equity finance, with an alternative. It is lightly regulated, which means that both the admission process and the ongoing requirements for companies are less onerous than those for more senior markets.

At the time of writing, there were 19 lines of stock trading on ShareMark, which includes equities and loanstock. In 2004 ShareMark was appointed 'market operator' to Investbx, the West Midlands regional stock exchange, which was launched in summer 2007.

How ShareMark works

ShareMark is designed specifically for companies whose shares are infrequently traded. One of the most common problems affecting these companies is wide bid–offer spreads, caused by a lack of liquidity. Wide spreads can disadvantage existing shareholders and potential investors. This problem becomes significant when wide spreads disadvantage those whom the share issue was originally intended to benefit or incentivize, ie employees, customers, members or supporters, and could result in those audiences turning against the company when the ultimate aim was to encourage loyalty.

ShareMark aims to overcome this problem by trading shares at a single price, through an auction process. There are no market makers, and shares may be dealt on a daily, weekly, monthly or quarterly basis. The frequency will depend on how much trading there is expected to be.

Prior to admission, the company will set its 'start price'; ShareMark is not involved in this process. The 'start price' will act as guide for the very first people to enter orders. Thereafter, the price will be determined by supply and demand.

In the build-up to the auction, people who want to buy or sell shares can enter their order through their existing stockbroker or through the Share Centre. The last traded price is available on the ShareMark website, www.sharemark.com, or through the ShareMark dealing team. An indicative price may also be available. People may choose to use either price to help them work out what price they want to buy or sell at. The ShareMark website also provides access to a company's announcements and report and accounts.

Placing an order on ShareMark is very similar to placing an order on any other market, although ShareMark can only accept limit orders. The order is entered into the auction and will be visible on an anonymous basis on www.sharemark.com.

The single price is calculated by working out where supply for shares meets demand. In the build-up to the auction, an indicative price will show, subject to there being matching buy and sell orders in the system. This is the price the shares would trade at if the auction took place at that precise moment in time.

One hour before the auction takes place, the order book is closed and a compliance review is conducted.

The auction then takes place and the settlement process begins. Orders are filled on a price and time basis. So if there are more sellers than buyers, those who entered their sell order at the lowest price will sell their shares in priority to those who have entered their order at a higher price. If orders are entered at the same price, then the earliest order will take priority. All buyers and sellers pay one price. Only those who were prepared to buy at or above, and sell at or below, the final price will stand a chance of successfully completing their order. Unfilled buy orders are carried over to the following auction, and unfilled sell orders can be resubmitted.

Settlement may be via CREST or in residual format, but all trades are settled on a T+3 basis.

Regulatory status

The ShareMark dealing facility is operated by The Share Centre Limited, a stock-broking firm. The Share Centre is a member firm of the London Stock Exchange and is authorized and regulated by the Financial Services Authority. Although ShareMark is not a 'recognized investment exchange', it constitutes an alternative trading system. Consequently, ShareMark must comply with certain regulatory requirements to ensure that there is adequate protection for investors and that the potential for financial crime is minimized. Shares on ShareMark are not 'listed', which gives certain tax advantages that are also available to AIM and PLUS Markets companies.

Advisers

Most companies are introduced to ShareMark by their professional advisers and it will help to have an adviser involved in the application process. However, the application for admission is not made by a corporate adviser; furthermore, companies do not have to retain the services of an adviser on an ongoing basis. ShareMark benefits from an advisers' network; however, companies will not be forced to work with a member of the network, although if required they can go to the network for assistance.

The ShareMark admission process

It is important when joining any market or trading facility to ensure that the needs of the company and existing and potential shareholders will be met. Achieving admission may require a period of consultation and discussion, and this should be factored into the admission process.

Whatever the underlying requirements of the company, all applicants must comply with *The ShareMark Code of Practice*, the rule book that governs the operation of the facility. This sets out the criteria a company must satisfy for it to be eligible for admission to ShareMark. In summary, these are:

■ *Legal status.* A company must be incorporated in the United Kingdom in either limited or public company form. A company intending to raise finance through a public offer must be a plc, as required by the Companies Act 1985.

■ *Track record.* Companies applying to ShareMark must have at least one year's audited accounts, without any statements as to fundamental uncertainty. Accounts should have been made up to a date no more than six months prior to the date of admission to ShareMark.

■ *Share valuation on admission.* There are no minimum or maximum share valuations for companies applying to have their shares traded on ShareMark. At the time of writing, the market capitalizations of ShareMark companies ranged from £500,000 to in excess of £60 million.

■ *Shareholding in public hands.* Companies must be able to demonstrate they have sufficient securities held in public hands to ensure buy- and sell-side demand. This requirement does not apply to companies that require a closed market for their shares. Whilst the ShareMark Code of Practice does not stipulate a minimum requirement, companies with fewer than 50 shareholders will be required to demonstrate a commitment to increasing the number of shareholders before admission is approved, eg through the introduction of an employee share plan.

■ *Working capital.* Companies applying to ShareMark are not required to make a working capital statement. However, the ShareMark Admission Committee will review the company's accounts prior to admission and will expect there to be sufficient working capital for the company to continue operating at current levels for at least a year.

■ *Additional factors.* The ShareMark Admission Committee will also consider the following factors in making a decision as to the suitability or otherwise of the company for admission to ShareMark:

  – Does the company have management information systems appropriate to its size?
  – Is there a high-quality management team with no obvious weaknesses in any one area?
  – Does the company have at least one non-executive director?

Information required

If a company is confident that it can fulfil these criteria, it will be required to provide ShareMark with a variety of documents. The ShareMark admission process is designed to be as simple as possible, whilst also ensuring compliance with the requirements of operating as an alternative trading system.

Documents required include completed ShareMark application forms, including directors' declarations, a certified copy of the company's memorandum and articles of association, and the company's report and accounts for the last three years, or since incorporation, if later.

Companies applying to join ShareMark are not required to provide a prospectus unless legally required to do so, ie if the company is also conducting a public offer.

The majority of companies applying to ShareMark are required to publish an 'admission statement'. This is designed to ensure that existing shareholders and potential investors are able to make an informed assessment of the assets and liabilities, financial position, profits and losses and prospects of the company. It should also include reference to any controls relating to who can and cannot purchase the company's securities and any limits pertaining to purchases. This document is unlikely to constitute a financial promotion and as such should not require verification or sign-off by a professional adviser.

The ShareMark Admission Committee

All companies applying to have their shares traded on ShareMark are approved for admission to ShareMark by the ShareMark Admission Committee. This process is usually completed at least 10 working days prior to admission, but ShareMark will be able to provide a firm indication of suitability prior to the commencement of the admission process.

Costs and time involved

Generally, a well-organized company could complete the ShareMark admission process in under a month. The time taken will be affected by a variety of factors, including the need for structural reorganization, ie a demutualization, and specific requirements of existing and potential shareholders.

The quarterly fee includes the cost of independent research coverage by *Alternative Markets Review*, two mailshots per annum to company shareholders and all announcements. The frequency or infrequency of auctions does not affect the ShareMark fees.

ShareMark charges do not include professional advisers' fees, although these should compare very favourably with the fees charged by advisers to a company joining PLUS Markets, AIM or the Main Market.

Shareholder communication and meeting ongoing shareholder requirements

ShareMark will help with shareholder communication prior to admission. This may include mailshots, PR campaigns, web communications and presentations to existing and potential shareholders.

Ninety per cent of deals in ShareMark traded shares are done through the Share Centre. The Share Centre can provide a company's shareholders with access to a dedicated customer service number, broking team, online portfolio valuations and management information.

ShareMark publishes a monthly e-mail bulletin, which may help shareholders and potential investors keep abreast of company news and price fluctuations. ShareMark prices can also be monitored through the Share Centre dealing team or on the website at www.sharemark.co.uk. Where required, ShareMark can also provide an indicative price line, which provides shareholders with constant access to a live share price.

Ongoing requirements

Companies must publish annual accounts prepared in accordance with UK or International Accounting Standards no later than six months after the end of the financial period to which they relate. Companies are also expected to publish a half-year report in respect of the first six-month period of the financial year. This must be published not later than three months after the end of the period, although it does not have to be audited.

Conclusion

ShareMark is still comparatively small. However, the recent admission of new companies such as Countrywide Farmers, a leading farmer and rural supplies business, and City Lofts Group Plc, a residential and mixed-use property developer, suggests that ShareMark is establishing itself as a niche provider of a simple, flexible share-trading facility to companies whose shares are infrequently traded. This steady growth is expected to be further boosted by the growth of the ShareMark advisers' network and the launch of Invest BX in 2007.

10

The Irish Enterprise Exchange

Daryl Byrne, Irish Stock Exchange

Your company is small to mid-sized and needs funding to expand and develop its business, now and in the future. You want to boost the profile and visibility of your company with investors, suppliers, customers, employees and other stakeholders. You have decided that a quotation on a public market is the best option for your company. If this scenario describes you and your company, then you should consider the Irish Enterprise Exchange.

The Irish Enterprise Exchange (IEX), launched by the Irish Stock Exchange in 2005, combines the benefits of a public market quotation with a regulatory regime tailored specifically to meet the needs of small to mid-sized companies.

The steady stream of new companies joining IEX since its launch has resulted in the market becoming increasingly cross-sectoral, with property investment, property management, outsourcing, specialist pharmaceuticals, telecommunications, financial services, software and exploration industries, among others, now represented on the market.

Market performance

The capitalization of the IEX market increased from 532 million on launch to 850 million by the end of 2005, and to 2,464 million by the end of 2006.

*A market designed by the
Irish Stock Exchange for small to
mid-sized companies, combining the
benefits of a public market quotation with
a regulatory regime tailored specifically to
meet the particular needs of its companies.*

Irish Stock Exchange
28 Anglesea Street
Dublin 2
Ireland

Tel: **+ 353 1 6174229**
Fax: **+ 353 1 6174289**
Contact: Daryl Byrne
e-mail: **daryl.byrne@ise.ie**
website: **www.ise.ie**

Table 10.1   IEX companies

	2005 (year)	2006 (year)	April 2006 (4 months)	April 2007 (4 months)
Number of IEX companies (at year/period end)	13	23	14	26
Money raised by Irish companies (€m)	132	941	115	339
Turnover (€m)	584	1,256	380	1,369
Daily average turnover (€m)	2.3	5.0	4.6	16.5
Number of deals	18,076	40,408	13,680	34,304
Market capitalization (€m)	850	2,464	1,225	3,101
Number of companies with market cap of:				
– less than €100m	11	11	10	14
– €100m to €200m	1	9	2	7
– more than €200m	1	3	2	5

The benefits of an IEX quotation

IEX offers small to mid-sized companies a number of advantages, including:

■ Trading on ISE Xetra®, the electronic trading system of the Irish Stock Exchange, ensures visibility across Europe and enhances liquidity through a euro-denominated quote facility.

■ There is access to capital from a pool of institutional and private client investors at the time of IPO and in further fund-raisings.

■ All eligible IEX companies participate in the ISEQ® Overall Index, thereby increasing their visibility to institutional and retail investors in the domestic and international markets.

■ Investor loyalty, as well as broker and analyst support, so as to maintain a liquid and stable market in your shares.

■ The IEX regulatory regime has been designed specifically for smaller companies.

■ There is increased financial flexibility, as shares can be offered as consideration to vendors when making an acquisition.

■ There is the capacity to give your employees a direct stake in the success of your business.

■ The IEX Rules for Companies are complementary to the AIM Rules for Companies, facilitating the coordination of admission to both markets.

Key features of the IEX regime

Admission

- A trading record is not required.
- The company is not required to be incorporated in Ireland.
- There is no requirement for a minimum number of shares to be in public hands.
- The company is required to appoint and retain an IEX adviser at all times.
- The company is expected to have a broker at all times.
- The market capitalization of the company must be at least 5 million upon admission.
- The securities of the company must be freely transferable.
- There are two methods of entry to IEX. The first method requires the preparation of an admission document involving four steps, as explained below in 'The admission process'. The second method is open to companies quoted on certain designated markets and does not require the preparation of an admission document – the 'fast-track route'.

Post-admission

- There is a disclosure-based continuing obligations regime, requiring disclosure of price-sensitive information to the market on an ongoing basis, as well as periodic publication of annual and interim accounts within set time limits.
- There is no requirement for prior shareholder approval for transactions (except for reverse takeovers and disposals resulting in a fundamental change of business).

The admission process

Step 1: Appoint an IEX adviser

All companies seeking admission to IEX must appoint an IEX adviser. An IEX adviser is a firm of corporate finance professionals who have been approved by the Exchange to act as an adviser to IEX companies. IEX companies must have an IEX adviser at all times – both before and after admission. The IEX adviser:

- acts as the principal point of contact between the company and the Irish Stock Exchange;
- assesses the company's suitability for IEX;
- draws up a detailed timetable and coordinates the activities of other professionals who are involved in bringing the company to the market;
- assists in the preparation of the IEX admission document; and
- is available at all times to advise and guide the directors of an IEX company about their obligations to ensure compliance by the IEX company with the IEX Rules for Companies.

Step 2: Submit a pre-admission announcement

At least 10 business days before the expected date of admission to IEX, an applicant company must provide the Exchange with a 'pre-admission' announcement, which sets out the company's intention to join the IEX and contains information on the company and its securities, directors and significant shareholders.

Step 3: Submit an admission document

A new company seeking admission to IEX is required to prepare an admission document disclosing information required by the IEX Rules for Companies and submit this to the Exchange at least three business days before the expected date of admission. However, there is no pre-vetting and approval of admission documents by the Exchange (other than where a public offer prospectus is required to be approved by the Irish competent authority under the Prospectus Directive).

The admission document must remain publicly available, free of charge, for at least one month from the date of admission to IEX. Its purpose is to provide prospective investors with sufficient information to make an informed decision on whether to invest in the shares. This admission document contains all the relevant information investors might need on the company and its activities, risks relevant to the business, accounting information, details of directors, including their past records and their interests in the company, and information on matters such as major shareholders and working capital.

Step 4: Submit supporting documents

At least three business days before the expected date of admission, the company must submit to the Exchange the IEX fee and a completed IEX application form.

The fast-track route to IEX

Where a company has securities already traded on one of a number of markets designated by the Exchange ('IEX designated markets') prior to the date of admission to IEX, it can apply to have its securities admitted to IEX without having to publish an admission document. Instead, at least 20 business days before the expected date of admission to IEX, a company using the fast-track route to IEX must provide the Exchange with a detailed pre-admission announcement. The pre-admission announcement must include:

■ confirmation that it has adhered to any legal and regulatory requirements involved in having its securities traded upon the IEX designated market;
■ details of its intended strategy following admission;

- a description of any significant change in the financial or trading position of the company that has occurred since the end of the last financial period for which audited accounts have been prepared;
- a statement that its directors have no reason to believe that the working capital available to it or its group will be insufficient for at least 12 months from the date of its admission;
- a brief description of the arrangements for settling transactions in its securities;
- a website address detailing the rights attaching to its securities;
- any other information that would be required for an admission document that is not currently public;
- a website address of a page containing its latest published annual report and accounts, which must have a financial year end not more than nine months prior to admission.

Companies taking the fast-track route must appoint an IEX adviser and submit the relevant forms to the Exchange.

The current 'IEX designated markets' are the main markets of:

- Official List of the Irish Stock Exchange;
- Official List of the FSA;
- Alternative Investment Market of the London Stock Exchange;
- Euronext;
- Deutsche Börse;
- NASDAQ;
- NYSE;
- Stockholmsbörsen;
- Toronto Stock Exchange.

Admission countdown

The timetable below gives an indication of the stages of the admission process to IEX:

- *24 weeks before admission:*
  - Appoint advisers and issue them with detailed instructions.
  - Prepare and agree a detailed timetable.
  - Determine that the company will have a market capitalization of at least 5 million on admission.
  - Identify and review problem areas.
- *12 weeks before admission:*
  - Draft the admission document and other necessary documentation for admission.
  - Consider pricing issues.
  - Prepare PR presentations.
  - Prepare and host an analysts' presentation.

- *6 weeks before admission:*
  - Continue the documentation drafting process.
  - Verify the contents of documents with the company and appropriate advisers.
  - Hold PR meetings and investor roadshows.
  - Submit the 10-day pre-admission announcement to the Exchange.
- *Week prior to admission:*
  - Finalize all necessary documentation for admission.
  - Finalize pricing and allocation of the offer.
  - Submit admission and application documents to the Exchange.

Life after admission

From a regulatory perspective, an IEX company is subject to a range of continuing obligations, mainly disclosure based, including the following:

Disclosure of price-sensitive information

Once a company is quoted on IEX it is required to keep the market informed of any developments (regarding its financial condition, activities, past performance and future prospects) that could have an impact on the share price of the company. All price-sensitive information must be notified to the market without delay, including corporate transactions and related party transactions. An IEX company must also notify the market of matters such as directors' dealings, changes in significant shareholders and changes in directors. Directors and certain employees are prohibited from trading prior to the release of the company's annual, half-yearly or quarterly results and during any period when the company has unpublished price-sensitive information.

Information on the company's website

Each IEX company must from admission maintain a website on which information is available to the public, including the following:

- a description of its business and, where it is an investing company, its investing strategy;
- the names of its directors and brief biographical details of each;
- a description of the responsibilities of the members of the board of directors and details of any committees of the board of directors and their responsibilities;
- its current constitutional documents (eg its articles of association);
- the number of IEX securities in issue (noting any held as treasury shares) and, insofar as it is aware, the percentage of IEX securities that is not in public hands, together with the identity and percentage holdings of its significant share-holders;

- its most recent annual report published and all half-yearly, quarterly or similar reports published since the last annual report;
- all notifications the IEX company has made in the past 12 months;
- its most recent admission document together with any circulars or similar publications sent to shareholders within the past 12 months.

Periodic accounts

An IEX company must publish half-yearly and annual accounts within specified time periods – within three months after each half-year end and within six months after each financial year end.

For companies incorporated in the EEA, consolidated financial statements must be prepared under IFRS. Companies not preparing consolidated accounts can prepare their financial statements in accordance with IFRS or in accordance with accounting requirements applicable in the country of incorporation.

IEX companies incorporated in non-EEA countries, on admission and when preparing their half-yearly and annual reports, may use IFRS, US GAAP, Canadian GAAP, Japanese GAAP or Australian GAAP (or any third country's national accounting standards that are equivalent to IFRS).

Acquisitions and disposals

In most instances, an IEX company is not required to obtain prior approval of shareholders or to produce a further admission document when effecting acquisitions and disposals. Instead, the company must notify the market about any substantial transactions or related party transactions entered into.

Conclusion

IEX allows small to mid-sized companies to benefit from the advantages of a public quotation whilst observing a set of rules that are designed specifically for their needs. IEX companies enjoy an enhanced profile in European markets and increased liquidity in their shares through a euro-denominated quote and trading facility.

Further information on IEX, including the IEX Rules for Companies and application forms, is available on the Irish Stock Exchange's website, www.ise.ie. Alternatively contact the Corporate Listing Department of the Irish Stock Exchange on +353 1 617 4229 or at companylistings@ise.ie.

The flotation process

Selection of advisers

Andrew Black, Pinsent Masons

Introduction

The flotation of a company requires carefully coordinated teamwork by the company and its professional advisers.

This chapter seeks to provide a description of the company's advisers and their respective roles. The more specific documents for which each adviser is normally directly responsible are set out in detail in the appendix at the end of the chapter.

As soon as a company has decided on a flotation, the directors' first step should be to identify and appoint the sponsor for the listing. The sponsor will coordinate the company's entry to the market. The board will also need a corporate broker, which may or may not be the same firm as that sponsoring the issue. Further advisers needed for the flotation include reporting accountants, solicitors and tax specialists (usually accountants or lawyers), and the directors will also probably decide to use both public and investor relations advisers.

Selection of advisers

Choosing good-quality corporate advisers is one of the first and most important things that a company must do in preparation for a listing. It is also one of the most difficult.

The sheer range of different aspects on which the company needs advice means that it requires an equally wide range of professional advisers, all looking after their own specific area of specialization. Some areas of responsibility, such as the roles of sponsor and corporate broker, can potentially be combined by a single firm. However, many directors feel it is actually in a company's best interests to have separate advisers for each area, since it may lessen the potential for conflicts of interests in the event of any problems or unforeseen developments.

The natural starting point in the company's directors' search for suitable professional advisers to guide them through the listing process is to talk to the company's existing advisers, usually accountants and solicitors. The directors should start this process at least a year before they intend to join the market, although they may ultimately find that the process takes less time than they expected. The company's existing solicitors and accountants may already possess the necessary expertise, experience and resources to act for it on the flotation. If not, they will certainly be able to recommend and introduce the directors to suitable firms of advisers that can provide independent guidance.

Many companies approach the appointment of advisers by holding 'beauty parades' with a series of them, asking each about their expertise and fees and getting a feeling for what it would be like to work closely with them over an extended period. The directors will be spending a considerable amount of time (and money) with their chosen advisers, and the relationship may well continue after the flotation, so it is crucial that they can get on with them on a personal level. The directors should also investigate the potential scope for negotiation on costs and areas of responsibilities.

Advisers' roles

The sponsor

The first concrete step towards flotation is to identify and appoint a suitable sponsor for the listing. The sponsor takes a central role in the flotation process, advising the company on a wide range of issues, probably including the appointment of other professional advisers. An investment bank, stockbroker or other adviser such as a corporate finance house or accountancy firm can take on the role of sponsor, provided they are approved by the UK Listing Authority (UKLA) to do so. A full list of approved sponsors is published on the FSA website.

Since acting as a sponsor also requires a high degree of commitment from the firm taking on the role, the appointment process is essentially two-way. The board will certainly want to look at the potential sponsor's expertise, experience and likely fees. However, the sponsor will also want to have a good look at the company's business before agreeing to take on its flotation. It is a good idea to prepare in advance a summary briefing on the company's business and financial history for each prospective sponsor.

Although the precise valuation of the business will not be decided until the eve of the flotation, many better-informed companies make a discussion about company valuation a part of the beauty parades for their sponsor. It is also sensible for the directors of the company, as a would-be issuer, to conduct research into the quoted companies in their own sector, to give them some idea of the methods of valuation and the kind of rating they might expect from the market. This will ensure that the management can have a meaningful discussion with the parading sponsors.

It is also advisable at this stage for management to question the sponsor about the likely investor base for the issue. If the sponsor is well prepared, it should be able to discuss the proportion of the issue that should go to investors specializing in the company's sector or perhaps to funds with an international flavour, and will have the evidence to back up its opinions. Much of this advice can apply to the appointment of the broker as well.

If the board and the potential sponsor are still interested in one another after the initial meeting, the sponsor will then require more detailed financial information, and will probably want to come and look at the company's operations and premises before accepting the business. Essentially, the sponsor will want to be sure that the company's business and its management are appropriate for a listing, and that the flotation stands a very good chance of success. So, it is the job of the directors, as well as assessing the sponsor's abilities and fees, to convince them of their own company's strength and prospects.

The sponsor's pivotal role, and its responsibilities both to the company and to the UKLA, means it has to undertake a wide range of duties all the way through the flotation process. Many of these duties will overlap with the company's own assessment of its suitability, in areas such as management depth and financial controls. First of all, the sponsor will assess the company's general suitability for a listing, in the light of its organizational structure and capital requirements. It will then advise on the structure and make-up of the board, the best method of flotation for the company, and the flotation timetable. It will also assist (if required) with the appointment of other advisers, and coordinate their activities once they are on the team. As the flotation approaches, the sponsor will advise on the pricing and under-writing of the shares, and the relevant marketing strategy for the issue.

In an AIM flotation, the role of the nominated adviser, or 'nomad', is very similar to that of a sponsor to a full listing. The nomad is responsible for confirming to the London Stock Exchange that the applicant is suitable for admission and that the AIM Rules (on admission and continuing obligations) are complied with. Like the sponsor to a full listing, the nomad will coordinate the entire application process and, following admission, will continue to provide advice and guidance generally as the company's financial adviser.

The main differences between the obligations of sponsors and those of nomi-nated advisers are as follows. First, while both nominated advisers and sponsors are required to confirm that the relevant requirements have been met, a sponsor is also required to confirm that all matters known to it regarding suitability for admission are disclosed in the prospectus or have otherwise been disclosed to the FSA. Second, a sponsor is required to give specific comfort to the FSA in relation to the reasonableness of the issuer's working capital statement and financial reporting procedures.

The corporate broker

The corporate broker acts as the board's main interface with the stock market and potential investors. The firm of brokers appointed will assess the current conditions in the stock market and provide vital feedback on investors' likely response to the issue. If the appointed sponsor is an integrated firm offering both investment banking and stockbroking services, then the directors may decide that they also want it to take on the role of corporate broker. Again, the sponsor will help and advise on the selection of the right firm, although it may be advisable to see a number of firms to compare their fees and approach. A useful guide is to look at the other companies that the prospective broker has acted for, which will give the board some idea of its standing and areas of expertise. For example, if the company is in the high-tech sphere, it may want a broker that has a solid track record in stimulating investor interest in technology businesses. The board may also want to be sure that its chosen broker appears in the league tables of leading research houses for the company's particular sector.

As well as advising the board and its sponsor on market conditions and the likely level of demand, the corporate broker actively markets the shares to potential investors and can advise on the best method, size, timing and price. It can put in place market-related arrangements such as sub-underwriting and placing agreements. It will also help the company meet the applicable listing requirements and usually continues to work with the company after the flotation to maintain its shares' liquidity and profile in the aftermarket.

Similarly, in an AIM flotation, the broker will provide a point of contact with the investment community, will help in fund-raising and will be responsible for creating and maintaining a market in the company's shares.

The reporting accountant

The role of reporting accountant in a flotation is separate from that of the company's existing auditors, but can be (and often is) fulfilled by a separate team in the same firm if the directors so choose. The sponsors may want to appoint a different firm to ensure the highest-possible level of detachment and independence in this key role. Essentially, the reporting accountant is responsible for reviewing the company's financial record for potential investors, and thus has an influence on their decision as to whether to buy the shares.

As the company goes through the flotation process, the directors will hear a lot about 'long-form' and 'short-form' reports. The difference is quite simple. The 'long-form' report, as the name suggests, is a detailed financial and management history of the business. It is not published, but does provide the management and sponsors with the information needed to draft the prospectus. It also serves as the basis for the reporting accountants' 'short-form' report, which is published as part of the prospectus itself. The reporting accountants will also usually prepare a report for the sponsor on the company's projected working capital position over the 12 to 18 months following flotation. They may also advise on the tax implications of the flotation, or the board may have decided to appoint separate tax specialists to do this.

Lawyers

Most flotations involve two separate sets of lawyers – one to advise the company and its existing shareholders, and the other to advise the sponsor or nominated adviser. The responsibilities of the company's lawyers, with whom the directors will of course have the most contact, include preparing a legal due diligence report on the company, advising the board on their potential liabilities in relation to the prospectus and their continuing obligations as directors of a listed company, drafting new articles of association and directors' contracts, and possibly re-registering the company as a plc or reorganizing its group structure. The lawyers will advise on the legal and regulatory content of the prospectus and prepare the painstaking 'verification' questions, which are used to confirm that every single statement in the prospectus can be justified as fact. The rigours of this process mean that management will get to know their lawyers very well. The company's lawyers will also work alongside the sponsor's lawyers on the necessary agreements between the company, the sponsor and the existing shareholders, covering aspects like underwriting and tax. The board might also want them to draw up share option schemes for staff, to be introduced with the flotation.

Other advisers

Depending on the method of the flotation and the specific circumstances of the company, the directors might also decide to use a number of other advisers in particular areas. The most likely is a firm of financial public relations consultants to maximize the degree of positive awareness of the company and its products or services among both the general public and the professional investment community in the run-up to the flotation. Companies coming to market often underestimate the importance of public profile and press contacts. The company's financial PR advisers should also help ensure that any public statements and press releases are permissible under the relevant disclosure regulations. The board will find that, by helping to generate ongoing press interest and publicity, its financial PR advisers can play a key role in sustaining awareness and liquidity after the listing. The management might consider media training for those key directors who will be under the spotlight.

The company may also require a number of other advisers. These include registrars to manage the company's share register; chartered surveyors or valuers to assess property values; specialist financial printers for safe, accurate and speedy production of documentation; actuaries to assess the position of company pension schemes; receiving bankers to handle share applications (only in a public offer); and insurance brokers to check that all risks are adequately covered.

Appendix: List of documents for a flotation

Set out below is a typical list of documents required for an offer, indicating the professional adviser primarily responsible:

■ *Sponsor/nominated adviser:*
  – pathfinder prospectus;
  – prospectus;
  – mini-prospectus;
  – administration document – timetable, list of parties and documents;
  – application form/preferential application form;
  – newspaper advertisement(s);
  – abridged advertisements/formal notices;
  – Model Code for directors' share dealings;
  – letter for publication on profit forecast (if applicable);
  – declaration/confirmations/comfort letters to the UKLA or London Stock Exchange;
  – press announcements;
  – consent letter;
  – expenses estimate.
■ *Stockbroker:*
  – marketing logistics;
  – research material;
  – presentation material for investor presentations;
  – directors' declaration questionnaires;
  – application for listing;
  – particulars of securities being listed;
  – declaration as to filing of documents;
  – sub-underwriting/placing letters;
  – letter of derogation and non-applicability;
  – comfort letters.
■ *Solicitors to the company and to the issue:*
  – memorandum and articles of association;
  – capital reorganization documents;
  – company resolutions;
  – letters of allotment;
  – re-registration as a public limited company (if applicable);
  – memorandum on directors' responsibilities;
  – directors' responsibility statements;
  – powers of attorney;
  – placing/underwriting agreement (including warranties and indemnity);
  – employee share scheme documents (if applicable);
  – directors' service agreements;
  – legal due diligence report;
  – certificates of incorporation and re-registration;
  – certificates of titles to properties (if applicable);

    – verification notes;
    – completion agenda;
    – board minutes for completion meeting;
    – documents for display;
    – comfort letters.

■ *Reporting accountants:*
    – long-form report;
    – short-form report (if applicable);
    – statement of adjustments (if applicable);
    – indebtedness statement;
    – confirmation of bank facilities;
    – memorandum on working capital;
    – memorandum on profit forecast (if applicable);
    – letter for publication on profit forecast (if applicable);
    – consent letter (if applicable);
    – tax clearances;
    – comfort letters.

■ *Public relations consultants:*
    – presentation material for press and analyst presentations;
    – statutory and corporate advertising;
    – artwork for prospectus/covers;
    – press announcements.

■ *Receiving bankers and registrars:*
    – receiving bankers' agreement;
    – letter of acceptance;
    – share registration.

■ *Other:*
    – pension scheme valuation (if applicable);
    – property valuation (if applicable);
    – market, environmental and other specialist reports (as applicable).

forest

Making more possible

12

The role of the nomad

Justin Jones, Hoare Govett

Introduction

The nominated adviser or 'nomad' sits at the centre of the UK's AIM market fulfilling important roles for the companies quoted on it and the London Stock Exchange as a whole.

When AIM was launched in 1995, the creation of the nomad, with its related responsibilities and obligations, was arguably the most distinctive feature of this new market. In seeking to launch and operate its 'lightly regulated' market for young and dynamic companies, free from many of the rules and processes of its Main Market, the London Stock Exchange delegated much of the day-to-day regulatory responsibilities to the nomad. In simple terms, every company quoted on AIM must have a nomad at all times and, in the first instance, it is for the nomad to determine, both at the time of seeking admission to trading on AIM and thereafter, whether it is appropriate for that particular company to be quoted on AIM. While the proposed application to trade on AIM will be reviewed by the London Stock Exchange, this is very much at the end of the process. Up to that point, it is for the nomad to judge and assess the suitability of a company to be admitted to trading on a UK public market.

Given the great degree of responsibility delegated to a nomad, it is not surprising that the eligibility, conduct and activities of nomads are closely regulated by the London Stock Exchange. Recently, the degree of regulation has been strengthened and formalized with the introduction of separate 'AIM Rules for Nominated Advisers' in February 2007. While this new rule book includes the previous AIM

Rules as they apply to nomads, new guidelines have been included on the responsibilities of nomads and the work they should undertake to discharge the responsibilities (particularly with regard to due diligence on the company and its management),
together with the review and disciplinary procedures available to the London Stock
Exchange in the event of rule breaches by the nomad.

As a result of these recent developments, new companies applying to AIM, as
well as existing AIM companies, should expect much greater scrutiny and super-
vision by their nomad than has sometimes been the case in the past.

Who may act as a nomad?

All nomads are approved by the London Stock Exchange, such approval being in
addition to any other relevant legal or regulatory approvals that may be required,
and subject to an annual review by the AIM regulation team to ensure their
continuing eligibility. In order to gain and retain approved status, a nomad must be
a firm that is able to demonstrate that:

- it is independent from the AIM companies for which it acts and has no related
  conflicts of interest;
- it has a two-year track record in providing corporate finance advice as its principal business activity;
- it has acted as lead corporate finance adviser on at least three relevant transactions (that is, a public fund-raising requiring a prospectus; or a public bid, on
  behalf of the bidder, requiring an offer document; or a transaction requiring an
  admission document) during that two-year period;
- it employs at least four qualified executives (that is, full-time, experienced
  corporate finance advisers who have each led on at least three relevant transactions during the last three years).

As well as requiring that a nomad meets these eligibility criteria, the London Stock
Exchange will consider whether the approval of a nomad or qualified executive
might endanger the reputation and integrity of AIM as a whole. It is by ensuring that
there is a robust framework for the approval of nomads that the London Stock
Exchange seeks indirectly to regulate the workings of the AIM market.

Clearly, from a company's perspective, these eligibility criteria represent only a
minimum and, when appointing a nomad, a company should probably look for one
with a longer track record of transactions, including, where relevant, specific sector
knowledge, together with an appropriate depth of experience and resource within
the firm to service the company's requirements properly.

Most nomads are investment banks, specialist corporate finance advisers or
brokers: this reflects the important crossover between obtaining admission to
trading on AIM, raising new equity from institutional investors and ensuring appropriate liquidity levels in the secondary aftermarket. However, both accountants and
lawyers may also act as nomads. There is often some debate within companies at the
time of appointing a nomad as to whether the firm appointed as nomad should also

be its broker (appointment of a broker being another mandatory requirement for AIM companies). Clearly, while this is a matter of preference for the board, for many smaller companies this integrated banker and broker model is more efficient in terms of both management time and expense.

What a company should expect from its nomad

It is a mandatory requirement of the AIM Rules for Companies that every company quoted on AIM must have a nomad at all times. Failure to comply with this key AIM rule will result in the immediate suspension of trading in a company's shares and subsequent cancellation of its admission to AIM if left unresolved for more than a month. However, notwithstanding this mandatory requirement, it would be wrong for a board to view the appointment of its nomad as simply a compliance requirement to maintain the company's admission to AIM.

A company's nomad should be available at all times to assist and advise its board regarding their responsibilities and obligations to their shareholders, potential investors and the London Stock Exchange.

There are two elements to this role: firstly, on a new company's application for admission to AIM; and, secondly, once admitted, on meeting its continuing obligations as an AIM company.

On admission

Seeking admission to trading on a public market is a major landmark in any company's life: it is a complex, time-consuming, pressurized and expensive process. The nomad should be there, working alongside its client, directing and managing that process, supervising the work of other advisers and, importantly, explaining and assisting the company and its management towards a successful admission to AIM.

A proactive, hands-on approach by the nomad to project-managing the admission process is even more important when you remember that the directors also have to keep managing the business and delivering the equity story to be sold to new investors.

As part of the admission process, there will be numerous interconnected work streams that the nomad should supervise in close consultation with its client, including, amongst others, financial and legal due diligence investigations, legal documentation, composition of an appropriate board and related corporate governance matters, working capital projections and financial reporting procedures, as well as advising the board on the application of the AIM Rules for Companies and what is the expected behaviour of an AIM quoted company and its board.

For many companies and their management teams, the admission process will be a new experience and, in this context, the nomad has a vital role to play in ensuring the process is properly understood by the board and that admission is efficiently executed with due skill and careful enquiry.

Post-admission: continuing obligations

As important a landmark as admission to AIM is, the responsibilities and obligations of being an AIM company only increase post-admission. The AIM Rules for Companies apply at all times, and the nomad should act as the principal adviser to the company and its board, guiding them as to the application of these rules, together with related disclosure requirements and developments in best market practice. Not surprisingly, this role is especially important in the early stages of a company's life on AIM. However, regular dialogue between the company and its nomad should become a feature of both parties' normal working week.

It is important to recognize that, unlike the company/sponsor relationship on the Main Market, the post-admission relationship between company and nomad is not just event driven, for example at the time of a corporate transaction or fund-raising, but is a constant interaction throughout the year.

Summary

In overview, the AIM Rules for Companies set out the responsibilities of companies admitted to trading on AIM. The rules cover all aspects of both a company's application for admission to AIM and its continuing obligations thereafter, including, amongst others: the admission document; general disclosure requirements (particularly price-sensitive information); corporate transactions (including those with related parties); annual and interim accounts; dealing restrictions; directors' responsibilities; maintenance of orderly markets; and disciplinary procedures.

While the nomad must ensure that the board understands how these rules govern the company's actions, so the board should know to seek the advice of its nomad as and when required. Without this mutual commitment, both parties will struggle to fulfil their obligations to the London Stock Exchange as a whole.

What the London Stock Exchange expects from a nomad

So as to understand better what underpins this close and ongoing relationship between a company and its nomad, it is important to recognize the responsibilities and obligations that exist between the nomad and the London Stock Exchange. The responsibilities to the London Stock Exchange somewhat complicate the normal client/adviser relationship and should be formally acknowledged in the nomad agreement entered into between a company and its nomad at the time of appointment.

Under the AIM Rules for Nominated Advisers, the nomad remains responsible at all times to the London Stock Exchange for assessing the appropriateness of a company to have its shares traded on AIM. This obligation even extends to contacting the London Stock Exchange should the nomad consider the company, its own client, is no longer so appropriate.

Clearly, this is a position to be avoided where at all possible and explains why nomads spend so much time working closely with their clients to ensure they comply properly with their continuing obligations under the AIM Rules for Companies and conduct their affairs in line with best market practice. The London Stock Exchange views this work as an important responsibility of a nomad and will hold the nomad to account for the actions (or inactions) of its clients. As nomad, the firm is obliged to cooperate fully with the London Stock Exchange in this regard. The execution of this role by the nomad will be monitored closely by the AIM regulation team and taken into account at the time of a nomad's annual review.

The new AIM Rules for Nominated Advisers have formalized and strengthened these obligations, with the London Stock Exchange now setting out the specific responsibilities of nomads and the expected work to be undertaken by nomads in order to fulfil these responsibilities properly. The nomad's responsibilities, contained in Schedule Three of the AIM Rules for Nominated Advisers, consist of a number of principles, together with related actions, which nomads are now expected to follow in determining the appropriateness (or otherwise) of a company to be traded on AIM. Furthermore, the work undertaken by the nomad in satisfaction of these obligations should be documented and retained to demonstrate the basis of the nomad's assessment of a company's suitability. Importantly, the responsibilities set out in Schedule Three now represent a clear yardstick against which the London Stock Exchange will assess a nomad's performance in compliance with the AIM rule books.

In overview, the responsibilities of nomads cover all aspects of the nomad's role and, amongst others, include gaining a thorough understanding of the company's business and its markets (including the use of external experts, if necessary, and site visits); assessing the suitability of the board; overseeing the financial, legal and, if necessary, technical due diligence investigations undertaken by appropriate professional experts; considering the future working capital requirements and financial reporting procedures; ensuring compliance with the AIM Rules for Companies; and supervising the preparation of shareholder documents, such as the admission document and announcements to the AIM market. As well as introducing the AIM Rules for Nominated Advisers, in March 2006, the London Stock Exchange published specific due diligence and disclosure guidelines it expected natural resources companies and their nomads to follow on admission to AIM and thereafter.

While these new developments broadly seek to formalize previous best market practice followed by nomads, companies and their management need to recognize that the new framework will now drive the work streams their nomad will require to be undertaken in the future.

It is important to recognize that the formalization of these practices is in part a response to increasing investor concerns as to the quality of some companies admitted to trading on AIM and, by implication, the role played by the nomad on such admissions. While inevitably every stock market will have its successes and failures, it clearly is in everyone's interest to ensure that the quality threshold applied to AIM companies is properly monitored and assessed. The obvious benefit for the company and its board going forward is the enhanced confidence investors will have based on their nomad and the way that the nomad fulfils its responsibilities.

Choosing the right nomad

Given that the appointment of a nomad represents a major decision for new and existing AIM companies, what should the board be looking for?

The choice of nomad should weigh the following factors:

- commitment to understanding the dynamics of your business;
- relevant experience and the depth of resource made available to you;
- demonstrable understanding of the transaction and the level of work involved;
- confidence that the nomad can efficiently project-manage the transaction;
- interaction with brokers: the investor-facing team has to work well together;
- a proven track record of getting the transaction done.

Finally, and perhaps above all, there should be the right personal chemistry between the board and the nomad's team: both teams will spend many hours in each other's company and so that aspect of the relationship must be right.

Conclusion

The role of the nomad remains at the centre of the AIM market, acting as an AIM company's principal adviser while supervising its conduct with the market as a whole. The relationship between the company and its nomad is unique in the context of UK public markets and facilitates the intended 'light regulatory' touch of the London Stock Exchange that characterizes the AIM market.

However, to appreciate fully the role of the nomad, it is important to recognize that nomads have responsibilities both to the AIM companies they act for and to the London Stock Exchange. Of itself this should not present particular issues to either party but may explain why the admission process for trading on AIM, and subsequent continuing obligations, sometimes seems far from 'light'.

The introduction of the AIM Rules for Nominated Advisers is likely to lead to greater involvement by nomads in supervising the activities of AIM companies, in doing so, and existing and new investors should gain confidence in those companies and the AIM market overall.

13

The role of the lawyers

Rob Hutchings, Pinsent Masons

Introduction – general role

The role of the lawyer in the flotation process will cover many different areas, including the preparation and review of documentation and general advice on complicated areas of law. The principal responsibility of the lawyer is to prepare the necessary documentation, to ensure compliance with the applicable law and regulations and to assist (specifically on the legal aspects but not exclusively so) on the project management of the transaction. The work of the lawyer will be essential in meeting the target timetable for the project and ensuring the smooth running of the process.

Though obviously not able to advise in detail on the commercial advantages and disadvantages of each of the principal stock exchanges available to a company for fund-raising, the lawyer can be a sounding board to determine the merits, compliance requirements, documentation and other issues that apply to each market and to highlight the differences between a full listing and listing on AIM, Ofex or any of the other recognized exchanges – and even to give a view on other international exchanges (eg Paris, New York or Japan). Often, the identification of the correct market is determined on the balance of the legal and financial requirements to be met against the level of funding required. An experienced adviser may also assist on whether an offer of shares to the public is the appropriate route for the company or whether other sources of funds, such as venture capital, should be considered. A comparison of the regulatory frameworks relating to flotations is made in Chapter 5.

The general role of the lawyers in a flotation will be to provide advice on a number of issues including:

- the advantages and disadvantages of obtaining a listing from the point of view of legal requirements;
- the choice of appropriate stock exchange;
- the suitability of the constitution of the company for flotation and the compliance of the company with listing requirements;
- the flotation procedure and timing;
- the preparation, publication and verification of a prospectus, listing particulars or an admission document as appropriate;
- the compliance of the officers of the company with their ongoing responsibilities;
- the continued compliance of the company with the Listing Principles; and
- the legal consequences of going public and the legal restrictions on the businesses that arise.

In Chapter 11 the process of selecting your legal adviser was discussed. There are a large number of factors involved in determining this, but in the main it is a balance of two factors, which are not necessarily mutually exclusive, being first the need to select and instruct an experienced and competent legal adviser who is capable of carrying out the wider range of complex legal work required, and second ensuring that the legal adviser provides a value-for-money service.

The particular role of the legal advisers

Corporate lawyers are principally retained to guide companies effectively through the particular legal aspects of the fund-raising process. However, a client may rely on his or her corporate lawyers for advice on a range of commercial issues, not necessarily relating to purely legal aspects of the process. Although a few lawyers would be reluctant to advise formally on any matter other than legal issues, those corporate lawyers who have considerable experience in dealing with flotations and other public issues of securities are often able from experience to give straight-forward common-sense assistance to clients who are encountering certain problems for the first time.

In particular, the legal adviser can provide advice and guidance on the initial steps to flotation and the basic conditions for listing set out below:

- Are the securities eligible for listing?
- Has a sponsor been appointed?
- Have the requirements of the listing authority been satisfied?
- Is the company in compliance with its governing legislation and is its business undertaken in accordance with the constitutional documents by which it is regulated?
- Do the company's constitutional documents comply with the provisions of listing legislation?

- Is sufficient share capital of the company available for distribution to the public to meet the requirements of the relevant stock exchange?
- Is there a controlling shareholder? If yes, has an agreement been entered into regulating its position if this is required under the appropriate listing regulation?

In working through the above questions with senior management and the other advisers, the legal adviser will assist the company to reach the major decisions about its business and the proposed flotation.

Legal advisers to whom?

A typical flotation will involve:

- a company whose securities are to be listed and that may be raising capital by the issue of new shares;
- shareholders of the company who may be selling shares in the flotation to realize all or part of their investment;
- a merchant bank, which may underwrite the share offer and act as sponsor (these roles are sometimes assumed by a broker alone where a merchant bank is not involved);
- a broker who is responsible for the marketing of the offering, with a view to identifying those who wish definitely to acquire securities as placees and/or those who are prepared to sub-underwrite the offering;
- investors who may be institutional or private clients of the broker or members of the general public;
- the relevant stock exchange.

It is possible that lawyers are advising the first four of those parties identified above in respect of the flotation.

Nevertheless, there are two sets of legal advisers who play the dominant role in a flotation. The company's solicitors will normally be responsible for the preparation of legal documentation in relation to the issue, for advising the directors of their responsibilities both in relation to the prospectus and following the flotation, for conducting a review of the company's existing contractual and other legal relations with third parties, and for advising the company in relation to any agreement entered into with the nominated adviser. They will also deal with the verification of the whole of the prospectus as well as producing the information section or so-called 'back end' of the prospectus.

A different firm will act as solicitors to the issue, primarily to advise the broker/merchant bank in relation to matters where the company's solicitors would have a conflict of interest, such as any placing agreement relating to the broker/merchant bank's obligation to identify new shareholders for the company.

The solicitors to the issue are also responsible for ensuring that all legal requirements associated with the issue are met and that verification of the prospectus with the assistance of the company's solicitors is thoroughly undertaken.

Specific role of lawyers to the company

The specific role of the company's lawyers will require them to:

- ensure compliance with the regulatory framework appropriate to the market on which the shares will be listed;
- examine the company's memorandum and articles of association to see if they are appropriate for the transition of the company to a quoted company – for example, any anachronistic voting structures or restrictions will need to be removed;
- assist the company in creating the group structure appropriate for a listing;
- assist the company in re-registering as a public company in accordance with sections 42–47 of the Companies Act 1985;
- support the company and the financial adviser in structuring the offer, and document this structure;
- work with the company on verification of the offering document, ensuring that (wherever possible) statements are justified by reference to objective sources;
- assist in the production of the flotation documentation, preparing, where appropriate, wording to comply with listing requirements;
- advise on the ongoing compliance requirements under the rules of the relevant stock exchange, including the Listing Principles and under the general law.

The company may consider setting up an employee share scheme if it has not already done so. The purpose of this would be to incentivize employees at a time when their commitment to the company is crucial. The company's lawyers will generally advise the company in the setting up of any such scheme.

Although the role of overall project manager of the flotation should normally be that of the sponsor, the legal adviser will project-manage the legal aspects of the transaction and will assist in the overall project management process.

Due diligence

A flotation cannot progress without due diligence being undertaken. The legal due diligence process revolves around a detailed questionnaire prepared by the legal advisers to the company and revised by the legal advisers to the sponsor, the answers to which form the basis of the legal due diligence report, again prepared by the company's legal advisers and reviewed by those of the sponsor. There will be a great deal of time spent in putting together and reviewing the information for this report, both verbal and written. Depending on the nature of the company's business, the main headings to be covered will include title to the company's properties, environmental issues, litigation, intellectual property ownership and licences, pension schemes, banking arrangements, material contracts, employment terms, constitutional documents, share capital, competition and trade regulations, licences and insurance. The report will highlight the areas that are made known to the general public in the offer document under existing legislation and also any particular areas of concern to which reference should be made.

As well as gathering together the information required for the prospectus, the company's legal advisers should be checking that the company has proper title to the key assets of the business. They will also be looking out for any unusual obligations or liabilities that might affect the company's value. For example, any unresolved litigation, for which no provision has been made in the accounts, should be highlighted, as should any unduly heavy reliance on a particular supplier or customer.

The second form of due diligence is the verification process. The company's solicitors will prepare a detailed series of questions seeking objective evidence of the correctness of each statement made in the flotation document. The directors will then take responsibility for those statements through their answers to these questions and produce, where possible, independent evidence of the factual basis for those statements. Through this process, directors can obtain comfort that each statement made by them in the offer document can be independently verified. The questions and answers are reviewed by the legal advisers to the sponsor to ensure that evidence is provided wherever practicable.

Documentation

There are a large number of documents to be drafted, negotiated and finally settled for flotation. The principal documentation to be provided will include:

- *The offer document* – the precise nature of this will vary depending on the nature of the offer and whether it is to be underwritten by any sponsor or broker. Its principal terms will be to ensure that the sponsor or broker obtains shareholders for the new shares to be issued or transferred (or possibly to take up the shares itself if it fails to obtain shareholders). The offer document may also contain warranties and indemnities from the directors of the company to the sponsor or broker on their own behalf and on behalf of the shareholders they identify, together with restrictions on future sales of shares by directors and by major shareholders.
- *An application form* under which prospective shareholders may undertake to take up the shares, or a placing letter under which the sponsor or broker will place shares with prospective new shareholders.
- *A raft of additional supporting documentation* to effect the flotation in compliance with the rules of the relevant exchange, including directors' declarations, powers of attorney, directors' responsibility letters, appointment letters for agents/bankers/ merchant bankers, verification notes and board minutes.

The above list is not exhaustive and depends on the nature of the flotation. In particular, the company's lawyer will advise and negotiate on its behalf the offering agreement with the issuing house, especially the warranties and indemnities sought by the sponsor from the directors and/or principal shareholders.

The sanctions for negligently or dishonestly raising finance through the issue of shares are great and, therefore, extreme care must be taken in preparing all of the above documentation.

Continuing obligations

Following flotation, the company and its directors will be subject to continuing obligations on which its lawyers will advise. These include:

- the requirements of the listing rules and disclosure rules of the relevant stock exchange on general and specific disclosure obligations;
- the content and timing of the release of circulars, press announcements, communication with shareholders and other information concerning the company;
- the requirements of the Model Code on directors' dealings, if a listing is in the UK on the Official List, or other relevant best-practice guidelines;
- the preparation of annual reports and accounts in compliance with the relevant listing rules and statutes.

A more detailed discussion on these continuing obligations is provided in Chapter 21.

14

The role of
the reporting
accountants

David Main, Hazlewoods LLP

Introduction

The reporting accountants take a central role in the flotation process. This role is very similar, whether a company is seeking admission to AIM or a flotation on the Official List of the London Stock Exchange. The role has three principal elements:

- providing an independent opinion on financial information included in the document published by the company at the time of flotation;[1]
- providing private letters and reports to the sponsor/nominated adviser[2] and directors of the company to assist them in assessing whether the company is suitable to have its shares admitted for trading on a public market and to provide comfort that certain statements made in the circular have been made with due care;
- providing taxation advice – whilst this is not part of the reporting role of the reporting accountants, it will often be expected that the reporting accountants will provide guidance on taxation issues.

Thinking about floating your company?

Let Hazlewoods steer you in the right direction

Get on board for expert, honest advice that can help steer you towards a successful flotation. Our team has many years of experience in navigating companies though the flotation process, providing expertise in all accounting, taxation and corporate finance matters.

Don't miss the boat,
call David Main on 01452 634800
www.hazlewoods.co.uk

HAZLEWOODS LLP

BUSINESS ADVISERS & CHARTERED ACCOUNTANTS

Authorised and Regulated by the Financial Services Authority

Recent changes

In recent years, there have been a number of changes in the statute and regulations that govern the flotation process and information to be included in the circular. The changes include:

■ The issue in 2003 of the European Prospectus Directive, which was implemented in the UK with effect from 1 July 2005. This changed the rules relating to the financial information to be included in prospectuses. These changes have been reflected in the rules for circulars required at the time of flotation.
■ New Standards for Investment Reporting were issued by the Auditing Practices Board (APB) in 2005 and 2006. These standards contain the basic principles and essential procedures for reporting accountants.
■ In October 2006, the APB issued an Ethical Standard for Reporting Accountants. This standard sets out detailed rules to ensure the independence and objectivity of the reporting accountants.
■ In most cases UK companies will need to restate financial information previously reported in accordance with UK Generally Accepted Accounting Practice (UK GAAP) in accordance with International Financial Reporting Standards (IFRS).
■ The Committee of European Securities Regulators (CESR) from time to time issues recommendations. In 2005, it issued recommendations in respect of financial information to be included in prospectuses and in October 2005 issued technical advice in respect of companies with complex financial histories. All companies are required to follow the CESR recommendations.

It is essential that the reporting accountants have a working knowledge of all of the recent changes so that they are able to guide the company through these often complex requirements.

Are you ready for flotation?

The flotation process brings with it costs in terms of both fees payable to the professional advisory team and a significant amount of time engaged by the company's directors and management. Preparation is the key to ensuring that the process runs as smoothly as possible. Lack of preparation could lead to otherwise avoidable costs and in the worst case could lead to the whole process being aborted.

It is suggested that the reporting accountants should carry out an initial review with the directors of the company in order to identify at an early stage whether there are any likely 'deal breakers' that could lead to the flotation being aborted. This process should also identify any issues which might be resolved prior to the flotation process commencing, to avoid undue delays in the timetable.

The following points will typically be considered:

■ *Financial reporting procedures.* The reporting accountants might discuss the control procedures in place and consider any reports made by the company's auditors on the financial reporting procedures of the company. The directors should ensure that these procedures are sufficiently robust for a company whose shares are to be publicly traded.

■ *Audited historical financial information.* The circular must include a three-year audited track record of the company's historical financial results, except that applicants to AIM must produce that information for the period that they have been in existence if less than three years. An issue that can arise, particularly in the case of AIM applicants, is that the company might have taken advantage of the small-company exemptions from audit. If this is the case, a retrospective audit of the historical results will be required. If any particular problems are anticipated in carrying out this audit, this should be considered at an early stage. For example, if the company holds physical stock, it may be impossible to form an independent opinion as to the existence of those stocks retrospectively.

■ *IFRS.* The rules relating to financial information included in the circular require that the last two years' historical audited financial information must be presented and prepared in a form consistent with that which will be adopted in the company's next published annual financial statements, having regard to the accounting standards and policies and legislation applicable to such annual financial statements. This effectively means that many UK companies will need to convert their previously audited financial statements to comply with IFRS. The challenge of converting historical information prepared under UKGAAP in accordance with IFRS should not be underestimated. The APB Ethical Standard does not permit the reporting accountants to carry out this conversion exercise on behalf of the company.

■ *Financial resources.* The company will need to ensure that it will have sufficient financial resources following flotation. The reporting accountants will discuss with the directors how the directors plan to fund the company.

■ *Re-registration as a public limited company (plc).* The company must be registered as a plc. In order to re-register an existing limited company, the company must obtain a report from its auditors confirming that it has net assets that exceed the total of its share capital and undistributable reserves, based on a balance sheet dated not more than seven months prior to the re-registration. This is not possible if the company has accumulated losses. There are possible solutions to such problems that should be discussed and agreed with the company's professional advisers.

■ *Complex financial histories.* If within the last three years there has been a group reorganization or significant acquisition, this can provide particular challenges in presenting meaningful financial information in the circular. This might mean presenting pro forma information or aggregated audited financial information for entities that did not in fact form a legal group prior to the reorganization or significant acquisition. A thoughtful approach is required and should be agreed with the sponsor.

■ *Taxation.* A review of the company's taxation affairs should also be considered at the planning stage to address major issues that might cause difficulties or delays.

Financial due diligence

Probably the largest part of the work of the reporting accountants will be to carry out a detailed investigation into the business and financial affairs of the company. The reporting accountant will produce a detailed report that is referred to as a 'long-form report'.

The principal purpose of this exercise is to provide detailed information to the sponsor so that it can fulfil its duties to the Stock Exchange in ensuring that the company is suitable for flotation.

The scope of the report will be agreed in advance with the sponsor and the directors of the company, and this will be confirmed in writing.

The reporting accountants will issue a detailed list of the information required in order to carry out the due diligence exercise. The reporting accountants' team will require access to directors and management in order to carry out a series of interviews to obtain a thorough understanding of the dynamics of the business.

The reporting accountants' team will be alert to problems identified during the due diligence process and should discuss any such issues firstly with directors and management and with the sponsor so that these can be tackled at an early stage.

Typical content of the long-form report might include the following:

- executive summary;
- history and background – including major developments in the history of the company;
- nature and conduct of the trade – a detailed analysis of the business and its dynamics;
- management and employees – giving details of the management team to enable an assessment to be made of the quality of management, and to provide details about the workforce;
- financial reporting procedures, accounting systems and internal controls – giving a description of systems and controls in place within the company;
- accounting policies – description and assessment of the major accounting policies adopted by the company;
- trading results – a detailed commentary and analysis of the last three years' trading;
- net assets – a detailed commentary and analysis will be provided on all elements of the company's balance sheet;
- cash flow – a commentary on cash flow movements for the previous three years;
- taxation – a detailed review of the company's corporation tax history, consideration of any ongoing matters that might affect future tax charges compliance with other taxation regulations, such as VAT, PAYE and National Insurance will also be considered.

The long-form report is of assistance to the sponsor in drafting the circular.

Working capital requirements

The directors of the company will be required to make a statement that the company will have sufficient working capital for its present requirements, that is to say at least 12 months from the date the company's shares are admitted for trading.

The directors will need to compile detailed financial forecasts that should usually extend to at least 18 months after the expected date of flotation, supported by a list of detailed assumptions. The directors should formally adopt the working capital forecasts.

The reporting accountants review the basis on which the forecasts have been prepared and confirm to the directors and sponsor that they have been compiled on a basis that is consistent with the stated assumptions and that, in the opinion of the reporting accountants, the directors' statement about working capital has been made after due and careful enquiry.

The reporting accountants will produce a report setting out the results of their enquiries. This report will include a sensitivity ('what if?') analysis in respect of the principal assumptions. This report is a private report to the sponsor and directors. The reporting accountants will not provide an opinion in respect of working capital for publication in the circular.

Other comfort letters

In addition to the working capital and long-form reports, the reporting accountants typically provide other letters to the sponsor and directors that provide assurance that they have each properly fulfilled their respective responsibilities. Again, these letters are not for publication. Typically, the reporting accountants will provide the following:

- *Significant change.* Any significant changes in the financial or trading positions of the company must be disclosed in the circular. The reporting accountants will carry out a review to establish whether any such changes have arisen and will provide a letter confirming that they are not aware of any such changes or highlighting such changes identified.
- *Financial reporting procedures.* The directors must confirm to the sponsor that they have established procedures that will give them a reasonable basis on which to make proper judgements on an ongoing basis as to the financial position and prospects of the company. The sponsor will seek assurance from the reporting accountants that this is the case. The directors should support the basis for their confirmation to the sponsor in a board memorandum. The reporting accountants cannot give any assurance on the day-to-day effectiveness of the procedures that are in place. The comfort letter is intended to give comfort only that the directors have gone through an appropriate process to ensure that their confirmation is made after due and careful enquiry.
- *Other financial information.* The reporting accountants will usually check that extracts from audited financial information included in the circular have been

properly compiled, and will provide a comfort letter to this effect to the directors and sponsor.

■ *Tax disclosures.* The circular will include a summary of the tax legislation that will apply to investors in the company. The reporting accountants usually provide a letter to confirm that this provides a fair summary of the relevant legislation.

Published historical financial information

As indicated above, the circular will include at least three years' historical financial information that must have been independently audited or reported upon.

In theory, a company can merely reproduce its previously published annual financial statements in the circular. In practice, however, this approach is not usually adopted because, although less costly, it produces a rather cumbersome document. Furthermore, relatively few unlisted UK companies have chosen to adopt IFRS early. This means that most companies now seeking a flotation are likely to have to go through the process of restating at least their last two sets of audited results in accordance with IFRS.

It is likely, therefore, that in most cases a new three-year historical financial information table will be included in the circular, presented in columnar format. The information will appear very similar in format to published financial statements, except that there will be three years' information rather than two.

The reporting accountants provide an independent opinion as to whether, for the purposes of the circular, the financial information provides a true and fair view of the state of affairs as at each of the three balance sheet dates and of the profits, cash flows, recognized gains and losses and changes in equity for each of the three periods then ended. The format for this report is specified in Standards for Investment Reporting 2000 issued by APB.

The reporting accountants are not permitted by the APB Ethical Standard to participate in the preparation of the historical financial information. This contrasts with the previous situation that existed whereby the historical financial information was often compiled by the reporting accountants, who also provided an opinion thereon.

The financial information included within the circular must cover a period ending not more than nine months prior to the date of publication of the circular. Some sponsors adopt a house rule that such information should not be more than six months out of date. If information is more than nine months old, then interim financial information must also be included.

Any interim financial information can be unaudited and must cover at least the first six months of the financial year and include a comparative profit and loss account and cash flow statement for the same period in the prior financial year. In many instances however, the reporting accountants will be instructed to include the interim results within the scope of their opinion. Careful consideration will need to be given as to how the comparative profit and loss account and cash flow information will be presented for the interim period and whether such information can be readily compiled.

The reporting accountants are required to obtain sufficient appropriate evidence to support their opinion. It is, however, permissible for the reporting accountants to use audit evidence obtained by the auditors of the company's annual financial statements. If the reporting accountants conclude that the auditors' work is not adequate, if they do not have access to the auditors' working papers or if an audit has not previously been performed, the reporting accountants should perform procedures to compensate for this.

If the auditors are from a different firm to the reporting accountants, the auditors will normally, in accordance with the relevant professional guidance, make their working papers available to the reporting accountants. Such access would normally be given on the basis that the auditors accept no responsibility or liability to the reporting accountants.

Pro forma financial information

Pro forma financial information must be included in the circular to indicate the effect of transactions that cause a significant gross change to the company's business in the case of a company being admitted to the Official List of the Stock Exchange. A significant gross change is a transaction that causes a variation of more than 25 per cent relative to one or more indicators of the size of the issuer's business.

If the company is applying for admission to AIM it is not a requirement that pro forma information is included in the circular, unless the circular is also a prospectus as defined by legislation.

Where pro forma information is required, this must be accompanied by a report by the reporting accountants. The report will provide an opinion as to whether the pro forma financial information has been properly compiled on the basis stated and that the basis is consistent with the accounting policies of the company.

Forecast financial information

In relatively rare instances, a company might include forecast financial information within the circular. The reporting accountants will be required to report on any profit forecast or estimate. The opinion required in the report is that the forecast has been properly compiled on the basis of the stated assumptions made by the directors and that the basis of accounting used is consistent with the accounting policies applied by the company.

Conclusion

The reporting accountants have a wide range of responsibilities. The skills required include a high level of technical expertise, commercial awareness and taxation knowledge. The last few years have seen considerable change in applicable regulations. It is therefore essential that any technical issues are carefully considered at the outset and the approach agreed by all parties.

Notes

1. The type of document published will be determined by whether the company is seeking a listing on the Official List of the London Stock Exchange or seeking admission to AIM. It will also depend on whether a prospectus is required. For convenience the document to be issued will be referred to as 'the circular' throughout this chapter.
2. In the case of a company seeking a listing on the Official List of the London Stock Exchange they will appoint a sponsor whereas if seeking admission to AIM a nominated adviser will be appointed. For convenience this chapter will refer to both roles as 'sponsor'.

15

The role of the broker

Tim Davis, Charles Stanley Securities

Definition

A broker is a securities house that is also a member firm of the London Stock Exchange. Under the AIM Rules, an AIM company must retain a broker at all times to manage dealings in the company's ordinary shares. The London Stock Exchange maintains lists of nomads and brokers on its website (www.londonstockexchange.com).

Brokers engaged in fund-raising are usually *institutional* specialists: on the one hand, they have corporate clients (such as the prospective IPO candidate) and, on the other, institutional clients.

In this case, institutions are defined as those specializing in investing in AIM and small-cap companies, be they fund management groups, the investment arms of insurance companies and pension funds, hedge funds, specialist inheritance tax (IHT) funds or venture capital trusts (VCTs).

Nomad/broker relationship

Whilst companies can opt to use separate firms for nomad and broker, the majority of AIM specialists tend to provide both roles. In practical terms, the two sides of the business are subject to clear rules and restrictions and are run independently and divided by a so-called Chinese wall.

The benefit of using one integrated firm for the IPO is the nomad or advisory team's immediate proximity to the broking team, which tends to be much more efficient in terms of time, communication/reporting, management of expectations, administration and cost to the company.

Typical structure

The nomad/broker will have a corporate finance department that advises corporate clients on all regulatory and nomad-related matters.

On the other side of the Chinese wall is equity research and sales. This is where the equity research analysts publish research coverage (including comprehensive analysis and forecasts) on quoted companies, be they corporate clients or non-clients of the firm. Typically, they will be industry sector specialists with extensive expertise. Their research is in turn used by the broker's equity sales team to sell investment ideas on particular companies, or indeed industry sectors, to institutional clients.

The equity sales team will work closely with the sales traders, who provide timely and efficient execution of transactions within the stock market. The firm may also have a market-making facility, which will work separately from the rest of the equities team.

Areas of responsibility – summary

In broad terms, the broker's role in the IPO is to:

■ assess the appropriateness of the company as an IPO candidate;
■ assist in determining a valuation range for the shares, possibly with the benefit of test marketing;
■ provide comprehensive equity research analysis on the company;
■ identify likely investors and arrange the fund-raising roadshow; and
■ take overall responsibility for the actual fund-raising and provide input on pricing.

Post-IPO, it is the broker's responsibility to:

■ manage the secondary market, ie the market for the company's shares trading on AIM as opposed to its IPO role of selling new shares to investors;
■ help manage relationships with existing institutional investors;
■ provide equity research coverage;
■ match buyers and sellers of shares;
■ identify and educate potential investors; and
■ manage subsequent institutional fund-raisings by the company.

Role in preparing for the IPO

The broker's role is arguably the most important in the IPO process as, without its fund-raising capability, the efforts of the remainder of the client's professional team count for nothing.

The broker will be involved at the earliest stage in the planning of the IPO. Its view on whether the company is a viable IPO prospect – what it believes the stock market *will* buy and at what price – is fundamental to the whole process; hence it will provide this in the very earliest stages of the planning.

The broker will consider the following: the type of business, the industry space in which it operates, its stage of development and the outlook for the business and the market(s) it serves. Within this, the broker will consider:

■ the perceived quality, ability, ambition and track record of the management team;

■ management's ability to grow the business, profitably, and to capitalize on the company's opportunity;

■ the perceived ability of management to operate in the public arena;

■ management's approach to corporate governance, including non-executive directors;

■ the overall structure of the business, from board and management composition through to robustness of IT systems and financial controls;

■ the robustness of the company's business plan and strategy;

■ the financial health of the business, specifically with regard to debt levels, cash flow and its ability to generate appropriate profits both to reinvest in the business and to pay dividends;

■ the historical financial track record of the business and anticipated profits in the current and next two years (brokers typically forecast two to three years out);

■ the company's competitive position or uniqueness within its own marketplace and the outlook for the marketplace itself;

■ the scalability of the business, be it via organic growth or acquisition;

■ the performances and valuations of any companies already quoted and perceived as comparable;

■ the amount of new money the company wishes to raise and the use of the proceeds;

■ the amount of old, or existing, shares to be sold and how those sales relate to the continuing management team;

■ dilution of existing shareholders;

■ the likelihood and timings of subsequent fund-raisings;

■ any discount in valuation that will need to be applied in order to attract investors;

■ optimum timing for the IPO, taking into account stock market and prevailing industry conditions, the reporting (and audit) cycle of the company and the most appropriate timing for the company, the latter typically determined by a balance of sales growth, visibility of profits and need for funds; and

■ which institutional clients are likely to be interested in investing, both initially and medium-term, and their typical 'unit size', ie units of investment, whether measured in tens or hundreds of thousands or millions of pounds.

Following this part of the process, the broker will also arrive at a likely valuation range, which will help determine both viability of the IPO and its timing.

Preparation for IPO

Although the primary responsibility for the content of the admission document rests with the nomad, the broker will have input, specifically as to how the company is presented and the investment proposition articulated. Bear in mind that this document, with its extensive verification, serves as a lasting benchmark to which investors will continue to refer back – sometimes even years after the IPO.

The broker's analyst will prepare a pre-IPO research note on the company, which will encapsulate the investment proposition, describing in detail the business, its management, the competitive environment in which it operates, its strategy and reasons for IPO, together with detailed analysis of its historical financial performance – mirroring information that will be in the admission document. This note is purely for the benefit of potential institutional investors.

Similarly, the broker will have extensive involvement in the development of the marketing presentation (itself also derived from the draft admission document) that will be used at the meetings with potential investors. The importance of this cannot be stressed enough. Fund managers are spoilt for choice when it comes to companies wanting their money, so the presentation must be both persuasive and highly informative (explaining the business, the opportunity, why the company is floating and how much it seeks to raise and why) and be delivered confidently and professionally. At all times, it must reflect the content of the admission document and not inadvertently provide any additional information.

Equally, questions – often penetrating – must be answered. Dependent upon the uniqueness of the business, it may also be necessary to sell the attractions of the company's industry space and the potential it offers – all in, typically, 45 minutes to include questions and answers! The presentation will be subject to extensive development, rehearsal and verification, as will the likely questions and suggested answers.

With the admission document developing and with a reasonably refined presentation, the broker is likely to engage in some limited test marketing with potential institutional investors. This is as much to do with testing the appeal of the investment proposition as it is giving the management team – typically executive chairman or chief executive but definitely finance director – the opportunity for some first-hand practice. Most of all, the meetings provide vital feedback on the likely reception to the particular proposition, together with early indications of the valuation range.

A placing agreement – between company and broker – will be required. This sets out the terms and conditions of the placing and the broker's undertaking of the fund-raising. It usually contains warranties and indemnities to protect the broker in respect of information in the admission document and other information that will have been provided by the company's management.

Role during IPO

With this in hand, the formal contact with potential institutional investors can commence.

In some cases, in addition to the pre-IPO research note, a pathfinder prospectus may be available. This is effectively the admission document but without the final information such as pricing and related share statistics. The distribution of this document is strictly limited to 'appropriate' individuals, ie institutional investors.

In a typical fund-raising and IPO, the roadshow will equate to a two- to three-week period spent at meetings in London, with a few days in Scotland also likely. In the earlier stages, feedback from the fund managers will again help to mould the message. All meetings are followed up and interest in investing and, importantly, at what price, gauged – the first step in so-called 'book building'.

At the end of this part of the process, the broker will be able to determine likely demand, the pricing range at which institutions will buy shares and the amounts they are interested in investing.

The final pricing and share allocation is determined by company and nomad, but with input from the broker. The pricing will also reflect the need to maximize proceeds whilst balancing the need for new money versus dilution of existing shareholders.

Liquidity in the aftermarket is also an important consideration: the issue will be priced so that there is a positive reception by the wider stock market – usually resulting in a marginal increase in the share price in the first few days of trading.

With pricing and allocation agreed, the broker issues 'placing letters', irrevocable agreements between the broker and new investors to buy quantities of the company's shares at an agreed price. Key to this is allocation: ideally the company will start life as a quoted company with as wide a spread of institutional investors as is possible, not least of all to help with aftermarket liquidity.

The broker is also responsible for collecting the new funds and for ensuring that the new shares are issued correctly.

Role post-IPO – the secondary market

The broker's primary role is to provide a conduit between the company and institutional investors, ensuring that the company and its performance are at all times fully understood and appreciated, with a view to maintaining existing investors' support for the company.

In parallel, the broker will 'bring on' what could become the next generation of investors, in the event of existing shares becoming available or new shares being issued.

As a basis for this, the broker will assist the company with the formulation of an ongoing investor relations programme. Quoted companies are bound to report full- and half-year results and to communicate with the stock market on a continuing basis, so as to ensure that the market is aware of their financial position and prospects at all times. Similarly, a company is bound by continuing obligations to ensure an orderly market in its shares, the main one being to notify the market immediately of any developments that could impact – positively or negatively – on the company's share price.

The annual programme will be designed to maintain the company's visibility with existing and potential investors and to demonstrate continuing progress in line with market expectations.

Typically, it will revolve around the full and half-year results announcements, with update or introductory meetings offered at that time to existing and potential institutional investors respectively. Again, a tailored presentation will be required, covering both the period under review and an update on current trading.

At the same time, usually via its financial public relations advisers, the company will meet with the financial, investment and industry trade press and may also meet a mix of other brokers' analysts and interested private client investment managers. Interest from the latter can be very helpful in terms of stimulating marginal liquidity.

The company broker's analyst is likely, off the back of the company's half-yearly results announcements, to publish a research note updating the stock market on the company's performance, both in terms of the period under review and in the context of his or her published forecasts for future performance, which, from time to time and dependent upon the company's performance, the analyst may update. He or she will probably also publish occasional newsflow-driven updates on the company and provide coverage of comparable companies so as to help with the understanding and evaluation of the corporate client.

The broker will also work with the company and its financial public relations advisers to ensure that it remains visible between results announcements. Ideally, this will equate to two or three additional announcements made on the regulatory news services in each six-month period. Announcements may include news of acquisitions, disposals, joint ventures, senior management appointments, contract wins and suchlike.

The broker may also feel it necessary to hold occasional update or introductory meetings for fund managers, or to hold an annual facility visit – an opportunity for investors to experience operational aspects of the business at first hand and to meet divisional management.

The broker is also responsible for managing the process of company directors selling shares (or indeed purchases), once any lock-in arrangements have expired. Typically, these shares are sold to fund managers that may be existing holders, or non-holders that have got to know the company and have expressed interest in buying stock.

The broker's equity sales team will also provide a day-to-day information conduit between stock market and company, providing updates on anything relevant to them and their shares, such as general stock market conditions, market reaction to their own and competitor news, share price movements, activity in the company's shares, to include any information on share volumes, or feedback from fund managers.

It is important to stress that an investor relations programme is exactly that: it is an agreed and proactive approach to looking after the interests of this critical audience, with the main activity milestones agreed in good time, but with inbuilt flexibility. More, it is a discipline for the company's management to enter into right at the start of the company's life as a quoted company, and is expected of them by the stock market. From the company management's perspective, it need not take excessive amounts of time if planned well and in advance.

A common adage within the stock market is that companies must always meet, or just exceed, stock market expectations. In doing this, remaining transparent at all other times and maintaining a sensible investor relations programme, the company should be properly understood and valued accordingly.

Achieve more.

KBC Peel Hunt is the investment bank for growth companies.
Two things make us special. Being part of the KBC Group gives
us enormous strength. But strength means nothing without
commitment. We never let our clients down and won't give up
until we succeed. Two words sum us up – can do. Which means
you'll achieve more.

For more information please go to www.kbcpeelhunt.com

CRICKET
TEST MATCH

ENTRANCE
500 metres

◄——

KBC Peel Hunt
www.kbcpeelhunt.com

16

Key issues for the company, the nomad and the broker

David Davies, KBC Peel Hunt

Introduction

Selecting a nominated adviser (nomad) and broker for an AIM IPO and to look after your company afterwards is one of the most important decisions that will be made in the company's publicly listed career. Choosing the right partner(s) can make the difference between success and failure, so it is vital that boards understand what they should be looking for and what they can expect from their investment banking partner, as well as how this relationship will develop.

Responsibilities

In short, a nomad will be guardian and driver of the IPO process and afterwards assist the company in its new life as a publicly listed company. It is responsible for coordinating all the other advisers and ensuring the float proceeds safely and successfully. The nomad will also have responsibilities to AIM, explained in further detail at the end of this chapter.

The broker, which may or may not be part of the same investment house, is in charge of finding a home for the shares that will be issued to raise the funds needed, primarily amongst institutional investors.

An integrated broker and nomad?

Brokers invariably have two clients: the company and the institution/investor in the shares to be offered.

Nomads without broking arms claim that they are independent from the broker selling the shares, removing any conflict of interest in pricing. Companies are sometimes concerned that the broker will underprice the shares to give a cheap deal to its institutional clients. This fear is rarely proven, because there is generally a price at which investors will agree to buy the shares and no end of argument will persuade them to buy at a higher price. The 'book-building' fund-raising method that is widely used, where investors state how many shares they will buy at various prices, allowing the shares to be sold to those offering to pay the most, also negates this concern.

It is worth noting that the large majority of companies listed in the UK use integrated houses for their fund-raising and associated advisory work, eliminating a huge overlap of work, reducing fees and generally increasing efficiency.

> *Myth*: However much a nomad might say that your shares should be priced at xp, in fact it is the investors who decide

What a company should look for from its broker and nomad

Track record

A healthy and strong track record in completed transactions for your size and sector is vital and will give an indication of how well the broker and nomad could perform for you. Don't just check the success of completing IPOs; the continuing relationship after the float is just as important.

Check the reputation of a nomad or broker by taking references from its other clients, which should be given to you or listed on its website.

Consider approaching other trusted advisers, including accountants, lawyers and PR professionals, to canvass their opinions. If they have an expertise in your sector, they will be able to provide a clear insight into the workings and past successes and failures of the nomad or broker and its reputation in the market.

A number of broking organizations have market-making departments, which stand in the market and offer to buy and sell shares from all comers. Companies should actively consider this when selecting their stockbroker, because market-making often aids liquidity in the company's stock, especially for smaller, AIM listed companies, which may be less actively traded.

Note: Track record is important. If nomads and brokers are associated with companies that have been successful, then institutions are more likely to support their issues.

Sector knowledge base

Do your nomad and broker understand your business, or are you constantly going to have to explain everything and put it in context? If they don't understand your business, how can they sell it to investors?

What you should be looking for is an adviser with a sound knowledge of your sector, but with a wide enough base of clients and contacts to mitigate any possible conflicts that might arise. Chinese walls between corporate finance advisers and the analysts/salespeople are in place to protect you from leaks of confidential information to your competitors.

Note: If you and a competitor are both advised by the same adviser and want to make the same acquisition or raise funds at the same time, it will be impossible for the adviser to act for both of you.

Service levels

When selecting a broker or nomad, keep in mind that the relationship is not just for the IPO but on an ongoing basis post-IPO. Every AIM company is required to retain a nomad and broker at all times. You need to be happy that the advisers will not pocket the IPO fee and then ignore you and let your share price drift.

While the nomad's role in ensuring that you are well advised on compliance with the AIM Rules is important, the broker's role is key to ensure ongoing interest in your shares and to act as a liaison between you and your new investors.

For the IPO, the nomad will field a corporate finance team to work on the float, usually made up of director, assistant director, manager and executive. There will be other individuals from the broking team working on the account, including an analyst, institutional salespeople and possibly a corporate broking representative.

The intense work will be led by the corporate finance team, acting as ringmaster to coordinate the IPO process, with the fund-raising the responsibility of the broking team.

The IPO timetable and responsibilities

A regular dialogue will be maintained throughout the IPO process between the company and its advisers, towards the end of the process on a daily basis. The nomad will keep a timetable and monitor delivery of key documents from the rest of the advisory team and the company in order to deliver the IPO when promised. Companies tend to forget that they have a business to run during the time-consuming IPO process, and need to ensure that they are capable of keeping to the timetable themselves without unduly stressing the business. This is because the finance director and the chief executive will effectively be doing two jobs during a typical three- or four-month IPO.

Companies may need to respond to the broking analyst's queries to allow a research report (independent to the AIM admission document) to be written. This report, which contains forecasts for the business, is provided to potential investors and is a key factor in an investor's decision whether or not to invest.

Towards the end of the process, before the roadshow to raise the funds, the broking team will assist in honing the roadshow presentation, which is then made to possible investors during an intense period when up to 10 investors are met each day. After the money is raised it's back to the corporate finance team, which confirms investor commitments and secures the funds.

Post-IPO

Once a company's shares are listed, it will continue to have contact (although less regular) with its nomad and broking adviser. Contact relating to day-to-day trading in the shares will be mainly with the broker's sales team; they should be working on finding buyers and sellers of shares to satisfy market demand.

The broker's analyst will write research notes for the institutional and private investor audience whenever there is a corporate action and/or every half-year on the publication of results.

The nomad should keep in touch on a regular basis to assist with compliance with the AIM Rules and generally to monitor how things are going. The company should openly discuss any possible corporate activity, such as an acquisition or fund-raising, that it is planning, to ensure that it receives appropriate advice.

Note: Whilst a comparison of fees will doubtless be a part of the selection process, advisers offering the lowest fees may not provide the best service. Nomads and brokers that are most sought after may well charge more than others, as they offer more expertise, leading to a more efficient transaction and a better likelihood of success.

Pitching process

Key questions for companies to ask themselves during the pitch process for brokers and nomads are:

- Have I met all of the team and are they all fired up by my company?
- Do they understand my business?
- Have I determined who will be the team working for me at the nomad/broker and can I work with these people?
- Do they have a track record of success, to deliver what I need (the IPO)?
- Have the references received been positive?
- Will they achieve the promised valuation for the company or have they inflated this value just to win my business?
- Is their aftermarket service strong?

Take advice

You are employing your nomad and broker to give you the best chance for a successful IPO. They see many companies and know what will be best received by investors, so it is not unusual for changes to the structure or operation of the business to be suggested. This can be difficult for a company to accept, but it is worth bearing in mind that advisers generally don't make companies jump through hoops without good reason. Advisers will work hard to ensure the best chance of a successful IPO, and they also know what is suitable for the AIM market. If the company doesn't like the advice that it is receiving, then it should have a full and frank discussion with the advisers, talk with its non-executive directors (who should have had some experience of operating in a listed market) and discuss the experience with other advisers (such as accounting, legal and PR). While failing to take this advice may not necessarily mean that an IPO is impossible, it may affect the will of the nomad or broker to handle the process or result in a lower valuation being achieved.

> *Note*: If a nomad or broker has taken the trouble to establish a specialist team to focus on a particular sector, then its understanding of that market should be significantly better than that of a generalist. Institutions are more likely to show interest in issues from a specialist, as they are better placed to pick the winners, thereby improving the chances of a successful IPO.

Potential problem areas

At the early stages in the process, companies, brokers and nomads agree to work together after relatively little information has passed between them, on the assumption that things are more or less going to turn out as expected.

If a company at an early stage paints a different picture from that which the nomad and broker discover when they complete their due diligence, this could affect your relationship with them. The advisers might have thought they were floating a formula one car, but in fact it is a formula two car! It doesn't mean that a float is impossible but does mean that the indicative valuation that was originally indicated may be wrong.

Market conditions also have the tendency to change on a frequent basis. A valuation indication on a given day for a float six months in the future may prove inaccurate (especially if the valuation or the broker's ability to raise funds has been exaggerated). Such events may alter the willingness of either the company or the adviser (or both) to proceed with the transaction, and the IPO could be delayed until more positive market conditions arrive.

Golden rules for companies when dealing with advisers

1. *Present a fair and balanced picture of the company.* Sometimes a company will be tempted to 'talk up' its business and make optimistic promises at a fairly early stage. However, be wary. If they are seen to be or proved false within a relatively short time, this will be a serious concern for the adviser. The key for any company is not to promise too much – preferably under-promise and over-deliver.
2. *Stick to your forecasts.* A cardinal sin is to miss a forecast. For example, if a company meets an adviser or broker six months before the IPO and says that in three months it will report profits of £10 million and then the profits come in at £9.6 million – irrespective of whether this is an impressive 50 per cent growth instead of 60 per cent – this will knock the confidence of the broker. It is much better for the company to act conservatively and say that it will come in at a £9.5 million profit level and then beat that by reporting £9.6 million profits.
3. *Make sure you can work with your advisers.* It is very important to keep the personal aspect in mind when you are selecting an adviser and a broker. These are people you are going to be working with on an intensive basis both up to the IPO and thereafter. It is important that you get on with them. Once you have shortlisted those with the right credentials, a large amount of your decision will be down to whether you can work with the team and whether you trust them – everyone has a different style.
4. *Be prepared and be open.* You should field the chief executive and finance director for the pitch to your prospective nomad and broker. It is uncommon for an AIM company to field many other representatives, possibly apart from a senior non-executive director, especially if they have quoted company experience. Both the chief executive and finance director also need to be available for all meetings with investors and advisers leading up to the IPO. Be expert on your financial information, both historical and future. Nothing is less impressive than

a company coming into a meeting where relatively straightforward questions on the numbers or on the business can't be answered.

What the nomad is looking for

- To generate fees from this company both during the IPO and ongoing.
- To ensure that the company will take appropriate advice – it is a key service that is provided by the nomad, so to have it ignored will give rise to concerns on compliance with relevant rules.
- To ensure that the company will be honest and open in disclosing its business and plans and can be trusted to follow the AIM Rules.
- That at the time of the IPO and afterwards it can fulfil its ongoing responsibilities to the market and LSE to look after that company.
- That the business will meet the expectations set by the directors.
- That the company will not damage its reputation.

The AIM Rules set out guidance on what is expected of a nomad – this includes checks on directors and the efficacy of the board, visits to the company's premises to verify that it is what it says it is, a sound understanding of the company and the business, and carrying out due diligence on the business (which can be subcontracted to lawyers, accountants and commercial due diligence providers).

What the broker is looking for

- Similar answers to those sought by the nomad.
- To ensure that the company has a story that will be supported by investors, both at the time of the IPO and afterwards.
- To ensure that the management will be capable and available to present to investors when necessary.
- That the company will not disappoint investors post-IPO.

Helping your ideas to blossom

In recent years H W Fisher & Company has emerged as a leading force in transaction services. And over those years, we have had the satisfaction of watching our clients grow and prosper.

The success of these businesses is primarily due to the energy and talents of their management. But we like to think we also played an important role.

Our transaction services cover financial due diligence, reporting accountants, commercial and market due diligence, and company structuring. In every area, we combine a high level of technical expertise with an absolute commitment to personal service.

If you would like to learn how we can help your own ideas blossom, contact Gary Miller. We look forward to hearing from you.

H.W.FISHER & COMPANY
CHARTERED ACCOUNTANTS

Acre House, 11-15 William Road, London NW1 3ER
Tel: **020 7388 7000** Email: **info@hwfisher.co.uk**
www.hwfisher.co.uk

CREATIVITY ENTHUSIASM ENERGY VISION

Part of The Fisher Organisation

17

Due diligence: what it is and what it should cover

Gary Miller, H W Fisher & Company

Studies often show that when a company acquisition fails it is frequently because of problems that were identified only after the transaction was completed. If this is true, it suggests that the due diligence process tends to be less diligent than it might be.

In this context it is sometimes argued that standard due diligence techniques rely excessively upon historical data. Audited accounts provide a record of the target company's recent past, but tell us little about its immediate prospects. For that matter, any financial information, even current management accounts, can reveal only part of the picture. Key issues such as the exact nature of the relationship between the company and its customers (or suppliers) are often obscure. Matters such as the company's reputation in the marketplace or the threat posed by new competitors are seldom understood in detail.

If this is so, the apparent solution might be to make the due diligence process much wider. The acquiring company or its representatives should get out into the field. They should interview customers and suppliers and carry out detailed analysis of brand shares and market trends. They should understand what effect the acquisition may have upon the workforce of the target company, particularly key staff whose support could be essential.

The problem with this is that the process could drag on interminably, sorely trying the patience of the vendors. Cost, too, is an issue: a due diligence process that left no stone unturned could mean hefty fees that might be difficult to justify. If the transaction is a very large one, and if there are no other potential buyers in the frame, then it may be reasonable to adopt this approach. But in many cases, acquirers will be under time pressure, and the deal is unlikely to be so large that the cost of due diligence is an insignificant factor.

Another important point concerns notification of employees of the target company. It is probable that they will not have been told, at this stage at least, of the impending deal. However, if the due diligence investigations are such that staff begin to suspect that something is afoot, they may well become uneasy about their jobs. Some might conclude – key employees among them – that they should begin to look for other employment prospects.

What is the answer to this dilemma? Is there a due diligence strategy that can satisfy the demands of rigour without putting the deal in jeopardy and without costing very large amounts? There is probably not one approach that is appropriate in all cases, but acquiring companies that decide at an early stage what information is crucial, and what is not, stand a much better chance of success.

Even before the process begins, acquirers should think carefully about these matters. Professional advisers sometimes complain that their due diligence instructions are rather vague and lack precision. It should always be remembered that due diligence is not an audit. In other words, there are no statutory requirements, and it can be as comprehensive or as thorough as the instructing company wishes.

Of course, advisers should be able to help their client to decide upon the nature of the brief. After all, they will have been through this process many times, whereas the acquiring company's management may be experiencing it for the first time. Ultimately, however, the decision over what to include and what to omit is one for the purchaser.

The vendor's perspective

In saying that, I am assuming that due diligence is always a matter for the buyer, something that may seem self-evidently true. Recently, however, a new phenomenon has emerged – vendor's due diligence.

Why would vendors wish to undertake due diligence of a business they already own and which, presumably, they understand in detail – warts and all? The reason is that, in today's highly competitive mergers and acquisitions market, due diligence carried out by the vendor might make the target company more attractive to potential purchasers. The aim is to create a package of information that – the seller hopes – may be relied upon. At the very least, it provides a dossier that covers most essential factors, saving the buyer time and money.

But if there are no clear rules governing the issues buyers' due diligence should cover, there is even less certainty when it comes to due diligence carried out by vendors. However, a full review should be able to assist purchasers in a number of ways. It will:

- provide useful information that can act as a starting point for buyers and help them to set priorities for their own investigations;
- reduce the time (and cost) of due diligence carried out by buyers;
- reduce the disruption to the vendor's business. This is particularly important if there are a number of potential buyers, all with their own sets of advisers who might wish to make site visits and trawl through the target company's books.

While vendor due diligence can be helpful, it also has its potential drawbacks. Chief among these is the extent to which the purchaser may rely upon the information, if at all. Remember that the information will normally have been drawn up by the seller's advisers, who will be keenly aware of any conflict-of-interest issues. They may therefore wish to confine their report to purely factual matters, and avoid giving any opinions or emphasizing issues that might discourage the buyer from proceeding.

Accordingly, any potential purchasers who are presented with a vendor's due diligence report will wish to satisfy themselves about the nature of the brief that gave rise to it. They may also wish to seek agreement with the vendor about information that can be relied upon, and put this agreement in writing.

What due diligence should cover

But to return to due diligence carried out by the purchaser, the investigation broadly aims to answer two questions: 1) Does the financial position of the business justify the assumptions that were made in arriving at the initial indicative offer? 2) What matters will require the protection of warranties or indemnities?

Above, I referred to audited accounts and other financial statements. Acquirers might tend to assume that these can be relied upon – the audited accounts, at any rate. But there have been a number of cases in which acquirers did so and subsequently found material errors in the figures. In these instances, they are unlikely to have any redress. The reason is that auditors owe a duty only to the company whose accounts are being audited, and not to any future purchaser.

As a result, purchasers should instruct their accountants to carry out financial due diligence in most instances. Their report will not amount to a complete audit, as noted, but will concentrate on matters that have a bearing on the deal, including assets, liabilities and tax liabilities.

The accountants' report will normally also consider matters such as the nature of the customers, particularly whether there is excessive reliance upon a relatively small number, and other broad business issues such as competitive activity.

Of course, the due diligence report will not exclusively concentrate upon financial issues. Legal due diligence (carried out by the acquirer's solicitors) is also vital, and there may also be a need to examine environmental and technical matters. As a result, several different professional advisers could be involved, and there may be grey areas where their responsibilities overlap. To avoid unnecessary duplication and confusion (which could conceivably lead to important matters being overlooked), each adviser should have detailed terms of engagement. It is also helpful to nominate a specific individual in the acquiring company to liaise with advisers and coordinate their work.

Books and records

Later in this chapter I will provide a checklist of the main matters that financial due diligence should examine. However, it is important not to become so immersed in detail that the overall picture is lost. The first questions that financial due diligence should ask are the following:

- Are the books and records up to date?
- Does the information contained in the books agree with the data held at Companies House?
- Are share certificates held by the target company, or can they be readily obtained?

Tax

Generally, the purchaser's accountants will review the target company's tax affairs, but this is an area where the lawyers sometimes become involved, so it is important for these advisers to liaise with each other.

Employment

Here, too, there could be an overlap between accountants and lawyers. The legal advisers might be responsible for ensuring that all employees have contracts of employment and that the implications of these are clearly understood. The accountants will want to evaluate the costs of taking over the contracts and to understand the possible consequences of bonus schemes, commissions, share schemes or other profit-sharing arrangements.

An important point in all of this is the nature of the acquisition. If the shares in the target company are being purchased, employees will continue to be employed by the target company after the transaction is completed. If the business is purchased as a going concern, contracts of employment will be transferred to the acquirer under the Transfer of Undertakings (Protection of Employment) Regulations Act 1981.

Pensions

As with employment issues, the consequences of any pension schemes will depend upon the nature of the acquisition. Due diligence should determine what type of pensions schemes, if any, exist and what the future costs of these will be.

Defined benefits (ie final salary) schemes are gradually disappearing. But many still exist, and these can be costly for the acquirer. Broadly, the employer meets the cost of providing the benefits over and above the contributions made by employees and investment returns. In defined contribution schemes and group personal plans, the benefits provided will depend upon the amounts accrued in a member's account.

It is essential that these issues are understood in detail. As the defined benefit scheme is open-ended, there are long-term financial liabilities.

The checklist

No list of matters to be examined in due diligence can ever be entirely comprehensive, if only because every deal will have its own peculiarities. Nevertheless, the following matters should provide a useful starting point.

Financial

- Year-end audited financial statements, covering the past three years.
- Most recent interim results, showing detailed figures.
- Monthly management accounts for the past year, including the most recent figures.
- Forecasts, including cash flow projections, profit and loss and balance sheet for the year ahead.
- Tax returns for the past three years.
- Copies of existing purchase orders covering future months.
- Details of principal customers, including their historical purchase patterns and sales volume.
- Three-year analysis of revenue broken down by products and/or services.
- Detailed description of fixed assets.
- Details of capital expenditure over the past three years.
- Details of accounts receivable, including days-outstanding information and an analysis of doubtful accounts at the most recent date available; summary of write-offs over the past three years; summary of product returns and credit notes over the past year, as well as details of any guaranteed price agreements that will affect future revenues.
- List of all financial liabilities, including loans, mortgages, leasing agreements and other relevant information.

General management issues

- Organization chart and CVs of directors and key members of staff.
- Copies of employment contracts and non-compete agreements; details of employee salaries, benefits and length of service.
- Lists of shareholders and details of holdings.
- Copies of any significant management reports, including documents prepared by outside consultants and letters to senior management concerning the operation of the company.

- Copies of product warranties and guarantees.
- Copies of key person insurance policies.
- Details of leases and letting agreements.
- Information on the company's principal competitors.
- All material contracts and agreements, as well as details of any contingent liabilities.
- A copy of the most recent business plan (if any). If none exists, this in itself can be significant.
- Copy of sales and marketing plan, if one exists.
- Customer lists, with full contact details.

Legal

Although a detailed commentary on legal due diligence is outside the scope of this chapter, it is worth highlighting some of the key points that it should cover:

- details of any pending or possible legal claims;
- details of any legal claims over the past five years;
- copies of all information concerning trademarks, copyrights, licensing agreements and patents;
- minutes of directors' meetings over the past three years.

Of course, a due diligence checklist is simply that – a summary of points to be considered. It is no substitute for careful thought and advance planning. It should also be emphasized that the process will become more difficult and less reliable if it is carried out under severe time constraints. Accordingly, it is important to agree the timing with the target company at an early stage.

This is likely to involve a good deal of negotiation. Naturally, the vendor will be keen to get the matter over with quickly. However, a reasonable seller will realize that something of this importance cannot be hurried.

To sum up, therefore:

- Begin to plan early.
- Decide which information is important and which is not.
- Brief professional advisers thoroughly and agree their terms of reference in detail.
- Appoint one person – a senior executive – to oversee the process.
- Ensure that different professional advisers liaise with each other when appropriate.

18

Valuing the company's shares

Mike Thornton, Grant Thornton Corporate Finance

Summary

- There are a number of ways to value a company's shares, principally earnings based, the discounted cash flow method or asset based.
- A company's valuation may be expressed as a multiple of anticipated earnings, often based on the price/earnings (P/E) ratio of a comparable publicly quoted company's shares.
- Discounted cash flow uses the principle that the value of an asset can be determined by applying an appropriate discount rate to the cash flows generated by that asset.
- A business may be seen as a collection of assets, whose value is based on the company's audited balance sheet. While an asset-based valuation may be appropriate for an asset-based business such as a property company, for most companies it is inappropriate, as this method does not take into account the company's ability to generate earnings and dividends.
- The flotation of a company will be considered successful if the offer or placing is oversubscribed and, following flotation, the shares start trading at a premium to the offer or placing price. Conversely, a certain stigma will attach to shares that go to a discount. Within reason, brokers will tend to price the issue on the low side, in order to ensure that the shares go to a premium.
- Most owner-managers will be selling a limited number of shares when floating a company. The float price will therefore affect dilution, which is the proportion of a company the owners have to give away to raise a fixed amount of money.

Owners will want the highest possible price to recognize the value that they have built up in the company and to minimize dilution.

■ Brokers will set a share price to balance the two conflicting requirements of minimizing dilution while ensuring that the shares go to a premium.

■ The value that analysts give to a company will influence investors but, in practice, can only be indicative. The market price ultimately will be the price that investors are prepared to pay for a company's stock.

Introduction

One of the most important questions for any business owner floating a business is 'How much is my business worth?' Usually, owners will not be selling more than a small percentage of their holdings, but will be creating new shares that will be offered to the public or placed with institutions to raise money for the company. In that way the company will have additional funds, which it can use to increase further the value of the company. Nonetheless, even though the owners may not be selling their own shares, they still have to bear a 'cost', namely dilution of their shareholding, which is the percentage of the company the owner has to give up to raise the required funds. The price at which those shares are placed or offered will determine the percentage of the company to be given up to raise the necessary funds and therefore the level of dilution. The higher the float price, the lower the level of dilution.

However, it is important that the shares, when listed, start trading at a premium to the placing or offer price or, at the very least, do not start trading at a discount. If shares go to a premium, the flotation will be regarded as a success, and satisfied investors who have made either a cash or a paper profit on their investment will be more likely to take shares in subsequent fund-raisings. When shares go to a discount, some of the investors in the placing or offer will try to sell their holdings in the company once the share price reaches the flotation price and they can recoup their investment. This may put a 'lid' on the share price until those investors have all sold their shares. Once a share trades at a discount, it can take a considerable amount of time for it to recover and to trade at above its float price.

The job of setting the price at which the shares are to be placed falls to the broker. The broker has analysts and sales people who have a detailed and up-to-date knowledge of the values being accorded to such businesses by those institutions that are likely to take shares when the company comes to market. The valuation will often be estimated using a market-based approach such as using the P/E ratios of similar publicly quoted companies, adjusted for the characteristics of the company less possibly a discount to make the shares attractive to investors. There is a potential conflict of interest between the broker and its client company. A broker's commission is usually based on the amount of funds raised. Thus the broker will tend to favour a price at the lower end of a possible range in order to make the fund-raising process relatively easy and to ensure, as far as possible, that the shares start trading at a premium. The company's owners will generally prefer a higher price, to maximize the company's value and to minimize dilution. An independent adviser –

a nominated adviser or a sponsor – can help to ensure a fair balance between these conflicting demands.

In determining the value of a company there are a number of methods that can be used, but in addition the valuation process requires experience and judgement.

The principles of valuation

Basic economic theory suggests that the value of a financial asset is a function of the cash flows it provides and the discount rate applied to those flows. The income from a quoted investment comes in the form of dividends and it is for this reason that dividends have a key role in the determination of quoted share prices. For an investor whose return consists of dividends and either a capital gain or a capital loss on selling the shares, then this may not be readily apparent. A capital gain or loss is, however, driven by the growth prospects for the company and hence for the future dividends available to the investor.

Earnings are of course the source from which dividends are paid and therefore earnings represent a basis for the valuation on the company, as it is the company's choice as to distribution policy.

This therefore leads to the methods by which most companies will be valued, focusing on its earnings and its cash flows.

Valuing a company

Valuation methodologies may broadly be classified into three main approaches, namely:

■ the market approach;
■ the income approach; and
■ the asset-based approach.

Earnings-based valuations

Earnings-based valuation methods are frequently used in practice and generally ascribe a value to a company by using a method that compares the subject business to similar businesses.

The method involves identifying the underlying maintainable earnings of the business and applying an appropriate price multiple. The method is thus straightforward; the difficulties lie in determining underlying earnings and deciding on an appropriate multiple.

Issues to consider with regard to underlying earnings include deciding which earnings to use as a basis (historical, current or future) and whether any adjustments need to be made to the reported information in order to establish a true underlying and maintainable level of profitability.

The pro forma or underlying earnings upon which the valuation is based must consider the following: past results, which are important as they are factual and offer a solid platform to compare with current trading and forecasts for future trading; and forecasts, which are clearly relevant, particularly where significant profit growth is forecast and must be factored into the calculation.

Having determined a view on the underlying maintainable earnings, the second issue is what multiple to apply to those earnings. The most common multiple is the P/E ratio, and this is often used by brokers in determining value. In order to identify an appropriate P/E ratio to apply to the company under review, P/E ratios for comparable listed companies can be used as a basis for determining a multiple, although the difficulty with this approach is in finding comparable quoted companies. In the absence of comparable companies, sector average P/Es may be helpful.

Having identified a suitable comparable multiple, adjustments may be made to reflect the individual circumstances of the business in question. Such adjustments may include the need to reflect particular aspects of the business, including:

- the size of the business;
- the quality of the management team;
- the growth prospects, and certainty of that growth;
- the vulnerability of the business to outside forces;
- other special factors such as dependency on contracts.

Other common measures of profitability that may be used in valuation calculations are PBIT (using profit before interest) and EBITDA (earnings before interest, tax, depreciation and amortization). EBITDA is becoming a more common measure of value on the basis that it ignores depreciation and amortization policy differences between businesses. Turnover multiples that assess the value of the business relative to turnover may also be considered. To the extent that these measures derive the enterprise value of the business, ie the value attributable to debt and equity in total, debt would need to be deducted to arrive at the value of equity.

Discounted cash flow

Discounted cash flow (DCF) techniques tend not to be as straightforward as earnings-based methods but they do look at the cash generated by business activities, not reported earnings, and therefore as a basis for valuation are not subject to the vagaries of accounting policies.

The DCF method requires an estimate of the amount and timing of future cash flows. The cash flows are then discounted to present value with an appropriate risk-adjusted discount rate.

Discount rate factors often include general market rates of return at the valuation date, business risks associated with the industry in which the entity operates, and other risks specific to the asset being valued.

The discount rate is usually derived from the cost of debt and the cost of equity using a weighted average approach to give an overall weighted average cost of capital (WACC) discount rate.

The cost of equity (ke) for a company is commonly derived using the capital asset pricing model (CAPM), and the formula is as follows:

$$ke = rf + (\beta \times MRP)$$

where:

rf =   the return on long-term risk-free securities, normally taken as government securities;

β =   beta factor, which represents the volatility of comparable companies or the sector (and a β value of 1 implies a level of risk typical of the market as a whole);

MRP =   the premium added for market risk.

The cost of debt (kd) is found using the following formula:

$$kd = (rf + cs) \times (1 - tax)$$

where:
rf is as above;
cs =   credit spread (the additional cost of borrowing for the company);
tax =   the tax shield available to the company on its borrowing.

A company's WACC is the result of applying the optimal gearing structure of the company to the cost of equity and cost of debt above. It is important to note that DCF calculation uses total cash flows and therefore debt must then be deducted to give a value for equity.

However, CAPM only allows for systematic risk, the risk associated with the market and macroeconomic factors, which is adjusted by beta. The greater risk of small-company shares may not be fully accounted and this may be adjusted through a small-company premium. Small-company premiums have been identified through studies examining the difference in returns between large companies and small companies.

The DCF method is useful, as it does focus on the cash generated by business activities, but it does require rigorous forecasting to be conducted for extended periods of typically between 5 and 10 years. In addition, the value is heavily influenced by the terminal value – the value at the end of the forecast period – which can be as much as 75 per cent of the total value.

Asset-based valuations

A business can be seen as a collection of assets, whose value is based on the company's audited balance sheet. While an asset-based valuation may be appropriate for an asset-based business such as a property company, for most companies it is largely irrelevant for the following reasons:

■ It is based on accounting policies, the choice of which may be subjective.
■ Accounts are drawn up on a going-concern basis; balance sheet values are not based on values that would be achieved in a break-up situation.
■ It may not deal adequately with intangible assets, particularly brand values, goodwill and intellectual property rights.

Publications such as the *Investors Chronicle* do compare a company's share price to the value of the company's underlying net assets, but the fact that the two valuations are usually quite different emphasizes the irrelevance, in most cases, of net asset value to a company's market capitalization.

However, asset values can underpin the market value of a company, particularly if balance sheet values do not fully reflect the realizable value of certain assets. This may be relevant if a company has significant property assets that have not been revalued for a number of years.

A company's assets are valuable to the extent that they enable the company to trade and to generate profits. Their value to a business is the value of the cash that those assets generate. For most investors, that cash flow takes the form of dividends.

As indicated above, there are certain types of business for which an asset-based valuation is appropriate. For a property company, whose value is represented by its underlying assets, an asset-based valuation is appropriate. A natural resource company, whether it is in production or simply exploring for oil, gas or minerals, may also be valued on the basis of actual or potential reserves.

Valuation in practice

Brokers' analysts are able to perform highly sophisticated calculations to determine the value of a business based on anticipated growth, cash flow, dividends and an appropriate discount rate. The P/E ratio, though, remains a widely used valuation measure.

P/E ratios reflect the market's expectations of growth. This can, however, vary by sector, so for example on 25 May 2007 the mining sector had a sector P/E ratio of 9.68, whereas one of the highest, healthcare equipment and services, had a P/E ratio of 32.18. This implies that the market expects faster growth in the latter sector, but P/E ratios can also be affected by reduced short-term profits.

A company can be growing faster than its peer group, and this will affect the valuation accorded to it. Faster growth may be a reflection of stronger and more dynamic management or of the stage of development of the business. The credibility of the forecast profits and the extent to which they influence valuation will depend on a number of factors, including the experience and perceived quality of management, management's track record, visibility of earnings and the quality of advisers.

Valuation can be affected by other factors:

■ Selecting the appropriate sector can make a significant difference. On 25 May 2007 the general industrial sector had a P/E ratio of 16.16, whereas the support services sector had a P/E ratio of 29.43. A company that provided services to engineering and other companies would probably achieve a higher valuation if investors were to perceive it as a support service rather than a general industrial business. A company cannot be portrayed as something it is not, but there is some flexibility, and perhaps a lesson for strategy.

■ Within a company, there could be a number of different income streams, each of which could be valued differently.

■ If a company is growing, other things being equal it will generally achieve a higher valuation if it delays flotation, thereby reporting higher profits on which a P/E ratio will be based.

■ Market sentiment changes over time and is crucial in determining both the price at which shares are offered and indeed whether the fund-raising will succeed at all. Market sentiment can therefore both amplify and negate the effect of delaying flotation (referred to in the previous point) on the flotation price.

Valuation techniques as discussed above may be used to support a valuation, and the value that analysts give to a company will influence investors but, ultimately, can only be indicative. The valuation of a company is the market price that investors are prepared to pay for a company's stock.

19

Indemnities and warranties from directors and shareholders

Philip Goldsborough, Pinsent Masons

Introduction

This chapter considers the warranties and indemnities generally given in the context of a flotation and, more specifically, those contained in an underwriting agreement.

The underwriting agreement is one of the principal documents that will be entered into in connection with the underwriting of shares on a flotation. The principal purpose of the underwriting agreement is to:

- define the obligations of the issuing house to the company and the selling shareholders in its capacity as underwriter;
- provide the issuing house with protection against potential liabilities from third parties;
- assist the issuing house in satisfying certain of its duties as sponsor and maintaining an orderly market in the shares post-flotation.

Function of warranties and indemnities

Invariably, an underwriting agreement will include a series of warranties and a tax indemnity, as well as an all-embracing indemnity in favour of the issuing house. Much time can be spent by lawyers advising on a flotation negotiating the terms of these provisions. It is important to consider the function of these warranties and indemnities and what they achieve (or, perhaps more importantly, do not achieve).

The company and its directors will normally be requested to warrant that the prospectus complies with the requirements of the Prospectus Rules and Part VI of the Financial Services and Markets Act 2000 and to give numerous specific warranties regarding such matters as the accounts, the absence of litigation and sufficiency of working capital.

In the context of an underwriting agreement, these warranties have a threefold purpose. The first is to act as a sort of checklist for the benefit both of the company and its directors and of the issuing house so as to concentrate the minds of all those involved on the principal issues that ought to have been addressed in the preparation of the prospectus. The second is to act as a trigger mechanism for termination rights that are normally vested in the issuing house under the terms of the underwriting agreement. The underwriting agreement will normally provide that, if any of the warranties are discovered to have been inaccurate or misleading at any time prior to commencement of dealings, or become so during that time, the issuing house may terminate the agreement and thus pull the issue. The third purpose of warranties, but one that is most commonly misunderstood, is as a method of loss recovery.

Loss recovery

In the context of the underwriting of securities, the giving of warranties is something of a blunt instrument as a means of loss recovery. The ability to recover damages for breach of warranty will depend upon the plaintiff satisfying the various hurdles that the common law places before a person who wishes to recover damages for contractual misrepresentation. A person seeking to bring a claim for breach of warranty is required to demonstrate that he or she has suffered loss in consequence of the breach, that the extent and nature of the loss suffered were sufficiently foreseeable and that he or she took reasonable steps to mitigate that loss. In fact, it will often be the case that the issuing house itself has suffered no loss at all, in that all of the securities that were underwritten have been passed to sub-underwriters who have themselves suffered loss by means of a diminution in the value of their securities but who have no direct ability to claim under the warranties. (However, they may have a right to compensation under the Financial Services and Markets Act 2000, although this is not certain.)

Various attempts have been made in the past to bridge the gap between the person who has suffered loss (for example, the sub-underwriters) and the person who has received the benefit of the warranties (the issuing house). One possibility is to state that the benefit of the warranties is taken by the issuing house as trustee for the sub-underwriters. Even if this is effective as a matter of law to allow the issuing house to bring an action for loss suffered by the sub-underwriters, characterizing the issuing house as trustee imposes fiduciary obligations on the issuing house that may add to its own liabilities vis-à-vis sub-underwriters.

An alternative possibility is for the issuing house to argue that, since the warrantors would always have foreseen that any loss suffered would be suffered by third parties with whom securities were sub-underwritten, the issuing house should be able to recover the loss of those third parties.

An issuing house may prefer simply to ensure that the underwriting agreement includes a well-drafted indemnity in favour of the issuing house so that the issuing house will be able to recover losses incurred by virtue of actions brought against it by third parties, including sub-underwriters. Unlike a warranty, an indemnity is an express agreement that, should the issuing house suffer loss of a particular nature, the indemnifier will meet those losses. An action brought under such an indemnity does not constitute an action for damages and would not therefore be liable to the various common law rules described above.

In the context of most underwriting agreements, the more important purposes that the warranties serve are that they provide a mechanism for enabling the issuing house to terminate its underwriting obligations, and they focus the minds of those persons giving the warranties (probably more so than verification notes) and thereby act as a further means of due diligence/verification to ensure that the prospectus complies with the statutory requirements.

Sponsor's indemnity

The most important protective provision in the underwriting agreement, so far as the issuing house is concerned, is the 'sponsor's indemnity'. This is an indemnity in favour of the issuing house against loss that it may suffer in connection with the flotation, for example as a result of an investor bringing proceedings against the issuing house alleging that the prospectus did not comply with the general disclosure requirements of section 80 of the Financial Services and Markets Act 2000 or was otherwise misleading or inaccurate. The indemnity is not likely to cover loss to the extent that it arises as a result of the issuing house's own negligence or wilful default, or its failure to comply with the Financial Services and Markets Act 2000 (or any regulations made thereunder) or the FSA *Handbook of Rules and Guidance* or any other applicable laws or regulations.

There is an ongoing debate at present between practitioners over whether or not the sponsor's indemnity to the extent given by the company may contravene the financial assistance provisions of section 151 of the Companies Act 1985.

Who gives the warranties and the sponsor's indemnity?

The question of who is to give warranties and the sponsor's indemnity is often the subject of extensive negotiations. The candidates are the company, its directors (both executive and non-executive) and the shareholders. Even though the company may give the warranties and the indemnity, in practice any claim against the company is likely to prejudice the company's new shareholders, and the issuing house will therefore prefer to look elsewhere in order to pursue a claim.

The issuing house is likely to insist on the executive directors giving the warranties and indemnity. It may, however, take a less stringent attitude towards the non-executive directors, especially if they have had only a very limited involvement with the company or if they have only recently been appointed to the board (which is frequently the case in the context of flotations). The directors of the company will, in any event, be persons responsible for the prospectus under section 80 of the Financial Services and Markets Act 2000, and it is often questioned why they should give contractual undertakings to the issuing house in addition to incurring statutory responsibility.

Whether or not 'non-director' shareholders may be required to be party to warranties and indemnities will differ according to the circumstances of each case. However, it is apparent that institutional shareholders, such as venture capitalists, are simply not prepared to expose themselves to a liability under these circumstances. Indeed, some profess that it would be contrary to their constitution to do so.

Tax indemnity

As part of the protection obtained for the benefit of investors on a flotation, the issuing house will seek a tax indemnity in favour of the company and its subsidiaries. This will either form part of the underwriting agreement or be a separate document. The issuing house will usually look to all or some of the shareholders to give such an indemnity.

In the past it was not unusual for the issuing house to obtain a full tax indemnity, very similar to the type given on the purchase of a private company's shares, to the effect that the company would be indemnified against any charge to tax not provided for in the last audited accounts save as arose in the ordinary course of trading since the last balance sheet date. The current trend, however, is for the issuing house to seek a more limited form of tax indemnity. The rationale is that investors must accept the risk of tax charges that arise in the ordinary course of the company's business and, in any event, the investors may have various statutory and common law remedies if a material liability has not been disclosed.

The more limited types of indemnity will cover tax liabilities that are primarily those of some other person but for which the company has a secondary liability (for example, non-deducted PAYE). The indemnity may also cover the impact of anti-avoidance legislation and certain other liabilities that arise from events not in the ordinary course of the company's trading activities.

Whichever form of indemnity is given, it will usually cover all relevant liabilities up to and including admission to listing of the company's shares.

The issuing house will normally be a party to the indemnity, in addition to the company, in order to be able to enforce the indemnity for the benefit of the company.

Limitation on liabilities

No limitation on the liabilities of the company under the underwriting agreement is likely to be acceptable to the issuing house and, until relatively recently, the same was true for directors and selling shareholders. However, it has become more common for there to be some forms of limitation for the directors (despite the fact that directors' statutory liability under the Financial Services and Markets Act is unlimited) and, if applicable, selling shareholders in relation to both the underwriting agreement and the tax indemnity.

The most important limitation is a monetary cap on the total exposure of each of the directors (and selling shareholders). Ultimately, this is a matter of negotiation. However, the following comments may be helpful.

Non-executive directors

The limit here is often calculated by reference to the annual fees that the director will receive as a non-executive director of the company. Two or three times the applicable directors' fees appear to be common, reflecting the different role the non-executive director is expected to play.

Executive directors and selling shareholders

There is no particular common practice here, but the cap is not infrequently calculated by reference to the value of the particular person's shareholding in the company.

Putting a time limit on the period within which the issuing house can bring a claim is another way of limiting exposure under the underwriting agreement and tax indemnity. Issuing houses are usually prepared to accept some form of time limit for bringing claims against directors and shareholders (but not the company). Commonly, issuing houses will concede that a claim must be brought against such persons within two or three accounting periods after admission, or six or seven accounting periods in relation to tax matters.

A further form of limitation for the directors, which is finding mixed reaction amongst issuing houses, is to provide that the issuing house will not be able to claim under the sponsor's indemnity or for breach of warranty against an individual director if that director can show that he or she would have had a defence to such a claim under Schedule 10 to the Financial Services and Markets Act 2000, if such claim had been made against him or her under that Act. The rationale for this is that a higher standard of care should not be imposed upon a director than that required of him or her by statute.

Rights of contribution

Whenever warranties and indemnities are given by more than one person (whether jointly, severally, or jointly and severally) those persons will (unless there is agreement to the contrary) have a right of contribution against one another in respect of any claim that is made against any of them under those warranties and indemnities (see the Civil Liability (Contribution) Act 1978). Therefore, if, say, a claim is made by an issuing house against a director under the sponsor's indemnity and that indemnity has also been given by the other directors and the company, the director against whom the claim is made will be entitled to a contribution from the other directors and the company unless there is express provision to the contrary.

As has been mentioned previously, the issuing house will not wish to make a claim against the company except as a last resort. Similarly, it would not want any of the directors to seek a right of contribution against the company. From the issuing house's point of view, therefore, it is desirable that the underwriting agreement should expressly exclude any such right of contribution against the company, although the issuing house will probably not be so concerned about a right of contribution between the directors.

The Civil Liability (Contribution) Act 1978 provides that the amount of contribution to which a person is entitled under that Act is whatever the court decides is just and equitable having regard to the extent of the particular person's responsibility for the damage in question. There is therefore no certainty over the quantum of any contribution that a director may be required to make. The directors should, consequently, consider whether they wish to enter into a separate contribution agreement so that any liability incurred by any of them is shared in the proportions agreed between them (irrespective of any particular director's culpability). Such agreements are permissible under the Act.

> *Corfin Communications' advice, expertise and considerable knowledge of the UK markets was of invaluable help in successfully floating the company on the London Stock Exchange. It proved a key component in allowing the business to achieve its ambitions.*

Ami Vizer - CEO
SimiGon

Floating your company may seem like an end in itself, but the first day of dealing is the start of a new life.

We are skilled at guiding companies through this transformation, helping them capitalise on the significant cultural change that is part of being a plc.

We help you to educate the market and achieve positive media coverage for your company, encourage institutional investor support and help create momentum for the after-market. Importantly, we help you conclude the IPO process with your company correctly positioned for the long term.

We take pride in our distinctive approach and high level of personal commitment to our clients.

CORfIN
COMMUNICATIONS

Specialists in media, corporate and financial public relations, based in the heart of the City of London

Email: ipo@corfinpr.com
www.corfinpr.com

20

The role of public relations

William Cullum, Corfin Communications

The flotation process

You will, by now, be under no illusion about the flotation process and you will recognize that floating is intense and adviser heavy. However, now comes one of the best bits, namely getting to know the people who will pull back the heavy red curtains and thrust you into the spotlight! Welcome to the world of public relations.

Public relations matters because it is how you tell the world about your business and its prospects. It is the mechanism whereby would-be investors, equity analysts, competitors, suppliers, employees, market commentators and, of course, family and friends learn about your plans for the future of the firm.

You increase the visibility of your business and the profile of its management and staff dramatically when you seek a listing. By floating, you expose your business to public scrutiny and market regulation. A flotation is not just about the money: when you go public people may actually own a part of you or feel as if they do. They will feel entitled to know about your affairs.

You will have seen the argument that private equity always uses when it seeks to buy an undervalued asset: 'Restructuring this business is best conducted out of the public eye.' Well, your position is the opposite of this. It should be: 'This business will flourish and grow with improved access to capital and enhanced visibility.' The public will own a part of you but in return you will get considerable benefits.

Hiring a PR company

So, public relations (PR) is a key part of the flotation process in London and on AIM. You will be expected to hire a PR company, and your nomad, lawyer or accountant may be able to advise. You may also know some people in the business or some may already have approached you. Either way, try to get a recommendation and then draw up a shortlist of three to five firms to see.

What to look for

Most PR companies will send in a team to see you, usually three people of varying seniority and experience.

Seek assurances that the team that is in front of you is the team that will be working for you. Some companies have 'pitching teams' who disappear once the mandate is secured. This is not helpful to you for the simple reason that PR is a surprisingly intimate activity: you are discussing confidential issues that can be about deeply personal matters such as your reputation, your wealth and your plans for the future. So, when looking at the team ask yourself three basic questions. These are:

- Do they get what my business is about and understand its issues and my ambitions?
- Do they have contacts with the media that matter and with equity analysts if need be?
- Can I work with them, ie do they seem to be reliable and trustworthy?

Time and expense

PR is not necessarily the most expensive part of the float business. You will, though, spend a lot of time with your PR advisers in the coming weeks and in the months and years after you have achieved your float.

Do not assume either that just because you are a small company (at least, for the moment, that is…) the PR effort will be commensurately small. In fact, PR for smaller companies is, relatively speaking, a great deal more difficult than for big companies – after all, it is a lot easier for a journalist to write about Johnnie Walker whisky than about Uncle Bill's Home Brew. So don't spoil the ship for a ha'p'orth of tar: it is the quality of the relationship that matters.

First steps

Having agreed to hire an agency, what happens next? Timeliness and preparation cannot be stressed enough when approaching a float. A float is a major cultural change for you and for your business.

On first meeting your PR company you will need to give them thorough instruction in your business and its targets and ambitions. You will tell them why you are floating, how much money is being raised or realized, what will happen to existing investors and how much you will be worth. You will need to explain the competitive background and will need to talk through any financial issues such as sales gains, declining margins, cost increases, cash outflows and the like.

If your business depends on some physical assets – like a new property development or a state-of-the-art factory, show your team around. They will find your enthusiasm infectious. Finally, do not be surprised if you are asked more awkward questions. Think of this session as a full and frank confession!

The reason for this initial download is that your advisers need it to build up a communications pack. They need to think about all the things that people will ask you or could ask you, good or bad. And then they need to advise you as how best to relay your story to the markets.

Whom should you be talking to?

Investors

Your nomad will have explained to you something about investors. Investment is like religion: people subscribe to differing views and some differences can seem very small indeed to outsiders, but very important to the practitioners.

With the help of your financial advisers, what you would like to achieve in an ideal world is a high-quality, stable investment base. For an AIM listed company, this ideal will be difficult. You will, doubtless, meet specialist AIM investors. That is good. You may also come across hedge fund managers looking for absolute returns over a short period of time (as opposed to steady capital appreciation and a dividend stream), and this can be frustrating and time-consuming.

You should also consider hooking up with some private client fund managers. These are people who manage the money of relatively well-off individuals and are often looking for decent capital appreciation. Their clients frequently sympathize with entrepreneurs like you and like to feel part of your progress.

Generally speaking, though, private investors are more expensive to service than institutional investors (as you have to send out more annual reports and have more entries on your share register), but they reflect your size and your investor appeal. A word of warning, though: you will meet investors who know little about your company and others who have studied it minutely. Be prepared.

Professional or institutional investors will be looked after by your nomad or financial adviser. Both your financial adviser and your PR company can help you to approach private client fund managers should you decide to go down that road.

Analysts

It is one of the jobs of equity analysts to value shares in companies in the sector that they follow. They write reports that give forecasts of the earnings of your business and they make recommendations as to what to do with the shares (buy, hold or sell). They frequently promote their views in the media. They need to get investors to trade shares with their firm and, accordingly, they are in a fierce struggle for investor time, attention and business – just like you.

Your financial adviser's company may have an analyst who follows your company but as you grow and develop it helps to have other analysts follow your shares. This can be a useful third-party endorsement and it also makes a market.

Try not to worry too much, though, if you cannot get lots of analysts to follow your company – as long as you get some. Analysts will not write research just because your business is interesting or you're a nice person. Analysts need to feel that they can make their firm money by following your company. It takes just as long to build an Excel spreadsheet on a small illiquid company as it does for a big liquid firm.

Analysts can sometimes be difficult. They are paid to explore the options and ask those awkward 'What if?' questions. Consequently, they can take a contrary view and sometimes might signal a sell on your shares. It is very hard to do this, but try not to take it personally. If their view is well argued and sticks to the approach that your shares are overvalued then the best reaction is to be philosophical and prove them wrong through performance. Sometimes it does feel as if the attack is more personal: usually it is not but, again, try not to make enemies. There is no point – the City of London is a small place.

A good PR firm should be able to help you deal with equity analysts, identifying which firms are most appropriate to target and how to talk to them.

Site visits and seminars are other appropriate tools for explaining your business to the markets. Having seen your business, your PR firm should suggest, for example, that you might need to arrange a visit to see one of your factories, a number of your stores, or your laboratories. Only so much can be learnt, after all, from building a spreadsheet from the annual report and the website. Your PR people will advise on what to show (and what not!) and how to structure the day. You should always make an announcement to the market that you are holding such an event and tell them what will be discussed. In this way investors who are not on the visit or at the seminar cannot claim they were kept away from newsflow about your company. It is important to be open and to be seen to be open.

The press media

Trade and regional press

You may already have had an introduction to the business media via your industry trade press. As we note below, some sectors of the market have a very well-developed business press that is read by companies, analysts and bankers and even by the business journalists on the daily and weekend business sections. Trade press can remain just as important when you have listed, maybe even more so, as you may now enjoy the halo of being an 'authority' on the industry. Your PR people will advise as to how to nurture this relationship.

There are, though, some new people that you will meet.

Let us start with the business wires. These are organizations such as Reuters, Bloomberg, AFX, Press Association (PA), Dow Jones and Citywire that provide stories and data electronically to subscribers in the print media and in financial institutions. They are very competitive to get the story first, and what they produce often ends up in the regional newspapers' business sections. Newswires are up and running – like analysts and brokers – early in the morning. They can help set the tone of the news about you for the day.

This brings us on to the regional newspapers (like the *Yorkshire Post*). If you have a major plant or outlet away from London, your PR people will advise you how to deal with them and build appropriate relations. Regional media can be very helpful in getting important messages across to staff and suppliers but, be warned, they have a strong focus on jobs. Restructuring activity is often met with little sympathy.

Financial press

Specialist financial publications like the *Investors Chronicle* and *Shares* magazine are often good shop windows. They are read by professional and private investors alike and often follow themes – like 'green' investing – or have special features on certain industry sectors. Again, it is worth taking some time with them, as they have the capacity to provide coverage of your business and sometimes have the space to write at some length.

You should recognize too that these publications are also a good breeding ground for talent: yesterday's *Investors Chronicle* writer is tomorrow's *FT* news editor. Journalists maintain their contacts over many years, so you can see the value in having a good relation with these writers.

The national newspapers

Your PR company should be able to talk you through the business sections of the national daily newspapers and those of the weekend press. The major business newspaper is the *Financial Times* (*FT*), but all the other newspapers run business sections, albeit with differing styles and constraints on space.

The difference here is that competition for space is intense. You can find yourself bumped out of the paper by a more apparently newsworthy story from a bigger company even though you may have spent half an hour on the phone to a journalist. Try to be philosophical: it happens, but there will be other opportunities.

Pictures

Whilst on the subject of the business press, it is worth thinking about pictures. Old-school business journalists are fond of saying that 'A decent picture is worth a thousand words.' By the same token, a rubbish picture of a grey-haired, grey-faced manager taken in a photo booth just opens you to ridicule. Better no picture than this sort of snap. A good picture can make the difference between getting a story published about your company and not. Your PR company will encourage you to spend some money on briefing a professional photographer to get the most out of your business. And the good thing about photos is that you can use them again, for example on your website and in your annual report.

The broadcast media

Television and radio are unlikely to want to get to know your business at listing – unless, that is, it is very big or in a consumer-oriented sector like easyJet, for example, or could possibly be part of a feature on, say, Chinese businesses raising capital in London.

Generally speaking, the broadcast media devote little of their time and attention to business and, when they do, their shows are often wronged-consumer related (think *Watchdog* here) or are focused on big restructuring, ie job loss issues. Nevertheless, there may well be moments when you will have to and may want to engage with broadcast. Your PR people will advise – but it is unlikely to be at flotation. Approach with caution.

Website and annual report

Anyone under the age of 35 goes straight to your website. They expect you to have an up-to-date and relevant website. Don't fight it: this is life. If your PR company does not do website work itself – and most do not – then they should know someone who does. They can advise on content and costs.

The same thing applies to the annual report. Do not underestimate the annual report: it is an important and legally required document and should reflect both what has happened in the year and also your aspirations.

In summary, your corporate identity is important and it should be the same on both website and report. Letterheads, typefaces and so on should all conform.

Internal communications

It might be tempting to be like Mr Burns in *The Simpsons* ('Money fight, Smithers?') and be an unreformed robber baron when dealing with staff, but we would not recommend it! In fact, it is a sad observation that most companies' communications with their own employees – potentially the best ambassadors for the business – are pretty indifferent.

Many of your employees will have seen 'City types' wandering around your business and have wondered what is up. Wonder quickly turns to worry and this is magnified by gossip. As a result, when it comes to listing there may well be lots of questions – and not a little fear – internally. We recommend that you take a little time to explain to your employees what is happening and how this may, in fact, benefit their lives, especially if they have an opportunity to become shareholders.

Suppliers

Going public is also an opportunity to enhance relations with your suppliers. By virtue of the fact that your suppliers will now be able to see the value of their relations through your published accounts there will of course be fewer secrets. But there may also be some nervousness, as they will recognize the pressure that you will be under from your investors to maintain efficiency. Nevertheless, for them to be able to share in your kudos – royal warrants, for example – could be a good marketing tool for them. Together with your PR people, think of ways in which you can use your listing to promote your business with your suppliers.

Trade groups

You may well find yourself in a similar position with trade groups, ie that your profile has become raised and your weight within the trade body may increase. It is not an immediate public relations step, but together with your advisers you may want to take a moment to review your approach to lobbying given your raised profile.

Web-based pressure groups

Much has been written about the power of the internet and its capacity to change business practices. You may be familiar with the story of a music player whose screen kept breaking and how an internet-based campaign encouraged the manufacturer to make changes. Others might know of various fair trade initiatives that have started on the web. It is clear that the web can be a powerful agent for change.

On the other hand, the web can also provide an excellent soapbox for bigots and, worse, can make such people appear more important than they are. If you think there may be an issue out there, consult your PR advisers. And, by the same token, if you are in a data-sensitive, eg R&D-based, industry, then chat rooms may well need monitoring. You do not want any false or misleading information to be relayed from the web to the press, so consult your PR people if there could be an issue.

How your PR company will help you prepare

Those then are your audiences – or at least most of them – so how do you prepare to engage? What are the deliverables?

Behind the scenes ahead of your float there will continue to be a lot of preparation and rehearsal. As we have seen, PR advisers will help you with photos and your website. They will also have input into your prospectus and into the presentation that you will have to make many times to existing and new investors.

They may suggest that you have some presentation training, as it is a simple truth that not everyone relishes standing up and speaking to anything from a handful to several dozen investors several times a week. Confidence and consistency are very important, and presentation trainers can teach you some tricks to help you both focus and relax.

Away from this, your PR company will be doing some drafting for you. The big piece will be your intention to float announcement (ITF), which will condense your prospectus. This should be supported with fact sheets that can be distributed to the media, photos (see page 161) and links to the website (see page 162).

In addition, before you speak to a journalist, you should be briefed as to the nature of the publication to which you will talk, some background on the journalist and the rationale for the approach.

Most important of all, you will have discussed and agreed what your 'key messages' should try to be and you should have had a thorough look through the Q&A document your PR company has prepared just in case there is the possibility of the odd 'googly' in the chat.

Hitting the news

Finally, after all this preparation, there may be an output in terms of an article in the business press, one that is, hopefully, enhanced by a suitably dynamic photograph. More may follow, and the aim is to get the attention of investors and would-be investors so that demand for your equity is enhanced and knowledge of your business ambitions increased.

The purpose of the media campaign should be to raise your profile ahead of and during the float so that investors' appetites are whetted. At the end of the process you will want to feel that your business has been positioned correctly and is valued properly for the medium term.

Of course, a float is a major milestone for you, your employees and your investors and you are to be congratulated. It is not, however, the end...

Living with the listing

Continuing obligations

Robert Moir, Pinsent Masons

Introduction

This chapter examines the continuing obligations contained in the FSA Listing Rules and accompanying Disclosure Rules and Transparency Rules (DTR) applicable to companies on the Official List following the listing being obtained. It then briefly examines the differences in the obligations imposed on AIM listed companies in these areas. Finally, it discusses the potential consequences of non-compliance.

In the case of both the Main Market and AIM, the continuing obligations can be divided into the following broad categories:

- requirements to ensure prompt and fair disclosure of information in relation to the company simultaneously to all users of the market, so as to maintain an orderly market in its securities;
- requirements as to transparency of information, including periodic financial reporting, the disclosure of changes in shareholdings and communications with shareholders;
- requirements in relation to certain larger transactions undertaken by the company, so as to give shareholders a power of veto over the decision of the board; and
- restrictions on directors and others in senior positions in the company with regard to dealing in the company's shares. This provides an additional tier of protection for shareholders and the market (over and above that given by 'insider trading' and 'market abuse' legislation) against any abuse and, perhaps more importantly, the perception of abuse by the company's directors and other senior employees.

Main Market

Provision of information

Basic obligation

The principal obligation with regard to the provision of information is to publicize, as soon as possible, any 'inside information' that directly concerns the company. This is information of a precise nature that is not generally available and that would, if generally available, be likely to have a significant effect, either downwards or upwards, on the company's share price. Examples of such matters could include the decision to buy or sell a significant business, the insolvency of a major customer, a major price hike by a supplier or the commencement of a challenge to a key patent.

Publication of the information must be effected through an FSA-approved 'regulatory information service' (RIS), which provides a mechanism for the orderly provision of company information to the market. Announcements submitted to an RIS are processed and then released to subscribers (which are mainly London Stock Exchange member firms and press agencies) via a data feed, so that those who make a market in the shares have equal access to the information as it is announced. Information announced must then be posted on the company's internet site by the close of the next business day, and maintained there for one year.

The company is, of course, obliged to take all reasonable care to ensure that the information it notifies to an RIS is not misleading, false or deceptive and does not omit anything likely to affect the import of such information. The company is not permitted to combine, in a manner likely to be misleading, an RIS announcement with the marketing of its activities. The company must also ensure that any disclosure is synchronized as closely as possible in all jurisdictions where it is listed.

The company may delay the public disclosure of inside information, such as not to prejudice its legitimate interests, where its omission to disclose would not be likely to mislead the public, and any relevant person who does receive the inside information owes the company a duty of confidentiality (which the company is able to ensure is maintained). This would cover matters in the course of negotiation and, depending on the circumstances, would permit disclosures to recipients who needed the information in order to perform their functions, such as the company's employees (and trade union representatives), professional advisers, lenders or major shareholders.

If the company anticipates a 'leak' of its confidential information, then a 'holding announcement' must be made containing as much detail as possible, the reasons why a fuller announcement cannot be made and an undertaking to announce further details as soon as possible. Otherwise, trading in its shares may be suspended.

If there is press speculation or market rumour that is false, no announcement will generally be required. However, if it was largely accurate, disclosure would have to be made in almost all cases.

Confidentiality arrangements

The company must establish effective arrangements to deny access to inside information to persons other than those who require it for the exercise of their functions.

The company must have in place measures to enable public disclosure as soon as possible if the company is not able to maintain the confidentiality of the inside information.

Coupled with the above is the requirement on the company to maintain and regularly update 'insider lists' of all those who may have access to inside information on a regular or occasional basis. Those persons must be apprised of their legal and regulatory duties regarding such information (ie, broadly, they must not deal or disclose) and the sanctions for breach of those duties. The insider list obligation extends to ensuring that the company's agents and advisers maintain similar lists in relation to inside information regarding the company.

Other requirements

The Listing Rules and the DTR provide further detailed requirements for the disclosure of information. The more significant of these are discussed below.

Corporate governance and directors' remuneration

This has been a much-debated area in recent years and an additional layer of regulation and indeed cost has been introduced. By way of background, as a result of the deliberations of the Cadbury and Greenbury committees and their reports, the 'Combined Code' was prepared, setting out principles of corporate governance and best practice for listed companies. Areas covered by the Code include board composition, directors' remuneration policy, relationship with shareholders and accountability and audit. The Listing Rules provide that a company must include in its annual report and accounts: 1) a narrative statement as to how it has applied the *principles* in such a way as 'enables its shareholders to evaluate how the principles have been applied'; and 2) a statement as to whether or not it has complied with the *provisions*, together with reasons for any non-compliance. There are also detailed requirements regarding the information to be included in the annual report with regard to directors' remuneration.

Financial information

An RIS must be notified without delay after board approval of the preliminary statement of annual results and dividends (and in any event within 120 days of the end of the period to which the statement relates). The Listing Rules and the DTR provide detailed requirements for the contents of a company's annual report and accounts. There is also a requirement to produce half-yearly results and detailed rules as to what they should contain. Clearly, this all results in additional significant cost and management time over and above that necessary for audited accounts.

The DTR apply to all companies listed on the Main Market with the exception of certain collective investment schemes. They implement the EU Transparency Directive and provide as follows from 20 January 2007 (subject to certain transitional provisions):

■ The company must publish its annual report at the latest four months after its year end, which must remain publicly available for five years after that. The annual report must include the audited financial statements, a management report and statements of responsibility; the rules prescribe the form and content of each.

■ Generally, the company must publish a half-yearly report (on a basis consistent with its annual report) at the latest two months after the end of the six months to which it relates, which must similarly remain publicly available. The half-yearly report must include condensed financial statements (which may be unaudited), an interim management report and statements of responsibility, again in the prescribed form. The company must also, unless it already issues quarterly reports, issue management statements on its financial position and performance during each six month period.

From 1 July 2005, fully listed companies must also publish an 'annual information update' within 20 days after publication of their annual results. The update must contain or refer to all information published in accordance with securities laws in the EU or worldwide in the preceding 12 months.

Profit forecasts/estimates

The Listing Rules control what a company may say about its profits prior to audited figures being made available. In particular, any such statement must be clear and unambiguous and include a statement of principal assumptions; and, where it is included in Listing Particulars, a Class 1 circular (discussed below) or circular on refinancing proposals, it must be accompanied by an accountants' report.

Rights as between holders of securities

The basic principle is that shareholders in the same position must receive equality of treatment. In particular, shares issued for cash must be issued on a pre-emptive basis, unless shareholders permit otherwise. (In practice, the general principles of company law will usually achieve the same result for shareholders.)

The company must also ensure that all necessary facilities and information are available to enable holders to exercise their rights, for example regarding notification of meetings (and proxy rights) and the issue of circulars.

Changes in capital and filings

A company is obliged to notify an RIS of certain specific matters in relation to its share capital, such as any proposed change in its capital structure (or the rights thereof) and changes in the ownership of its shares where notified to it pursuant to the relevant Companies Act or DTR requirements. Copies of circulars, notices and resolutions (other than for ordinary AGM business) must also be notified and made available through the FSA's document viewing facility.

Information in relation to directors

Any change in directors is to be notified, as is any change in their or their connected persons' ownership of shares or derivatives and details of the grant and exercise of options (the director must notify the company of any such change within four business days of it occurring). Directors' service contracts are to be available for inspection at the company's registered office and at its AGM.

Requirements in relation to transactions above a certain size

The Listing Rules provide for the division of transactions entered into by a UK listed company into certain 'classes', dependent on size, with different requirements applying for each. Further information on the precise requirements of these 'class tests' is provided in Chapter 24. It should be noted that any transaction of a subsidiary undertaking of a listed company is deemed to be that of the listed company and is accordingly brought within this regime.

Transactions of a revenue nature in the ordinary course of the company's business are excluded from the requirements, as are transactions that consist of the issue of securities or other fund-raising not involving the acquisition or disposal of any fixed asset.

Class 1 transactions

Basic principles

The articles of association of virtually every UK company delegate to its directors the power to effect an acquisition or disposal of any subsidiary, business or other assets owned by the company or to enter into other transactions; there is, in broad terms, generally no restriction as a matter of company law (in the absence of bad faith) on the exercise of those powers, even where this would constitute a fundamental change in the nature of the company's operations.

However, in the case of companies on the Main Market, the FSA considers that this does not give sufficient protection to shareholders. Therefore, shareholder consent is required before a transaction above a certain size, referred to as 'Class 1' transaction, can be completed by a listed company.

In broad terms, a transaction will be Class 1 where the assets being acquired (or disposed of) will increase assets, profits or turnover by 25 per cent (or decrease them by this amount if the transaction is a disposal) or where the consideration for the assets being acquired or disposed of has a value equal to or greater than 25 per cent of the listed company's market capitalization.

The Listing Rules provide comprehensive definitions as to precisely what is meant by 'gross assets', 'profits', 'consideration', etc, and a detailed and careful analysis and calculation need to be carried out by the listed company and its financial advisers to ascertain into which class any transaction falls for Listing Rules purposes. Where the bald application of the class test produces an anomalous result or where the calculations are inappropriate to the sphere of activity of the company, the FSA may modify the relevant rule to substitute other relevant indicators of size, including industry-specific tests.

'Exceptional' indemnities, etc

It should be noted that any 'exceptional' agreement or arrangement, such as an indemnity, pursuant to which a listed company agrees to meet the costs, losses or liabilities of another person (whether or not contingent) will constitute a Class 1 transaction unless there is a cap in the liability of the company. This cap must not exceed an amount equal to 25 per cent of the average of the company's profits for the last three financial years. Warranties and indemnities customarily given in sale agreements or to underwriters and advisers are expressly stated not to be 'exceptional'. Clearly, the applicability of this rule in other circumstances may be open to question and therefore consultation with the FSA may often be required.

Other Class 1 transactions

A break fee (or fees) payable by the company in respect of a transaction is treated as a Class 1 transaction if the total value of the fee(s) including VAT exceeds 1 per cent of the value of the company (if it is being acquired) or 1 per cent of its market capitalization (in any other case).

An issue of equity shares by a major subsidiary of a listed company that would dilute the company's interest in that subsidiary in such a way as effectively to represent a disposal of 25 per cent or more of the aggregate of the assets or profits of the group is also treated as a Class 1 transaction.

Aggregation

An individual transaction that falls below the relevant threshold stands to be aggregated with another transaction or transactions taking place over a 12-month period where they are linked, for example by being with the same person or relating to the same investment. Again, in the case of doubt the FSA should be consulted.

Preparation of the circular

The required procedure is for the listed company proposing to undertake a Class 1 transaction to negotiate and enter into the relevant agreement subject to the company obtaining the approval (in general meeting) of its shareholders to complete the sale or disposal (upon which the agreement must be conditional).

The directors of the listed company will then, with their advisers, prepare a circular to the shareholders containing a full description of the proposed transaction and explaining why they believe that it is in the best interests of the company. The circular will contain certain other matters prescribed by the Listing Rules; the purpose of this additional information is to allow shareholders to make an informed decision on the advisability or otherwise of the directors' decision. This information includes details of the following matters, both for the listed company and for the business or company being acquired or disposed of:

- material contracts (which does not include any contract that is entered into in the ordinary course of business), where required for making a properly informed assessment about the proposal;
- litigation or arbitration proceedings (whether actual, pending or threatened) during the previous 12 months, which may have or have had in the recent past significant effects on the group's financial position or profitability;
- risk factors relating to the company and the target;
- significant changes in the financial or trading position of the group since the last date to which audited financial statements or interims have been published;
- confirmation of working capital being sufficient for the company's present requirements and for the following 12 months (or, if such confirmation cannot be given, how it is proposed to raise such working capital);

- group prospects, consisting of general information on the most significant recent trends in production, sales and inventory, and costs and selling prices since the end of the financial year to which the last published accounts relate. This should also include information on known trends, uncertainties or events reasonably likely to have a material effect on the company's prospects for at least its current financial year;
- detailed financial information prepared by the company's auditors, including, for a typical acquisition where net assets of the undertaking being acquired will be consolidated, a comparative table or accountants' report and a statement of the effect of the acquisition or disposal on the earnings or assets and liabilities of the group;
- directors' (and significant shareholders') interests in the company's shares and information regarding directors' service contracts and any contracts entered into by the company in which the directors or significant shareholders have an interest.

The circular must comply with the provisions of the Listing Rules that are applicable to all circulars. These include both general and specific requirements – the circular has to provide a clear and adequate explanation of its subject matter and a responsibility statement confirming that the directors of the listed company collectively take responsibility for the accuracy of its contents.

Format of the circular

Preparation of the circular will typically commence as the negotiation of the transaction is being finalized, to allow the circular to be released to shareholders simultaneously with, or shortly after, the announcement of the conditional agreement.

The format of a typical circular for an acquisition of a business or shares is as follows:

- Front page: in bold letters, the nature of the proposed transaction, surrounded by legal/regulatory 'boilerplate'.
- Inside front page: timetable of events – principally the date of the EGM, the last date for receipt of proxies and the date for proposed completion of the transaction (after and subject to the passing of the relevant shareholders' resolution).
- Letter from the chairman: describing in more detail the nature of the transaction, the commercial rationale, the fact that it has the support of the board, and a recommendation for shareholders to vote in favour at the proposed EGM. This will be drafted in close consultation with lawyers and financial advisers and will be subject to 'verification' by legal advisers, ie the veracity of every statement must be capable of being demonstrated.
- Accounting information: typically an accountant's analysis of the financial performance of the business or company being acquired and a pro forma statement of net assets of the group going forward, on the assumption that the transaction is completed.
- Detailed summary of the conditional agreement with the seller/buyer.
- Additional information section: a miscellaneous gathering together of the other required information, again prepared primarily by the company's legal advisers and subject to verification.

- Notice of EGM and form of proxy: the final page of the circular will almost invariably be the formal notice constituting an EGM of the company, at which a resolution to approve the transaction will be proposed. Such a resolution is to be an ordinary resolution of shareholders, requiring only a simple majority of votes cast for it to be passed.

The circular must be approved by the FSA prior to its dispatch.

As will be seen, the production of the circular is very much a collaboration between the company's directors (one of whom is usually deputed to supervise) and its financial advisers, accountants and lawyers. The contents of the circular remain, though, the responsibility of the directors, and the circular will contain an acknowledgement of that responsibility by the directors.

Conclusion

In practice, it is extremely rare for shareholders to fail to approve a transaction in the face of a directors' recommendation, but the knowledge that shareholders' approval needs to be obtained is intended to (and probably does) act as an additional brake on any extravagant or high-risk transaction being undertaken by the directors.

Transactions with related parties

Basic principles

The Listing Rules provide certain safeguards against related parties taking advantage of their position. 'Related parties' include current or recent (within 12 months) directors of the listed company or any of its subsidiaries, substantial shareholders (holders of 10 per cent or more of shares), 50/50 joint venture partners, and persons exercising significant influence and their respective associates.

'Associates' has quite a complex definition (and detailed consideration to the Rules always needs to be given) but includes (in the case of individuals) family members, trustees of family trusts and companies where 30 per cent or more of votes attached to shares or a majority of the board are controlled by the related party and (in the case of a company) its group companies and any company accustomed to act in accordance with its directions.

Where any transaction is proposed between a listed company and a related party (or which benefits a related party), the prior approval of shareholders will be required following the receipt by them of a circular containing the relevant information prescribed by the Listing Rules. This prior approval is by way of a simple majority of those voting in favour of a resolution proposed at an EGM. The related party and its associates must not be permitted to vote at the meeting.

Exclusion of certain types of transaction

The Listing Rules exclude the following types of transactions from the related party requirements outlined above, subject to satisfaction of certain requirements:

- smaller transactions where all the relevant ratios (as referred to above) are less than 0.25 per cent;
- transactions of a revenue nature in the ordinary course of business;
- issues of new securities;

- employees' share schemes and long-term incentive plans;
- loans on ordinary commercial terms;
- indemnity/insurance arrangements for directors;
- underwriting on normal commercial terms;
- transactions involving an insignificant subsidiary (by reference to its profits and assets relative to those of the listed company);
- transactions with a 50/50 joint venture partner either not relating to the joint venture or where the joint venture is insignificant; and
- joint investment arrangements involving the company and the related party, where the amount invested by the related party is no more than 25 per cent of that invested by the company and the terms offered to the company are certified independently as no less favourable than those offered to the related party.

Where a transaction with a related party is of a size such that each of the percentage ratios referred to under 'Class 1 transactions' above is less than 5 per cent but one or more exceeds 0.25 per cent, there is no requirement for a circular/shareholder approval. The transaction may proceed subject only to: 1) the FSA being provided with written confirmation from an independent adviser acceptable to the FSA that the terms of the proposed transaction are fair and reasonable so far as the shareholders of the company are concerned; and 2) an undertaking being given to the FSA to disclose full details in the company's next published accounts.

For the purpose of determining size, the FSA can require aggregation over a 12-month period of transactions with the same related party (or its associates).

Contents of a related party transaction circular

The steps for preparation of the circular are as for a Class 1 transaction. The information to be included is, however, more restricted (unless, of course, because of its size the transaction is also Class 1). The main information to be included is as follows:

- full particulars of the transaction, including the name of the related party and the nature and extent of the interest of such a party in the transaction and a statement of why the shareholder is being asked to vote;
- a statement by directors (other than those who are related parties or their associates or directors of a related party) that the transaction is fair and reasonable so far as the shareholders in the company are concerned and that the directors have been so advised by an independent adviser acceptable to the FSA – typically this would be the company's usual financial adviser or stockbroker;
- a statement that the related party will abstain and has taken all reasonable steps to ensure that its associates will abstain from voting at the relevant EGM;
- in the case of a transaction where the related party is a director, or an associate of a director, of the company or any subsidiary, details of the following in relation to that director – his or her interests in shares in the company, his or her interests in any recent transactions entered into by the company and details of his or her service contract;
- the holders of major interests in shares in the company;

- material contracts, to the extent relevant with regard to how a shareholder should vote;
- significant changes since the end of the period to which the last published audited or interim accounts relate.

Class 2 and Class 3 transactions

A transaction is 'Class 2' where the assets being acquired will increase any of the assets, profits or turnover by 5 per cent (but less than 25 per cent in each case) or where the consideration for the assets being acquired or disposed of has a value equal to or greater than 5 per cent (but less than 25 per cent) of the listed company's market capitalization. A transaction is 'Class 3' where all of the relevant percentages are less than 5 per cent.

Class 2 requirements

While no shareholder approval is required for a Class 2 transaction, the company must notify an RIS without delay after the terms of a Class 2 transaction are agreed. As one might expect, the notification has to include not only key information in relation to the transaction itself – such as the name of the person from whom the company or business was acquired (or to whom it was disposed of), a description of the relevant business, the price and how it is being satisfied – but also other matters that the market might wish to know as potentially having an impact on the company's share price, being as follows:

- the value of the gross assets that are the subject of the transaction;
- the profits attributable to those assets;
- the effect of the transaction on the listed company, including benefits expected to accrue;
- details of directors' service contracts;
- in the case of a disposal, the application of the sale proceeds and, if shares or other securities are to form part of the consideration, whether such securities are to be sold or retained;
- details of key individuals important to the business or the company that is the subject of the transaction.

A further notification must be made if any significant changes in information provided occur, or any significant new matter arises that would have been disclosable had it arisen at the time of the preparation of the earlier notification.

Class 3 requirements

If the company agrees the terms of a Class 3 transaction involving an acquisition where the consideration for the acquisition includes the issue of shares for which a listing will be sought, the company must notify an RIS as soon as possible after the terms of the acquisition are agreed. The notification must include the amount of the securities being issued, details of the transaction (including the name of the counter-party) and either the value of the consideration and how this is being satisfied or the value of the gross assets acquired, whichever is the greater.

No notification is required for other Class 3 transactions, save that, if the company releases any details to the public, these details must also be notified to the

RIS. The notification must include basic details of the transaction, including the name of the counterparty and either the value of the consideration (and how this is being satisfied) or the value of the gross assets acquired/disposed of.

Reverse takeovers

Where one of the percentage ratios referred to under 'Class 1 transactions' above is 100 per cent or more, or where there is a fundamental change in the business or in board or voting control of the company, this circumstance is referred to as a 'reverse takeover'. Reverse takeovers are treated as Class 1 transactions and the requirements above accordingly apply to them. When a listed company undertakes a reverse takeover, the FSA will generally cancel the listing of its securities, and the company must reapply for its listing and satisfy the relevant requirements for listing afresh.

Purchase of own securities

The Listing Rules provide detailed requirements for a company wishing to purchase its own securities, whether on or off market. These are principally concerned with notification of proposed and actual purchases and the requirement for a circular to shareholders.

FSA approval

The Listing Rules provide that, unless a circular to shareholders is of a specified nature or complies with certain requirements, the prior approval of the FSA is required. In practice, the bulk of circulars for which FSA approval is sought are for Class 1 and related party transactions. It would be fairly rare for a listed company to want to do something other than this, the nature or manner of which would give rise to a prior FSA approval. All circulars have to be copied to the FSA.

Companies with particular characteristics

The Listing Rules vary or supplement the requirements in relation to the following types of company: overseas companies, property companies, mineral companies, scientific research-based companies, investment companies, investment trusts, unit trusts, public sector bodies and venture capital trusts. The details of the particular requirements for these entities are outside the scope of this book.

Restriction on directors and others dealing in the company's shares

The Listing Rules provide that a listed company must require every 'person discharging managerial responsibilities' (including directors) and every employee of the company or its group company with access to 'inside information' to comply with the Model Code set out in the Listing Rules.

It should be emphasized that this requirement is in addition to the requirements of common law (for example, the fiduciary duty of a director to act in the best interests of the company) and statute, such as the 'insider trading' and 'market abuse' legislation, which criminalizes trading in listed securities or disclosure of information in certain circumstances.

A summary of the key requirements and prohibitions contained in the Model Code is as follows:

■ The above persons must not deal in securities of the company at any time without receiving clearance to do so from the chairman or other designated director, or at all during 'close periods'.

■ Such persons must not be given clearance to deal when any matter exists that constitutes unpublished price-sensitive 'inside information' (whether or not the person is aware of the matter) or on considerations of a short-term nature, or otherwise when the chairman or designated director has reason to believe that the dealing would be in breach of the Model Code.

A 'close period' is the period of 60 days immediately preceding the preliminary announcement of the company's annual results or, if shorter, the period from the year end to the time of the announcement and:

■ (if the company reports half-yearly) the equivalent period preceding the publication of the interim report or, if shorter, the period from the end of the relevant financial period up to such publication; or

■ (if the company reports on a quarterly basis) the period of 30 days immediately preceding the announcement of the quarterly results or, if shorter, the period from the end of the relevant financial period up to such announcement.

During a close period the relevant person can be presumed to be in the possession of unpublished price-sensitive information regarding the forthcoming financial results.

These restrictions on dealings in the company's shares also apply to using them as security, the grant or acceptance of options, the exercise of options and dealings in options by the relevant person. They also extend to dealings of all such types by members of a director's or manager's immediate family and his or her connected companies and trusts. It is the duty of such a person to ensure that no dealings take place by the connected persons at times when he or she personally would be prohibited from dealing.

The chairman or other designated director may permit dealings in exceptional circumstances, for example a sale of shares to meet a pressing financial commitment in circumstances of severe financial difficulty, or an exercise of share scheme options where the final date for exercise is imminent and the relevant person could not reasonably have been expected to exercise the option at an earlier time.

AIM

Provision of information

Basic obligation

The AIM Rules are very similar to the Listing Rules in their requirement for disclosure of price-sensitive information to the market. There is no requirement, however, for an AIM company to maintain insider lists or to publish an annual information update.

Other requirements

The AIM Rules provide for specific disclosure of information on a more limited basis than the Listing Rules and DTR. Disclosure is, however, required of the following:

■ directors' interests and dealings in shares and the grant to or exercise of options by directors (and also connected persons);
■ changes in holdings of shares notified to the company pursuant to statutory requirements (principally for those holding 3 per cent or more);
■ resignation and appointment of directors;
■ annual audited accounts, within six months of the end of the financial period to which they relate;
■ a half-yearly report, within four months of the end of the period;
■ any material difference between actual and any previously published estimate or forecast of financial performance;
■ resignation of or other change in the company's nominated adviser or broker.

(Certain other more minor matters are also disclosable, but are not included here.)

Rules in relation to transactions

The key difference between continuing obligations in the Listing Rules and those in the AIM Rules is that there is no requirement for an AIM traded company to obtain prior shareholder approval for transactions above a certain size or with related parties, unless the transaction constitutes a reverse takeover or a fundamental disposal which exceeds 75 per cent in any of the class tests. Consequently, AIM traded companies are spared the attendant delay, cost and uncertainty of obtaining approval in these situations.

Instead, the AIM Rules provide specific requirements with regard to disclosure of the details of transactions to the market through an RIS. A brief summary of these requirements is given below.

'Substantial' transactions

A transaction is deemed to be 'substantial' if any of the class test percentage ratios, as discussed above, are greater than 10 per cent.

The RIS is to be informed without delay of the details of any substantial transaction as follows:

- particulars of the transaction, including the name of any company or business being bought or sold where relevant;
- a description of the business carried on by, or using, the assets that are the subject of the transaction;
- the consideration and how it is being satisfied (including the terms of any arrangements for deferred consideration);
- the value of the assets that are the subject of the transaction;
- the profits attributable to the assets that are the subject of the transaction;
- the effect of the transaction on the AIM company;
- details of any service contracts of proposed directors of the AIM company;
- in the case of a disposal, the application of the sale proceeds;
- in the case of a disposal, if shares or other securities are to form part of the consideration received, a statement whether such securities are to be sold or retained; and
- any other information necessary to enable investors to evaluate the effect of the transaction on the AIM company.

Transactions with a related party

A transaction with a related party in broad terms has a similar definition to that in the Listing Rules. Where any percentage ratio (as discussed above) is 5 per cent or more, then the requirement is to disclose the same information as for a substantial transaction, plus the name of the related party and the nature and extent of its interest in the transaction. The notification must also include a statement by the directors (excluding any director who is a related party) that, in their opinion, having consulted with the company's nominated adviser, the terms of the transaction are fair and reasonable so far as shareholders are concerned.

Details of any transaction with a related party where any percentage ratio exceeds 0.25 per cent must be included in the company's next audited accounts.

Reverse takeovers

As with a company on the Official List, the announcement of a reverse takeover (including the same information as listed above in relation to a 'substantial' transaction) will lead to a cancellation of the listing. An explanatory circular must be sent to shareholders and their approval obtained, and an admission document for the resulting entity must be prepared, before recommencement of the listing. The relevant acquisition or other agreement must be conditional on the shareholder approval.

Restrictions on directors and others dealing in the company's shares

The principles are similar to those for a company on the Official List.

Non-compliance

The first and most important point to make is that it would appear that material non-compliance with the Listing Rules is, perhaps surprisingly, pretty rare.

Clearly, the system of requiring applicants for listing to be sponsored (and therefore in effect thoroughly vetted by professional organizations known to the FSA) and the de facto monitoring of those companies by brokers, auditors and investors generally help in this regard – any infringement will almost certainly come to light eventually, with the potential negative consequences for the company's business, share price and, possibly most significant of all, the careers of those individuals involved.

However, where a breach does occur, the Listing Rules and DTR provide a range of sanctions (with the AIM Rules providing for similar sanctions):

■ enforcement, by requiring the publication of information (or, in an extreme case, by the UKLA publishing information itself);
■ private censure;
■ public censure;
■ suspension of listing;
■ cancellation of listing.

A censure may be of the company or any one or more of its directors. In the case of wilful or persistent failure to comply with the Listing Rules, the FSA may require removal of the director(s), failing which the listing will be suspended or cancelled.

Matters other than public censure, suspension and cancellation of listing are dealt with by the FSA's executives, with an appeal being possible to its Quotations Committee. Public censure, suspension and cancellation are determined by the Quotations Committee, with an appeal being possible to the Quotations Appeals Committee.

The Listing Rules indicate that the procedures for each committee can be determined and published by the FSA from time to time and that decisions are 'final'. However, the FSA is of course constrained by the rules of natural justice and the Human Rights Act and so its practices, procedures and decisions are, in theory, subject to control by the courts – though cases where this has been an issue are few and far between. Overall, despite the changing nature of the City and the greater possibility of challenges to regulations under the Human Rights Act, it seems unlikely, given the adverse negative publicity for the companies and individuals involved, that there will be a significantly greater role for the courts.

It should, however, be noted that breach of the Listing Rules, DTR or AIM Rules (for example, the rules on disclosure or dealings) may also constitute 'market abuse' within the Financial Services and Markets Act 2000 or 'insider dealing' within the Criminal Justice Act 1993. This may have criminal or civil penalties.

Expertise in every aspect of corporate finance

Floating your company could be one of the most exciting points in your business life.
Freeth Cartwright LLP can help you with all your corporate financial transactions
offering you advice, not options, and no-nonsense value for money.

Call: **Mike Copestake** on 0115 936 9369

Freeth Cartwright LLP, Solicitors, Cumberland Court, 80 Mount Street, Nottingham NG1 6HH
Nottingham, Derby, Leicester, Manchester ■ www.freethcartwright.co.uk

**Freeth
Cartwright
LLP**

22

Corporate governance

Mike Copestake and Bethan Davies, Freeth Cartwright LLP

What is corporate governance?

'Corporate governance' is a phrase that has evolved since the 1980s and means, in its very basic form, 'the system by which companies are directed and controlled'.[1] It encompasses many laws and regulations and has evolved into the regulation not only of how companies are directed and controlled but also of the interests of shareholders.

Where has it come from?

Corporate governance as an issue in the UK became prevalent following the collapses in the 1980s and 1990s of companies such as BCCI and Polly Peck and the issues surrounding the Maxwell pension funds and the controversy over directors' pay. There followed a number of important reports in the UK concerning corporate governance, namely:

- the Cadbury Report (1992);
- the Greenbury Report (1995);
- the Hampel Report (1998);
- the Turnbull Report (1999).

The Cadbury Report

The Cadbury Committee was set up in May 1991 to address concerns about a lack of confidence in the financial aspects of companies. It culminated in a Code of Best Practice, which concentrated on the three principles of openness, integrity and accountability and which developed to form the current Combined Code (see below).

The limitation of the Cadbury Report, however, was that it focused on the financial aspects of corporate governance.

The Greenbury Report

Following on from the Code of Best Practice established by the Cadbury Report, the Greenbury Report in July 1995 focused on directors' remuneration, particularly disclosure of remuneration in company annual reports.

The Hampel Report

One recommendation of the Cadbury Report was that a separate committee should be established by June 1995 to monitor how the Code of Best Practice had been complied with and what progress had been made on its other recommendations. The Hampel Committee was set up in November 1995 and looked at both the Cadbury Code and the Greenbury Code, resulting in the 1998 Combined Code.[2]

The Turnbull Report

This report, published in September 1999 by the Institute of Chartered Accountants in England and Wales, provided, and still provides, directors of listed companies with assistance on implementing the Combined Code. Listed companies have had to comply fully with the guidance set out in the Turnbull Report for years ending on or after 23 December 2000. The report was updated in October 2005, and the updated guidance applies for financial years ending on or after 1 January 2006.

The Higgs Review

The Combined Code never stands still. In April 2002, Derek Higgs was appointed to review the role and effectiveness of non-executive directors in the UK. The result, *Review of the Role and Effectiveness of Non-Executive Directors*, was published in January 2003 proposing changes to the Combined Code.

Smith Report

In 2002, the Financial Reporting Council set up a group, chaired by Sir Robert Smith, to look at the roles and responsibilities of audit committees. It published its Smith Report in January 2003, also proposing changes to the Combined Code in relation to the role of audit committees and their reporting to shareholders.

The Combined Code was, as mentioned above, revised in 2003 and has been further revised in 2006.

Corporate governance therefore has evolved since the early 1990s into a set of principles, regulations and guidance for listed companies on the way they are directed and controlled, their directors' remuneration, their audit committees and the interests of their shareholders. The Combined Code is at the cornerstone of corporate governance, but corporate governance is also about the application of established laws.

To whom does it apply?

All companies, both private and public, should have systems in place to ensure that they are governed correctly. The principles and provisions of the Combined Code, however, apply only to companies that are listed on the London Stock Exchange. Companies that are listed on AIM do not have to comply with the Combined Code. For AIM companies, the Quoted Companies Alliance has devised a set of corporate governance codes that are based on the Combined Code but specifically adapted for smaller companies.

What does the Combined Code say?

Directors

- Every company should be headed by an executive board, which is collectively responsible for the success of the company.
- There should be a clear division of responsibilities at the head of the company between the running of the board and the executive responsibility for the running of the company's business. No one individual should have unfettered powers of decision.
- The board should include a balance of executive and non-executive directors (and in particular independent non-executive directors) such that no individual or small group of individuals can dominate the board's decision taking.
- There should be a formal, rigorous and transparent procedure for the appointment of new directors to the board.
- The board should be supplied in a timely manner with information in a form and of a quality appropriate to enable it to discharge its duties. All directors should receive induction on joining the board and should regularly update and refresh their skills and knowledge.

- The board should undertake a formal and rigorous annual evaluation of its own performance and that of its committees and individual directors.
- All directors should be submitted for re-election at regular intervals, subject to continued satisfactory performance. The board should ensure planned and progressive refreshing of the board.

Remuneration

- Levels of remuneration should be sufficient to attract, retain and motivate directors of the quality required to run the company successfully, but a company should avoid paying more than is necessary for this purpose. A significant proportion of executive directors' remuneration should be structured so as to link rewards to corporate and individual performance.
- There should be a formal and transparent procedure for developing policy on executive remuneration and for fixing the remuneration packages of individual directors. No director should be involved in deciding his or her own remuneration.

Accountability and audit

- The board should present a balanced and understandable assessment of the company's position and prospects.
- The board should maintain a sound system of internal control to safeguard shareholders' investment and the company's assets.
- The board should establish formal and transparent arrangements for considering how they should apply the financial reporting and internal control principles, and for maintaining an appropriate relationship with the company's auditors.

Relations with shareholders

- There should be a dialogue with shareholders based on the mutual understanding of objectives. The board as a whole has responsibility for ensuring that a satisfactory dialogue with shareholders takes place.
- The board should use the AGM to communicate with investors and to encourage their participation.

Institutional shareholders

- Institutional shareholders should enter into a dialogue with companies based on the mutual understanding of objectives.
- When evaluating companies' governance arrangements, particularly those relating to board structure and composition, institutional shareholders should give due weight to all relevant factors drawn to their attention.
- Institutional shareholders have a responsibility to make considered use of their votes.

The principles of the Combined Code are supported by 'supporting principles' and 'code provisions'. Companies may depart from the Code but they must give a considered explanation if they do so.

Other rules to which public companies have to adhere

Whilst the Combined Code is a vital part of the corporate governance framework, public companies also have to adhere to:

■ *The Companies Acts.* The Companies Acts 1985, 1989 and 2006 govern almost every aspect of the regulation of private and public companies. When the Companies Act 2006 is fully implemented by 1 October 2008, it will replace virtually all of the Companies Acts 1985 and 1989.
■ *The Listing, Disclosure and Transparency Rules.* These rules apply to companies that are listed, or are seeking listing, on the Financial Services Authority's Official List and to their sponsors. They are contained within the FSA handbook.
■ *The findings of the Turnbull Report.* As mentioned above, this report was published in 1999, and provides directors of listed companies with assistance on implementing the Combined Code. The guidance focuses on the importance of internal control and risk management; maintaining a sound system of internal control; and reviewing the effectiveness of internal control and the board's statement on internal control.
■ *Guidelines produced by the regulators for the accountancy profession, insurers and pension funds.*

Notes

1. Cadbury Report.
2. The Combined Code applied to UK listed companies for years ending on or after 31 December 1998. The revised Combined Code came into effect for reporting years beginning on or after 1 November 2003.

23

Corporate communications

William Cullum, Corfin Communications

Congratulations! You have floated some or all of the equity in your business. Kick off your shoes, put your feet on the desk and light up a large cigar. Job done.

Sadly, no. And, to be honest, you knew that was coming – just as you know that you are not really the type to put your feet up anyway. A float can feel like the end of a process but in many ways it is more like the wardrobe in *The Lion, the Witch and the Wardrobe*: it is a portal to another world, the start of a new life in a different place.

A whole new world

The landscape of this new world is worth surveying. Whilst the float has been about you, you, you, a continuing listing is all about your obligations to 'them'.

Who is 'them'? 'Them' is the market, and the bad news is that to 'them' you are just one of several hundred relatively small companies jostling for continued investor attention. It may not feel like that – you are justifiably proud of what you have achieved and you know you are moving onwards and upwards – but look at it for a moment from the perspective of the people who manage investments or, indeed, the people who write about them.

If they can invest in or write about Diageo or Sainsbury's or Microsoft, for example, why should they continue to invest in or write about you? How are you going to help them achieve growth in the value of the capital you have raised?

Two questions then arise: why should you talk to the markets and how do you set about the task?

Why you should talk to the markets

The short answer to the first question is that you have to. It is part of the deal of being a quoted company.

As you will know by now, you are required to inform the market of any new, material and price-sensitive information relating to your company. Your broker, nomad or other corporate adviser will take you through the disclosure rules applying to AIM. You can also look them up on the AIM pages of the London Stock Exchange website at www.londonstockexchange.com.

When we say new, material and price-sensitive, the sort of announcements that are covered by this are any new developments that are not public knowledge concerning a change in:

■ financial condition;
■ activity;
■ performance of the business; or
■ expectation of performance.

(The latter is an interesting catch-all that means that you cannot mislead investors intentionally or otherwise about the expected progress of your business.)

You will also have to talk to the markets because your business has raised or realized capital and, capital being 'big money', it should come as no surprise to you that people want to know what you are doing with it.

How to do it

One of the reasons you employ PR agents is to take this sort of pain away; after all, it is your job to run the business. Yet you have now discovered that you have another job besides: you have to report on the progress of the business to the new owners of the company, the capital markets. This is a job you had not foreseen or had seen but dimly. You are now the custodian of other people's capital and you have to tell them what has been happening to it. Time to call in your favourite PR person!

The calendar gives you a structure

You and your PR person have a friend at hand, namely the calendar. You are required to report on the progress your company is making at least twice a year in the shape of full-year numbers or 'preliminary results' and interim results. Use these results not just to explain what has happened but to enhance your brand and your reputation.

Say, for example, your company has a December year end. Then it is quite likely that you will be in a position to report your results by the end of February or the beginning of March. Again, at the interim, you should be in a position to report interim results by mid-August. Of course, you may want to hold off at that time and do them in the first week of September, as everyone (including probably you and your advisers) will be on holiday in August. This gives you a second reporting opportunity.

There are other ways of creating opportunities, but for the moment let's look at how the day works.

Announcement day

So how does an announcement day work? The first thing to note is that it makes for a long day.

Whilst the markets may not officially open until 8.30 am and close at 4.30 pm, the reality is that brokers are expected to be at their desks at 7 am. Announcements start hitting the screens at 7 am and analysts are expected to have something pithy to say at their morning meetings within 15 minutes. (There is that time pressure thing again!)

What this means is that your announcement must also hit the screens at 7 am, and this in turn has other implications for you, for which the best bit of advice is preparation with a capital P.

Be well prepared

Make sure your announcement is ready in good time and is in any case signed off by close of play the night before. This means that in the weeks and days before you announce you should draft a statement and collate the numbers, discuss it with your board and agree a final version. Your PR company and advisers should be helping you to formulate what it is you need to be saying, explain why and then help you with drafting the release, preparing a Q&A document and any other materials you may require for your announcement day – such as an investor presentation and relevant photos.

One of the best companies we used to work with had a cast-iron discipline when it came to results. The chairman – after telephone conversations with his PR advisers – wrote a draft that he circulated to his board. They then commented on it and this resulted in the creation of draft two. This was circulated to financial and PR advisers and debate ensued, thus giving rise to a third and final draft. This was circulated to all parties with the warning that only under the most dire of circumstances would changes be tolerated!

You should not in any case be changing your announcement at the last minute or adjusting numbers. To be doing so suggests that:

■ your reporting systems need a good looking at;

- you are personally disorganized; or
- you are plain rude.

After all, it is neither wise nor polite for you and your advisers to be up half the night prior to what is, as we note above, rather a long day in your corporate diary. How can either you or they expect to function properly if deprived of sleep? Sign off early and get a good night's rest.

And, by the way, no one can release any data to the stock exchange until each page of the announcement has been signed by you. This is because of indemnity insurance; so, again, you cannot go home until this job is done.

Pay attention to the wires

Once your results are on the screen then you can start talking to the media and to analysts and investors.

But, first, have breakfast: don't be at a disadvantage during the day because of low blood sugar or caffeine levels. It may seem a small thing but you would be surprised by how many people get tetchy as the morning wears on.

Depending on how popular you are and on how good a job your advisers and PR people have done, you may have enquiries from all three groups, ie investors, analysts and media.

First thing in the morning you are most likely to get calls from the newswires and from analysts. It is helpful to pay attention to the wires, as they often set the tone of the news for the day. And, for a smaller company, they are a useful way of promoting your business to a broader shareholder base, especially when it is possible or, sadly, even likely that you will not get coverage in the *Financial Times* or the *Daily Telegraph*.

Analysts too may want a chat with you and with the CFO in order to clarify a statement or pick over some finer detail of your financial position. Remember, you cannot tell the analysts or investors anything that might be construed as inside information.

If you have lots of analysts following your company (lucky you), you might want to consider having a conference call and even once a year having a full-blown meeting for analysts and investors. If, however, you have only a few analysts to call following your interim results then you should be able to deal with them one on one over the phone.

Most newspaper journalists start late and end late so will not be available to talk until late morning. You may have lunch with a journalist or investor, and the afternoon could well be taken up with journalist calls and meetings with investors. Expect your day to run from 7 am to 6 pm and, as with all days when you are on parade, it will be tiring.

Getting the right words

For this big day, your PR company should help you draft your statement and also prepare what are called 'key messages'. These are a few short sentences that encapsulate what it is you need to say on the day. These are useful when dealing with the wires, for example. A conversation with a wires journalist usually takes less than 10 minutes, so you have to learn to be concise. Old-school business journalists used to say that you should be able to describe what your company does 'on the back of a fag packet'. This remains a good discipline (even if smoking does not!).

(A quick aside here on 'creating shareholder value'. Many senior executives in public companies say that they are committed to creating shareholder value: well, of course they are. Some even say that they are driven by the creation of shareholder value. These people are mistaken and, one suspects, are not really good long-term managers: they are just being politically correct. You as a director and driver of your business know that shareholder value is a by-product of doing what you do and doing it well. Shareholder value is an outcome – it is not a driver. So talk about your business and refrain, wherever possible, from discussing 'shareholder value' as a motive.)

Your PR people should also do you a Q&A and this should, specifically, allow you to rehearse how you might deal with less-than-friendly questioning on the day. If you have the luxury of time, you could rehearse with a Q&A session the night before your results, say at 6 pm in the evening.

There are two key pieces of advice with regard to dealing with journalists on your announcement day. The first one is: do not speculate. Stick with what you know, and if you are asked about other people's business – because everyone is looking for a 'read-through' to other companies as well – then simply reply that that is a question for them. Journalists love people who speculate.

The second point is: don't lose your cool. If something is not going quite the way you need it to in an interview, get back to your key messages, be polite and if necessary try to close the thing down.

No surprises, please

The truth is, though, that there should be no surprises. Your financial advisers should have told you before the results how investor sentiment lay. And your financial PR adviser should have warned you how the media and, if required, how the analysts are viewing your company. Make sure you ask your advisers to provide you with this feedback in good time, as it is important. Time spent in preparation is never wasted.

Other events, better relations

Talking to the markets twice a year may not be enough. You can use other events as a means to keep the market informed of your progress. Your PR firm should be able to advise you as to what constitutes 'news' but, remember, your view of news and theirs may not concur. This is because you are very close to your business and deeply involved: they should have a critical distance.

A good PR firm will encourage you to develop a campaign of communications for the next 12 months, and this should be reviewed every couple of months to see how you are getting along.

This campaign should, of course, include your preliminary and interim results but may also take on the issuance of statements or trading updates around your AGM (very popular) and around key seasonal trading peaks or major industry events. For example, if you are a retailer, your shareholders would quite rightly expect you to update the market as to how you got on over the Christmas holiday peak. On the other hand, if you were a semiconductor firm then an update at 3GSM might be appropriate. Your PR adviser should help you to think about your business calendar and use it creatively.

The sort of events that can prompt newsflow are as follows:

■ interim and preliminary results;
■ AGMs;
■ new appointments;
■ contract wins;
■ restructuring;
■ trading updates;
■ analyst and investor site visits;
■ mergers and acquisitions.

Remember too that you do not just have to go for the wires and the broadsheet press. In many sectors – property springs to mind here, for example, and also the pub and catering trade – there is a powerful trade press that is read by investors, analysts and the business writers on the national newspapers.

Dealing with journalists

You should expect your PR people to demonstrate an understanding of the media and to have some experience of and relationships with them. Many financial PR people are ex-business journalists. This does not immediately qualify them for a job in PR – the modes of thinking can be very different – but it can help in getting to an understanding of how you need to pitch your corporate story.

Journalists want (and need) to write stories. This is what they get paid for. For this to happen, they need news. Your chances of getting a favourable news story into a newspaper increase (so people in PR believe) if you have a relationship with that journalist. To this end, your PR person should advise as to how to approach journalists: a series of background briefings with a sector journalist – supported by fact sheets, links to websites and analysts' notes – should be useful. These may be held over lunch or in your PR person's office, but if the former do not relax over a long lunch and let down your guard. Never say anything you would not expect to see in print even if the meeting is 'off the record'.

Feedback

As we note above, your PR firm should be providing you with regular updates as to changes in the recommendations of the equity analysts and as to changes of personnel in the press.

When you go to see a journalist, your PR person should be telling you why you are seeing this particular journalist, and why now, and should also be able to provide some background on the individual. Essentially, you should feel confident that your PR person knows whom to talk to and how and that he or she maintains good relations. The same applies to your financial adviser when going to see investors: do not be afraid to ask the adviser 'Who are we seeing?', 'What is their investment style?' and 'Are they or have they been investors?' These are important questions.

And what if it all goes wrong?

Your experience as a businessperson will tell you that not everything goes according to plan. But here's the rub: when you were a private business (in those dark days before you floated), no one could see your pain. Now you are a public company, not only do your stakeholders see what has gone wrong but they will also expect you to diagnose yourself in public and recommend a course of treatment to get better again – all the while maintaining your managerial credibility.

A good PR company – and one with which you have built a satisfactory relationship – should see itself as the guardian of your corporate reputation. And this means helping you with crises.

A crisis is a great deal more common than it would appear, and we can say this with the certain knowledge that a good PR person may spend a considerable amount of his or her time and skill in keeping something *out* of the press. It is worth building a circle of friends, sympathizers, acquaintances and contacts whilst times are good – in the certain knowledge that they will not remain that way.

Summary

You will have concluded by now that living with the listing means having two jobs. The first is the proper job you always wanted, namely running a public company. The other job you hardly ever dreamt of is reporting to the capital markets, and this could take up a meaningful chunk of your time. Take it seriously, plan thoroughly and you will be rewarded with the proper rating and decent value for your equity. It will get easier as time goes on, and you may even find that you like doing it. More importantly, you will also build a store of value for continued success in this business or, most likely, in a bigger one. This is called your reputation and it has huge value. Employ a good PR company to help you take care of it.

24

Quoted company transactions

Sarah Cartwright, Bevan Brittan LLP

Introduction

So you have been through the flotation process – and made it to the other end. The investors seem happy, the market is strong, trading in the company's shares is healthy and you are now looking to grow by acquisition. As a private company you may typically have had to consult a small group of shareholders to seek approval of any potential acquisition or disposal, and the transaction could be completed out of the public domain. However, a company that has its shares listed on the Official List of the UK Listing Authority or admitted to trading on the AIM market or another exchange in the UK must consider a number of other regulatory issues when contemplating an acquisition or disposal of the company's shares or assets.

Regulatory environment

In addition to the requirements of the Companies Act 1985 and the provisions that have so far been brought into force under the Companies Act 2006, for a company with shares traded on a public market in the UK the following will also need to be considered:

- the Listing Rules (if the company's shares are listed on the Official List of the UK Listing Authority), the AIM Rules (if the company is on the AIM market), the Prospectus Rules and the Disclosure and Transparency Rules (the latter

Bevan Brittan

A breath of fresh air

Our corporate team is used to getting right to the heart of a client's business, protecting interests at every stage of development and providing expert advice to public and private companies and consortia, SMEs, owner-managed businesses and entrepreneurs, as well as institutional investors and finance providers

Our services are extensive and our practice expertise embraces mergers and acquisitions, corporate finance, private equity, joint ventures and IPOs and secondary fundraisings on both AIM and the Official List.

For further information, please contact:

Sarah Cartwright
T +44 (0)870 194 5012
sarah.cartwright@bevanbrittan.com

Adam Duthie
T +44 (0)870 194 7901
adam.duthie@bevanbrittan.com

having more limited application to AIM companies than to those on the Official List);

■ the requirements of any exchange on which the shares are traded (for example, the Admission and Disclosure Standards of the London Stock Exchange);

■ institutional investor views through the Investor Protection Committee (IPC) guidelines; and

■ the City Code on Takeovers and Mergers (which applies to both listed and unlisted plcs in the UK).

These additional regulations may impact greatly on the proposed timetable for the transaction, how it may be structured and ultimately whether or not it is right for the company in question.

The Listing Rules/AIM Rules

For a company that has its shares listed on the Official List of the UK Listing Authority then the relevant provisions of the Listing Rules relating to transactions are contained in Listing Rule (LR) 10 (significant transactions), LR 11 (related party transactions) and LR 13 (contents of circulars). In addition, if the company is an investment entity or venture capital trust there are additional and alternative requirements in LR 15 and LR 16.

For an AIM company, the relevant rules are AIM Rules 12, 14, 15 and 16, which set out detailed requirements in relation to the provision of information to the market in the context of a proposed transaction. In addition, AIM Rule 13 sets out the additional requirements where the transaction is with 'related parties'.

Transactions under the Listing Rules and the AIM Rules are classified according to the size of the transaction by reference to what are known as 'class tests', which are in effect percentage ratios.

Shareholder approval

Shareholders' consent may be required where a transaction exceeds a certain threshold by reference to the class tests. This will involve holding an extraordinary general meeting (EGM) and issuing a circular to shareholders (which in the case of a company that has its shares listed on the Official List of the UK Listing Authority must also be approved by the Financial Services Authority (FSA) prior to publication). Prior approval of a circular to shareholders by the FSA is not required under the AIM Rules. The production of a circular including a notice of EGM adds an additional expense to the cost of a transaction. There will also be additional timetable implications, particularly if the circular needs to be approved by the FSA.

So which transactions require shareholder approval? Well, it depends on the size of the transaction.

The class tests under the Listing Rules

For companies on the Official List of the UK Listing Authority, transactions are classified according to the 'class tests'. There are four such tests under the Listing Rules, which will when applied result in a percentage:

■ *The gross assets test*:

> the gross assets the subject of the transaction ÷ the gross assets of the listed company × 100

Note: Where shares are being acquired, the value of 'the gross assets the subject of the transaction' is the consideration payable for the shares being acquired and, for a disposal of shares, 'the gross assets the subject of the transaction' is the value of the shares being disposed of as stated in the listed company's accounts.

■ *The profits test*:

> the profits attributable to the assets the subject of the transaction ÷ the profits of the listed company × 100

Note: 'Profits' for the purposes of this test means profits after deduction of all charges save for taxation.

■ *The consideration test*:

> the consideration for the transaction ÷ the aggregate market value of all of the ordinary shares (excluding treasury shares) of the listed company × 100

Note: If there is an element of deferred consideration, the consideration will be treated as being the maximum amount payable or receivable, ie such amount as if all possible deferred consideration had in fact been paid or received rather than any element deferred. Also further note, if there is no cap on the deferred consideration payable or receivable, then under this class test the transaction is automatically treated as a Class 1 transaction (see later) irrespective of the class it would otherwise fall in.

■ *The gross capital test*:

> the gross capital of the company or business being acquired ÷ the gross capital of the listed company × 100

Note: 'The gross capital of the company or business being acquired' means the aggregate of the consideration payable and the liabilities (other than current liabilities) being assumed. 'The gross capital of the listed company' includes its liabilities (other than current liabilities) together with its aggregate market value.

For all of the class tests above, the figures to be used are those shown in the latest published audited consolidated accounts of the listed company or if the listed company publishes a preliminary statement of later annual results at the time of agreeing the terms of the transaction then the figures to be used are those taken from any such preliminary statement.

Classification of transactions

The class tests will determine whether the transaction in question is a:

- *Class 3 transaction* – where *all* percentage ratios are less than 5 per cent;
- *Class 2 transaction* – where *any* percentage ratio is 5 per cent or more, but *each* percentage ratio is less than 25 per cent;
- *Class 1 transaction* – where *any* percentage ratio is 25 per cent or more;
- *reverse takeover* – where any percentage ratio is 100 per cent or more or the acquisition in question would result in a fundamental change in the business of the listed company or a change in board or voting control of the listed company.

Class 3 requirements

A Class 3 transaction needs neither shareholder approval nor notification to a regulatory information service (RIS) unless the company releases details of the transaction to the public or the consideration includes the issue of shares by the listed company that will be listed.

Class 2 requirements

A Class 2 transaction requires notification to an RIS of prescribed details of the transaction as soon as possible after the terms of the transaction are agreed. No shareholder approval, however, is required and therefore no circular is needed.

Class 1 requirements

If the transaction is a Class 1 transaction, the Listing Rules require:

1. the listed company to engage a sponsor (see below);
2. prescribed details of the transaction to be notified to an RIS;
3. an explanatory circular to be sent to shareholders to obtain their approval; and
4. any agreement effecting the transaction to be conditional on shareholder approval being obtained.

A sponsor is a firm of financial advisers. On a company's IPO a sponsor will be appointed and the same firm may be retained to act again in relation to a transaction. The Listing Rules do not require the sponsor to be permanently appointed. The sponsor's primary duty is to guide the company and the directors through the Listing Rules and their application and to liaise with the FSA on the company's behalf.

Reverse takeover requirements

A company proposing a reverse takeover is required to appoint a sponsor for guidance.

A circular must be prepared and the approval of the listed company's shareholders obtained. On the announcement of a reverse takeover the FSA has the discretion to suspend trading in the listed company. Having the shares illiquid, albeit temporarily, is something to consider in this context. The listed company's advisers, particularly the sponsor, will be able to guide it through the process of whether suspension is appropriate and liaise with the UK Listing Authority on the company's behalf. The general rule is that suspension may not be required if there is sufficient information in the market about the proposed transaction.

When a listed company completes a reverse takeover, the FSA will generally cancel the listing and the company will be required to reapply for listing.

Related party transactions

Certain transactions of companies with shares listed on the Official List may also require compliance with LR 11 if the transaction involves a 'related party'. A 'related party' is:

■ A 'substantial shareholder', being a person who is at the time of the transaction or was in the 12-month period preceding the transaction entitled to exercise or control the exercise of 10 per cent or more of the votes at a general meeting of the listed company (or any of its significant subsidiary undertakings).

■ Directors or shadow directors of the listed company or any of its significant subsidiary undertakings and those persons who held such position in the 12-month period preceding the transaction.

■ A 50/50 joint venture partner of the listed company. Also note it is considered that an amendment to a 50/50 joint venture agreement, further investment into a 50/50 joint venture, or the exercise of an option of a right to buy a joint venture interest or to sell an interest in a 50/50 joint venture will be a related party transaction.

■ A person or entity exercising significant influence over the listed company.

■ An associate of any of the above.

A proposed related party transaction will also require the appointment of a sponsor for guidance.

Requirements for a related party transaction

A related party transaction must usually (save in certain circumstances in LR 11) be notified to an RIS. The announcement must contain prescribed details under the Listing Rules. An explanatory circular must be sent to shareholders, and shareholder approval must be obtained prior to the transaction being entered into or as a condition to completion (with the related party and its associates abstaining from voting).

Circulars

LR 13 governs the general content of circulars under the Listing Rules. Both Class 1 and related party circulars also need the approval of the FSA prior to publication.

In addition, Class 1 circulars must include certain information in order to provide shareholders with sufficient information to allow the shareholders to make an informed decision as to whether they will vote in favour of the proposed resolutions. The circular will also include the notice of EGM. All directors of a listed company are required to take responsibility for the information in the circular and there will be included in the circular a declaration of responsibility. By taking responsibility in such a way as to the content of the circular, directors subject themselves to potential liability if information in the circular is found to be incorrect or misleading or information or opinions given in the circular have not been given on a reasonable basis. The advisers to the company will guide the directors through the process to ensure that the content of the circular is true and accurate and not misleading and that opinions are made on a reasonable basis.

Typically a process called verification is undertaken to test the truth and accuracy of the contents of a circular. The company's lawyers will prepare a set of questions and answers on the statements within the circular and in any announcements.

If the consideration for an acquisition involves the issue of shares, the company may also have to issue a prospectus and ensure compliance with an additional set of rules, the Prospectus Rules. A prospectus will be required to be vetted by the FSA. A prospectus needs to be prepared when either: 1) there is an offer of securities to the public in the UK; or 2) securities are admitted to trading on a regulated UK market. Only the Official List in the UK is a regulated market; the AIM market is not. An AIM company may still be required to produce a prospectus, though, under 1) above, if it is making an offer of securities to the public in the UK and none of the applicable exemptions apply.

Requirements of the AIM market

There are certain similarities for companies on the AIM market proposing to undertake acquisitions or disposals to companies on the Official List. However, transactions involving AIM companies are governed by the AIM Rules rather than the Listing Rules. AIM is perceived to be less regulated, particularly in relation to transactions, and for this reason amongst others, acquisitive smaller growth companies often find AIM more attractive.

Substantial transactions under the AIM Rules

An AIM company must have a nominated adviser (nomad) at all times. Contrast this with the position of companies on the Official List and their requirement to have a sponsor only in relation to certain transactions. AIM companies are required to disclose to the market details of 'substantial transactions'. A substantial transaction for the purposes of the AIM Rules is one that exceeds 10 per cent in any of the class tests. The class tests for the purposes of the AIM Rules are set out later in this chapter. Transactions for these purposes include any transaction by a subsidiary of the AIM company but exclude any transactions of a revenue nature in the ordinary course of business and transactions to raise finance that do not involve a change in the fixed assets of the AIM company or its subsidiaries. As soon as the terms of any substantial transaction are agreed, an AIM company must issue notification of an announcement containing the information prescribed in the AIM Rules without delay.

Related party transactions under the AIM Rules

Transactions of an AIM company may also be related party transactions, and if such a transaction exceeds 5 per cent in any of the class tests then AIM Rule 13 applies and the AIM company must issue notification without delay as soon as the terms are agreed, disclosing the information prescribed by the AIM Rules.

Reverse takeovers under the AIM Rules

A reverse takeover for the purposes of the AIM Rules is an acquisition or acquisitions in a 12-month period that for the AIM company would:

- exceed 100 per cent in any of the class tests; or
- result in a fundamental change in its business, board or voting control; or
- in the case of an investing company, depart substantially from the investing strategy stated in its admission document or stated elsewhere.

Any agreement that would effect a reverse takeover under the AIM Rules must be conditional on the consent of the AIM company's shareholders being given in general meeting, certain prescribed information must be notified without delay and an admission document in respect of the proposed enlarged entity must be published that will include a notice of a general meeting. The admission document may also be required to be produced in accordance with the Prospectus Rules unless an exemption applies as mentioned above.

Disposals resulting in a fundamental change of business

This is a disposal by an AIM company that when aggregated with any other disposal or disposals over the previous 12-month period exceeds 75 per cent in any of the class tests. Such a disposal is conditional on the consent of shareholders, an announcement must be made without delay and it must be accompanied by the publication of a circular.

Aggregation of transactions under the AIM Rules

For an AIM company, certain transactions completed during the 12 months prior to the date of the latest transaction must be aggregated with that transaction for the purpose of determining whether the relevant AIM Rules apply.

Class tests for the purposes of the AIM Rules

There are five class tests under the AIM Rules:

■ *The gross assets test*:

the gross assets the subject of the transaction ÷ the gross assets of the AIM company × 100

■ *The profits test*:

the profits attributable to the assets the subject of the transaction ÷ the profits of the AIM company × 100

■ *The turnover test*:

the turnover attributable to the assets the subject of the transaction ÷ the turnover of the AIM company × 100

■ *The consideration test*:

the consideration ÷ the aggregate market value of all of the ordinary shares (excluding treasury shares) of the AIM company × 100

■ *The gross capital test*:

> the gross capital of the company or business being acquired ÷ the gross capital of the AIM company × 100

Where the class tests might produce anomalous results or where the tests are inappropriate to the sphere of activity of the AIM company, the London Stock Exchange may disregard the calculation and substitute other relevant indicators of size or industry-specific tests. The nomad's guidance on the class tests should be sought at the outset of any transaction.

Other rules and regulations for listed and AIM companies

The Disclosure and Transparency Rules

In the context of a significant transaction, 'inside information' may need to be announced. Inside information and its control and release are governed by the Disclosure and Transparency Rules.

Inside information is information of a precise nature that:

■ is not generally available;
■ relates directly or indirectly to one or more issues of qualifying investments or the qualifying investments themselves;
■ would, if generally available, be likely to have a significant effect on the price of the qualifying investments or related investments.

Companies on a UK equity capital market do need to be alive to these rules and the sensitivity and confidentiality of certain information and when and whether to release such information.

The Model Code

Listed companies must ensure that persons discharging managerial responsibilities (PDMRs) (for example, directors and senior management with regular access to insider information and with certain decision-making powers) comply with the Model Code. The Model Code requires PDMRs to obtain advance clearance to deal in securities of the listed company. Advance clearance cannot be given in close periods (usually a certain period before the announcement of inside information, eg accounts or a potential transaction). Mandatory compliance is required by Main Market companies. It is not mandatory for companies on AIM, but market expectations are that AIM companies will comply with the Model Code to the extent applicable for companies of their size.

Insider dealing

Part V of the Criminal Justice Act 1993 relates to insider dealing in listed securities. The offences of insider dealing are:

- dealing in price-affected securities by an insider;
- an insider encouraging another to deal in price-affected securities;
- an insider disclosing price-sensitive information.

Price-sensitive information is generally information that if made public would be likely to have a significant effect on the price or value of securities. The prospect of a significant transaction, particularly major acquisitions or disposals for a company on a UK equity capital market, is very likely to be price-sensitive information and therefore each of the Disclosure and Transparency Rules, the Model Code and the Criminal Justice Act 1993 will be applicable.

Takeovers

Any company may receive a takeover bid for its shares. A listed company (AIM and Official List), unlike a private company, may not simply refuse to have anything to do with an approach or offer for its shares. A listed company that receives an approach should immediately contact its financial advisers.

Takeovers in the UK are governed by the City Code on Takeovers and Mergers (City Code). Under the City Code, once an approach has been received it is the target company's primary responsibility to make an announcement to the market of the existence of the approach if its share price changes materially. The target company is also required by the City Code to take competent independent advice on any offer that is received and to communicate the substance of that advice to its shareholders.

The City Code applies to offers for all listed *and* unlisted public companies based in the UK, and is founded on a set of principles that underpin its more detailed rules. It is fundamental that, where there is any doubt as to the application of the City Code, the matter should be discussed with the Panel on Takeovers and Mergers, which monitors and regulates the operation of the City Code. Before entering into a transaction that would amount to a takeover or merger, a company should always seek professional advice to ensure compliance with the City Code.

Summary

In summary, transactions for companies on a public market are far more regulated than transactions for private companies and, before proposing to enter into a transaction, companies should seek the advice of the lawyers and financial advisers (sponsor or nomad as the case may be) at the earliest possible opportunity.

25

Making the most of your time on AIM

Patrick Booth-Clibborn, KBC Peel Hunt

Introduction

After the long slog of the IPO process and the public listing of your company on AIM, you should be feeling full of enthusiasm for driving the business forward and fully prepared to face your new audiences: shareholders, analysts, brokers, market makers, advisers and the media.

Floating on AIM is an extremely detailed and thorough process, and for many chief executives and finance directors this means working on two full-time jobs during the listing process.

Your corporate guardian

As well as being an important first point of advice, the nomad is effectively a company's City 'guardian', with a duty to know everything about what is going on within the client company. The nomad's involvement varies for each one: some like to attend every board meeting, most hold regular management meetings, many ask for quarterly figures and all like to maintain a regular dialogue. It is the duty of the nomad to ensure that the company keeps to its strategy for growth and, if there is a change in the plan (such as acquisitions or entry into new markets), then the nomad needs to advise the company as to whether a public statement is required and may recommend future financing options.

The aftermarket

Post-IPO, it is vital that the company and its brokers maintain the 'aftermarket' in the shares. Unfortunately, this is all too often forgotten, with many companies pausing for breath and failing to come up for air for some time afterwards.

Looking after the 'aftermarket' means making concerted efforts to facilitate trade in the company's shares; the key to this is ensuring that the business plan set out in the IPO documentation is delivered and that an orderly market in the shares is maintained, requiring all possible buyers and sellers to have access to the same information, and may mean regular announcements to apprise the market of the health of the business – both good and bad.

The AIM Rules apply to all companies and, while company directors are expected to have a working knowledge of these rules, it is up to the nomad – your corporate guardian – to make sure each company is aware of and follows them.

The importance of communication

Every listed company has a duty to maintain and keep the market informed about material movements in its shares. If the shares trade up or down, a company may need to let investors know why, especially if the trading is on the back of unconfirmed rumours. Most importantly, it should work at informing the market and managing investor expectations by keeping the City updated about trading and other corporate events.

Under the AIM Rules, every company is obliged to report any changes in its trading position. Therefore, if there is a material downturn in trade or profitability, the company must inform the market as soon as it is aware of this fact. Being quoted isn't just about creating positive newsflow to increase the share price, but also, when a company hits a bump in the road, which invariably happens, reporting this in a balanced manner.

'First' or 'maiden' results

The first set of results post-IPO is when a company needs to be the most proactive; this means visiting existing institutional investors and also meeting new retail brokers and other fund managers who have expressed an interest in the company. The story told at the IPO will need to be confirmed and updated, giving comfort that all is on track or explaining why it is not. The chief executive and finance director will normally present the results and, if necessary, the chairman gets involved as well.

If a company is good at communicating with the City, this will help to smooth share price movements on the back of a weak trading statement – and hopefully keep shares from plunging. An estimated 60 to 70 per cent of companies on AIM will make a profit warning at some stage – so be prepared!

The biggest problem faced by many AIM companies is that of maintaining information flow, particularly for early-stage companies where earnings are still some way off and thus significant trading news is lean. Milestones should be set publicly and achievements against these milestones should be reported. The temptation to 'puff' (put out unimportant statements to generate interest) should be resisted.

Do I need a PR adviser?

A pattern of steady newsflow will help liquidity. These announcements are the responsibility of the company (with advice from the nomad), but a public relations (PR) adviser can be of real assistance, and it is common practice for a marketing and PR campaign to be drawn up at the IPO and at the time of the first results and thereafter.

Communication with investors and the press is critical for the ongoing success of an AIM company's share price, and if a company fails to provide the City with the right sort of information at the right time then its credibility can be severely damaged.

Some PR firms provide an investor relations service to put you in front of key media and a number of private client and retail investors. Some stockbrokers also provide this service and will take you on regular roadshows around regional brokers. This can be a significant aid to generating liquidity and bringing the company to the attention of retail buyers.

AIM companies face considerable costs for being listed on the financial markets: nomad and broker fees, listing fees, legal, accounting and registrar fees, and fees for PR advice. It is usual for a company to try to minimize costs, but every listed AIM company generally employs all of these services, and some are mandatory, as set out in the AIM Rules.

Attracting shareholders

Attracting new investors to your company (as well as keeping existing ones) is vital to the success of the company's listing. This will be primarily the responsibility of the broker.

The company needs to make itself available for meetings to explain its business. Developing a comprehensive presentation so that companies can show investors why they should buy the shares is vital; this should include trading history, a growth strategy and management experience as well as detailed financials.

Leading up to the float, you will have visited numerous fund managers to present your company to them, in the hope of persuading them to invest in your business. It's a busy time – during the average AIM IPO, management meets 30 or more of these institutional investors. It is possible that you will have also carried out an active campaign among private client stockbrokers to interest retail investors – none of this activity stops after the float.

How many is enough?

You should be looking to increase your institutional shareholder base during your first few years on AIM; for example, if a company has 10 to 15 institutions on the shareholder register when it floats, it should be looking to try to double its institutional investors over the following two years. Some of these may have met the company pre-IPO but not invested, while others will be new investors attracted to the story.

Using tax breaks

One of the key drivers for the AIM market is the tax incentives that are available for private UK shareholders, either through the Enterprise Investment Scheme (EIS) or through venture capital trusts (VCTs). As a result, a lot of smaller floats have many tax-based investors, who take a long-term view and thus provide useful support to the stock.

However, having many long-term investors as shareholders can mean that there is limited liquidity in the market. VCT funds particularly like to hold stock for three years, and EIS funds are also long-term investors. A balance of investors with differing outlooks is key.

Venture capitalists

Usually a company coming to the market is owned by its founders, management or venture capital investors (VCs). Most VCs see the float as an exit for their holding and generally look to reduce their stake in its entirety at float or shortly thereafter. Founders and management should not look at the IPO as an opportunity to sell significant amounts of shares – why would someone invest when the people who know the story best are selling? Nevertheless, it is often possible to sell a small proportion of management's shares at the IPO – 5 to 10 per cent is not unusual – although the market likes to see founder/management shareholders still tied in to the company, to know they are committed to growing the business and to ensure that their interests are aligned with those of all other investors. They should be locked in for at least 12 to 24 months after the IPO before selling further shares and thereafter only with permission of the nomad and broker.

Corporate transactions

As with the IPO process, the management of the regulatory issues concerning corporate transactions is led by the nomad.

Companies can feel under pressure after they have floated to make acquisitions. This process can be difficult and distracting for a small company and so it is rare for a new AIM company to make an acquisition during its first year of trading, unless this is a stated part of its growth plan. Don't feel under pressure to buy something – investors are far happier to see annual results in line with expectations and a progressive acquisition policy going forward. A lot of good companies grow organically without buying other companies.

The nomad will consider whether the proposed acquisitions are in line with the company's stated strategy and will be well received by the market. The nomad will then advise on the appropriate sources for raising any necessary finance – either by issuing more equity or through raising debt.

At the early stages of growth, many companies don't think about making acquisitions, but it is important that you have a good relationship with your bank so that you can arrange financing for any sort of corporate activity at relatively short notice – many acquisitions are available with a short exclusivity period and so it is important that the right sort of finance is available. Fast-growing companies tend to issue a lot of equity but lack debt facilities, often owing to their lack of profits. Getting in place a debt finance facility to cope with growth means that a company doesn't have to rely on equity, which can be dilutive and costly. The nomad will also advise the company on how much information companies need to tell the market and when.

Liquidity

One of the main benefits of listing on AIM is that you can welcome new shareholders into the company and provide a currency for future growth by issuing equity. Problems can arise if there is a lack of liquidity in the stock and investors are unable to buy or sell the shares in the market.

There is no requirement in the AIM Rules to have a minimum number of shares as 'free float' in the market (the number of shares in public hands), but it is good practice to have a minimum of 25 per cent.

Brokers usually place most company shares with larger institutions and other long-term investors. However, ignore the retail and shorter-term investors at your peril – they can generate most of the liquidity in the stock. The problem with placing most of the shares with long-term institutions is that this doesn't leave many shares available for market makers to trade the stock. The ideal shareholder base is between 75 and 85 per cent long-term investors, institutions and company and 'insiders', with between 15 and 25 per cent retail investors.

It's floated – now what should I focus on?

- Let the market and your advisers focus on the aftermarket, but be available for meetings if necessary. The advisers will inform you what to do if there is an adverse share price movement in your company's shares. The most important thing is to focus on running the business and not on the share price.
- Focus on running the business. There will be some investor maintenance work that includes roadshows and investor events throughout the year. These will maintain interest in the stock and attract new investors.
- Remember that the rewards will come through on the back of good earnings. However good a PR campaign or broker, the critical success will be hitting the forecasts and milestones that the market is expecting.

What makes an unsuccessful company on AIM

- *One where the founders are exiting or the owner/chief executive is leaving.* The root cause of an unsuccessful float is often the management team. Management needs to be clear why it is undertaking a float, what this involves, why it is not undertaking a trade sale and that it is focused and incentivized through options and profit share to grow the business. If the management team leaves, investors get concerned that the company knows something the market doesn't.
- *Where there is no focus.* Not having a clear and coherent strategy that is understood by the market is a major mistake. The market needs to see where future growth is coming from and how the company is going to deliver it. This is generally a three- to five-year plan and will be laid out in the IPO prospectus. Companies are also advised to remind the market of this strategy when appropriate: results, trading statements and presentations. The company should not be looking to float and then exit AIM within a short period of time. Most companies that float should not have a limited shelf life and would be expected to be on the market for 5–10 years.
- *Lack of analysis.* Independent research on the company is key to help the understanding of investors. The lack of it can hamper growth. Institutions and private investors want to be able to monitor the growth of a company, assess the financials in digestible format and find out other vital financial information. A research report will provide a benchmark and expectations in the market, as well as telling investors whether to buy, sell or hold shares. Your retained broker should be writing a research report at least twice a year, and more if there is lots of corporate activity. However, attracting analysts from different investment houses to write on the stock can be very useful. If they initiate coverage on your company, this will provide an independent recommendation and should assist in generating additional liquidity.

Important corporate regulation

AIM companies have to announce their results twice a year. Some companies provide quarterly results, but this is not an AIM requirement for UK companies, only a requirement if US companies are required to file with the SEC. As a company you also need to make a trading statement at the AGM once a year. During the year the company has a duty to provide information to the market as soon as it becomes available if it could affect investors' assessment of the company's prospects.

The annual report needs to be published six months after the year end and interim results within three months of the period end. It is very important that companies meet these deadlines. If you fail to achieve them, the shares will be suspended and reputational damage will occur. For regular offenders, being delisted from AIM is possible. Also inform the market of the date you plan to announce results. Although you are not required to inform the market of the results date, it helps investors to get a sense of regularity on when to expect results and builds confidence that there are strong financial reporting processes in place.

V

Shareholders' and directors' considerations

Going public is an
exciting yet complex
process. Your company
requires professional
and pragmatic advice

flotation*

every stage. It's
these factors based
upon real experience
that lead to a
successful listing.

pwc.com/uk

*connectedthinking

PRICEWATERHOUSECOOPERS ⓡ

26

Shareholder/director tax planning

Steve Gilder, PricewaterhouseCoopers LLP

Summary

Tax planning can add substantial value as a company moves towards a listing. However, failure to address tax issues early may result in lost opportunities and potential barriers to the flotation itself against a tight flotation time line. The key tax points to focus into the flotation process are:

- Plan well in advance.
- Decide exactly what to float, and devise a method to extract any non-floatable assets tax-efficiently.
- Understand the tax consequences of different markets, and plan accordingly.
- Plan your employee incentives, and buy those staff into your long-term objectives to motivate them.
- Be flexible – events may alter plans.

Plan well in advance of any flotation

Flotation is often the final point at which tax issues can be addressed easily and effectively. If no tax plan has been devised until sponsors are appointed, it can be very difficult to rectify existing inefficiencies, and opportunities may be lost.

As a guide, a tax plan should be devised at least two and potentially up to six years ahead of any flotation – but later is better than never! – because:

■ personal capital gains rates may only fall effectively to 10 per cent two years after any shares have been acquired;
■ tax-efficient share option schemes may require ownership for at least two years and sometimes longer;
■ reliefs for shareholders such as Enterprise Investment Scheme reliefs require ownership and qualifying activities for several years; and
■ there are certain corporation tax anti-avoidance provisions that can tax transactions in the preceding six years.

Once flotation is proceeding, due diligence might identify tax problems to solve that may require either negotiations with the tax authorities or, at the very least, full indemnities from shareholders. This can cause complications but also potentially reduce the credibility of shareholder/directors in the eyes of the sponsors. If, however, the issues are identified early they can often be far less serious than they might appear and can be resolved thoughtfully, and then the tax issues on due diligence should be negligible and flotation can proceed smoothly.

If it is the intention to give equity to employees then valuations for small holdings will often be much lower when the company is unquoted, and any income tax charges will arise up to 22 months later. Once a decision to list has been announced, the valuation of minority interests will be much higher, and income tax is likely to be under PAYE, with employer and employee National Insurance (NIC).

With a corporate tax rate of 28 per cent (from April 2008) and a personal income tax rate of 40 per cent, plus 13.8 per cent NIC, tax is a major cost for any business or shareholder. As with any business issue, tax needs managing carefully, and applying sufficient thought and seeking proper advice well ahead of a listing will be one of the most valuable investments that any company can make.

Preparing for a listing: what to float

There will be a range of tax issues to address before a company should contemplate embarking on a listing.

For groups controlled by a single shareholder or family, there can often be private assets or expenditure in the company that need to be addressed. There will be tax consequences of removing assets from the company, and these can be complex. For example, a group may have to be broken up into separate businesses to facilitate the flotation of one part of it, and this could be by a demerger process, which typically can take six months.

The tax consequences of different markets

Following the introduction of taper relief and the abolition of indexation relief from 1998, the effective capital gains tax rates for UK shareholders (after an annual exemption for £9,200 of gains) are as displayed in Table 26.1.

Table 26.1   Effective capital gains tax rates for UK shareholders

Years held		0	1	2	3	4	5	6	7	8	9	10+
Business assets	Taper %	0	50	75	75	75	75	75	75	75	75	75
	Effective rate for 40% taxpayer	40	20	10	10	10	10	10	10	10	10	10
Non-business assets	Taper %	0	0	0	5	10	15	20	25	30	35	40
	Effective rate for 40% taxpayer	0	0	0	38	36	34	32	30	28	26	24

Business asset taper relief (BATR) is given for shares in unquoted trading companies/groups (over 80 per cent of activities must consist of trading) or for holdings in any company of less than 10 per cent of both votes and share class rights, by an employee or office holder. Where a company has been both trading and non-trading, taper relief will be apportioned pro rata. For listed companies, BATR will only continue where:

■ the holder is an employee or office holder of a trading company/group;
■ the owner holds more than 5 per cent of the votes of a trading company/group; or
■ the owner holds less than 10 per cent of both votes and share class rights and is an employee or office holder.

Put differently, a non-employee shareholder in a trading company/group will no longer accrue BATR after listing on a 'recognized stock exchange'. For example, a small non-employee shareholder of two years could sell on flotation and qualify for BATR at an effective 10 per cent tax rate. If, however, such a shareholder sells two years after listing, half the ownership period will have qualified for BATR and half as non-BATR, and the person's effective tax rate will be 23 per cent (half of 10 per cent and 36 per cent).

Whilst the London Main Market is a recognized stock exchange, AIM is treated for these purposes as unquoted, which means that non-employee shareholders can continue to obtain BATR for AIM listed trading groups. The same goes for a number of other smaller markets. This can make AIM more attractive than Main Market listings for ongoing non-employee shareholders, or to attract new, private shareholders. Similarly, venture capital trusts can invest in AIM companies, and the Enterprise Investment Scheme can be used to raise capital.

Shares in private trading groups qualify for exemptions from inheritance tax after two years' ownership. Exemption continues for AIM but not Main Market shares, which again can drive private companies towards AIM.

Employee incentivization

This is a complex area of tax, with tremendous opportunities but great risks, and needs a separate and thorough tax plan over many years. A different strategy is likely to be necessary for different staff levels, and each group needs to be bought into the plans. Done properly, this can incentivize and retain employees, save on staff turnover and training, and build a loyal and effective workforce. Too often, however, equity is given to staff without sufficient communication as to its value or plans for exit, with the consequential failure to motivate staff on the way through. For example, cash bonuses invariably motivate sales staff more than higher-value stock options.

Existing employee shareholders: tax risks

Most people will be aware that, if they give shares to employees, income tax will arise on any undervalue. What is less widely understood is that the legislation has a very wide reach and can include founders and non-executives; and income tax issues can continue to arise during share ownership. As these issues will often be under PAYE with NIC, both the company's primary responsibility, they can create unforeseen costs, and a less-than-optimal tax rate for employee shareholders.

For shares issued since April 2003, the rules for employee shareholders are complex and can only be summarized briefly:

■ Any person who obtains shares in connection with past, present or future employment will fall within the provisions, including founder directors (though this may not necessarily mean a tax liability).
■ If there is not likely to be a market for the shares, any income tax will normally be a personal liability due on 31 January following the end of the fiscal year; if, however, there is likely to be a market or the shares are in a subsidiary, the liability will be under PAYE with NIC.
■ Normally the market value of shares will take into account any restrictions imposed on the ownership of the shares, such as bad leaver clauses. This can reduce the initial income tax exposure, but result in more significant taxes on exit.

For example: An employee is given free shares worth £1,000, but they are subject to forfeiture if the employee leaves within a certain period. Three years later the company lists when the shares are worth £100,000 and the forfeiture provisions are lifted. Eighteen months after listing, the employee sells the shares for £150,000.

The employee will have an initial income tax liability on the market value of the shares less the price paid of nil. Suppose, in negotiations with HM Revenue & Customs, a 20 per cent discount is agreed for the forfeiture provisions. The initial income tax liability will be on £800 of income, ie £320.

When the forfeiture provisions are lifted the initial discount of 20 per cent will be applied to the then value of shares, giving rise to taxable income of £20,000 on listing. Because there will then be a market for the shares, the tax liability will be due under PAYE, with employee NIC of 1 per cent (£8,200) and employer NIC of 12.8 per cent (£2,560).

On the share sale by the employee for £150,000, the effective capital gains tax rate is 10 per cent on £150,000 less base cost (nil) and amounts assessed to income tax (£20,800), giving rise to a further tax liability of £12,920 ignoring annual CGT exemptions, and total tax of £24,000.

■ It is possible to make an election to disregard any restrictions when assessing the initial income tax. Thereafter, growth in value will be capital gains tax. The election has to be signed by the employee and the employer within 14 days of acquisition.

Suppose the employee and the company make an election. The employee is assessed initially to income tax on the unrestricted market value of £1,000, ie £400 tax. No tax charge arises when the restrictions are lifted on listing, and on disposal there is a capital gain at 10 per cent on £150,000 less £1,000 of cost. The total tax is £15,300.

■ Serious income tax issues can also arise where shares held by employees are convertible (ie potential income tax on the full value of the shares on conversion).

■ Shares issued between March 1998 and April 2003 could render what might appear to be a capital gains asset as in fact entirely within income tax. The rules are complex, but for example if there were forfeiture provisions that were not included within the articles of association – for instance, in a shareholders' agreement – then any eventual proceeds of these forfeitable shares could be taxed as income, probably under PAYE and NIC. Any company that issued shares to employees in this period needs to undertake detailed due diligence to identify whether complications will arise.

Valuations

Valuing shares is complex, the main complication being the discount to apply for a minority holding in an unquoted group. If there is no existing or likely market for shares and the company has no dividend history, discounts of 50–80 per cent can be obtained for small minority holdings. This can help incentivize employees for past as well as future performance. However, a dividend history or publicity about a prospective flotation will significantly lift the value of minority interests, as will any funding that sets a clear benchmark valuation. Great care therefore needs to be taken on the timing of external funding and publicity about a potential exit, as it may impact upon the reward structures for management.

Alternatively, there are several tax-efficient share option schemes, some suitable for senior executives and some for wider employees. For most private trading groups whose gross assets are less than £30 million, the Enterprise Incentive Scheme (EIS) is likely to be the preferred methodology to motivate management and staff with equity. So long as shares issued to any full-time employee are worth less than £100,000 on grant and the total value of EIS options when granted is less than £3 million, then EIS options can usually be granted. The main advantage of EIS is for the option holder, in that capital gains BATR will run from grant not exercise. Furthermore, options can be issued at a discount to market value with no immediate tax consequences, and on exercise only the initial discount will be charged to income tax.

Other schemes such as company share ownership plans may also be appropriate. Finally, an unapproved option scheme is simple in the sense that there are no restrictions over the rules, and normally no income tax issues arise on grant; however, on exercise the whole of any option gain will be liable to income tax.

For all option schemes, a corporate tax deduction is normally given to the UK employing company for the growth in value of the options. This can create significant deductions that can eliminate corporate tax charges for a number of years. This tax deduction needs planning for carefully, because if the deduction is greater than the profits in the year of exercise then the use of the loss can be restricted. If it arises on an exit then the deduction can be lost depending on the identity of the purchaser if the timing is not planned.

International employees are likely to require their own particular incentive plan appropriate to the tax laws in their local jurisdiction. Furthermore, a recharge agreement should be introduced between the UK parent, whose equity is being provided to employees, and the overseas operating subsidiary, entitling the UK company to make a charge for the option plan. In certain circumstances this can give rise to a one-sided tax deduction, in that the local operating company can obtain a tax deduction but the UK company will not be taxed on the receipt.

Employee incentives on listing

The company may want to introduce a more complex set of employee incentive provisions on listing, giving key management or staff a share in the future performance of the business. Often this consists of a long-term incentive plan (LTIP), which will bundle bonuses, options and shares, with defined performance criteria. The listing document will need to include details of any planned incentive schemes, and it can be difficult to go back to the market for revisions to any scheme, so this needs to be thought through carefully. Many companies introduce a fairly generic LTIP, but often these are not really suitable to the plans and requirements of the particular company, resulting in management being under- (or over-) incentivized against company performance or rewarded on the wrong measures. An LTIP should be bespoke to the needs of the individual company, taking into account the business plans and forward projections on performance if it is to motivate fully the key management.

Conclusion

Tax is complex, and the answer for shareholders is not always 10 per cent. However, with appropriate and timely tax planning it can be. There are significant tax opportunities to be obtained both for shareholders (for instance, in locking into the 10 per cent capital gains tax rate) and for the company (for instance, corporation tax deductions on exercise of options). There are also bear traps across a whole range of issues, particularly on employee share rewards.

But with a carefully thought-through tax plan, all of the issues should be soluble, and tax planning can add significantly to the overall value of a company.

Money spent on tax advice may be a cost but should be regarded as an investment; and failure to invest in a tax plan will almost certainly lead to significant tax costs and potential complications that may derail a flotation. There is much to be gained, and little to be lost, by devising and implementing a thorough tax strategy that is focused on the commercial objectives of the company and its shareholders.

Punter Southall
Transaction Services

Specialist pensions consulting in transactions

Delivering the highest quality service in the most demanding situations,
Punter Southall Transaction Services advise private equity houses, investment
companies and other corporate entities on the acquisition and disposal of defined
benefit pension schemes and the ongoing management of pension liabilities.

Transaction consulting:
- Full international pensions due diligence
- Advice on disposal, re-financing or floatation
- Assistance with the Clearance process
- Post-acquisition solutions

Corporate consulting:
- Risk and cost management of defined benefit arrangements
- Valuation negotiations between trustees and companies
- Advice relating to dealing with the Pensions Regulator

"In difficult situations where others hide behind 'if', 'but' and 'however',
these guys always find a pragmatic commercial solution. I've never
known them to be outdone."

Jon Moulton – Managing Partner, Alchemy Partners LLP

Punter Southall
TRANSACTION SERVICES

For further information call 020 7839 8600
email info@pstransactions.co.uk
or visit our website at www.pstransactions.co.uk

27

Pension arrangements

Richard Jones, Punter Southall Transaction Services

Background to pension arrangements

In the UK, employer-sponsored pension schemes tend to operate on a pre-funded basis rather than the pay-as-you-go approach adopted in many other territories and by the UK government. Pre-funded occupational pension arrangements can be divided into two main categories, those which operate on a defined contribution (DC) basis and those which operate on a defined benefit (DB) basis.

In a DC arrangement, the sponsoring employer pays a set level of contributions each year, usually expressed as a fixed percentage of salary, into each member's individual fund. The pension a member receives depends on the amount of contributions paid in respect of that member by both the employer and the member, the level of investment returns generated on those contributions and annuity rates at the time the member retires.

From an employer perspective, a DC arrangement has stable and predictable costs and hence presents little in the way of financial risk to the sponsoring employer. The financial liability in respect of a DC arrangement is limited to the set contributions payable each year whilst a member remains employed, and thus DC arrangements do not present any significant issues for businesses looking to raise capital.

A DB arrangement presents much greater risks to the sponsoring employer, as the benefits are defined by reference to a set formula typically based on salary and service. The employer remains responsible for ensuring that sufficient funds are available to meet the benefits. The sponsoring employer is exposed to fluctuations in costs due to investment returns, mortality experience and other experience such as salary increases, inflation and the exercise of member options. Within a DB arrangement, the assets are compared to the value of liabilities at regular intervals (every three years in the UK for cash funding purposes and every year for accounting purposes) in what is known as a 'valuation'.

The presence of these regular valuations creates a significant risk for sponsoring employers if the measure used to place a value on the liabilities is different from the asset classes in which the DB arrangement's assets are invested (known as a 'mismatch' risk). Most measures of the DB liabilities are based on bond yields, whilst most DB schemes invest in other assets, typically equities, creating a significant mismatch risk. The accounting and cash funding requirements can be extremely volatile in such a situation.

The assets held can be greater or lower than the valuation of the liability, and thus there will be a 'surplus' or a 'deficit' in the arrangement:

■ A deficit requires that the sponsoring employer make contributions to make good the deficit within the arrangement. The sponsoring employer may have a reasonably long period of time, often between 5 and 10 years, to pay down the deficit.

■ A surplus can often be used by the sponsoring employer to provide for new benefits for its employees at no cash cost. However, getting full value from a surplus is nearly always impossible, as the members usually have some form of claim on the surplus or part of the surplus.

A significant issue with DB arrangements in the UK is that they are nearly always established under trust, and thus the sponsoring employer has only a limited degree of control over how the arrangement is run. The trustees typically retain the powers over the investment of the assets and the contributions that are payable. The trustees have to act independently of the sponsoring employer and in the best interests of the members of the arrangement.

Under UK GAAP and IFRS, DB arrangements must be fully accounted for, with any deficit reflected on the balance sheet. The cost of the extra benefits granted to members in any accounting year is taken as a charge to operating profit. Outside of the EBITDA calculation is a notional financing charge, consisting of the difference between the interest on the total liabilities and the expected return on the assets, which serves to reflect the impact of the funding position of the arrangement on the profit and loss account.

Stock market valuation of pension deficits

The presence of a pension deficit indicates that the sponsoring employer will, all else being equal, be required to make additional contributions to its pension arrangements in the future. Thus the existence of a deficit should mean that investors place a lower value on a business than on an identical business with a fully funded pension arrangement or one with no DB pension obligations. However, the surprising reality is that the equity market does not tend to punish a company fully for running a pension deficit.

The academic evidence available, whilst limited and fairly US-centric, strongly suggests that public equity markets tend to place too low a weight on pension liabilities. The analysis suggests that this is due to the price/earnings focus of many analysts, with the deficit in the pension arrangement not being factored in until it starts to hit the profit and loss account, which may not happen until several years after the deficit has arisen.

Evidence of this phenomenon is supported by the behaviour of the UK stock market following key changes to legislation and taxation affecting pension obligations. A very good example was the government announcement on 11 June 2003 that all solvent employers would have to secure members' benefits in full with an insurance company in order to terminate their pension arrangements. This completely changed the nature of the pension promise, making it an inescapable obligation, and locked companies into continuing to fund for expensive DB benefits granted in the past. The expectation of most pensions professionals was that the stock market would suffer some damage from this announcement, with the market falling. In reality the market rose by 0.6 per cent that day and by 1.6 per cent the following day.

The budget announcement on 2 July 1997, which removed from pension funds the ability to reclaim tax credits on their dividend income, is another good example. One would have surmised that either pension funds were going to sell equities or, if they retained equity investments, equities would be a less tax-beneficial investment for pension schemes causing costs for companies to increase. Either way one would have expected the stock market to suffer some damage from this announcement, with the market falling. In reality the market rose by 0.4 per cent that day and by 1.4 per cent the following day.

The equity market has also behaved contrary to expectations following announcements made by individual companies. For example, when BAE Systems plc announced their preliminary results on 24 February 2005, one of the significant issues shown was an increase in the pension deficit. The *Guardian* reported 'BAE pension deficit hits £4 billion', the *Independent* said 'Hole in BAE pension fund grows by £1.2 billion', whilst the *Daily Mail* led with 'Gigantic pensions black hole dwarfs BAE's £1 billion profits.' The shares of BAE Systems of course rose on the day of the announcement and on each of the following two days, even though the non-pension aspects of the results were broadly in line with expectations.

In conclusion, when considering a public listing, the surprising reality is that the presence of a pension deficit does not impact on the share price of a listed company as much as might be expected when looking at the accounting position. This is not to say that the stock market prices the pension obligations incorrectly, just that it does not price such obligations in line with the accounting standards. This is probably because the stock market takes a very long-term view on pension obligations, recognizing the period of deferral that a company has when dealing with its pension scheme and the ability to take a long-term view on investment returns. Significantly, a large number of companies pay very high levels of dividends whilst also having a significant pension deficit.

Consequently, dealing with a pension deficit may not be as important as you might think, and in particular there may be more efficient uses to which management can put their capital to improve the way the market perceives the business and hence the price it is prepared to pay for shares.

Other markets

It is worth considering the treatment of alternative markets to the stock market and how the existence of a pension deficit might impact on those methods of raising capital, as even though the full deficit may not be reflected in the stock market valuation the views of other capital markets may be of relevance to shareholders and management.

Private equity buyers take a significantly shorter time frame on their investments and therefore do treat a pension deficit calculated under the accounting standards as being a debt of the business. Any pension deficit does therefore have an immediate impact on value when a private equity buyer is considering a takeover.

Therefore an indirect impact on the share price of a listed company can be that a pension deficit acts as a 'poison pill' defence from a private equity takeover. In an equity market being driven upwards by the expectation of significant takeover activity by private equity firms, a pension deficit may cause a company's share price to lag behind that of similar companies that do not have the same hurdle for private equity firms to get over.

Another related consideration is the attitude of the debt markets. The major credit rating agencies treat an accounting deficit in a pension scheme as a form of debt when assessing the creditworthiness of companies. Therefore a pension deficit could increase the cost of raising debt in the bond markets.

These second-order impacts are worth considering when making decisions as to whether to clear a pension deficit before floating.

Equity analysts

Most equity analysts take the view, similar to that of private equity and the debt markets, that an accounting pension deficit should be treated as a debt of the firm when considering value. However, they find that this position is difficult to sustain when compared against actual market pricing and the movement of share prices when new pension information becomes available. Therefore they tend to take a hybrid view of pension deficits.

The area of pension deficits is becoming one upon which analysts are increasingly focusing. Although the magnitude of the accounting deficit might not be fully reflected in pricing, they will tend to mark down the shares of those companies where it is perceived that the pension scheme is a 'problem'. Generally, therefore, analysts like to see that company management is on top of its pension position and is taking proactive steps to minimize the impact on shareholder value.

Thus positive newsflow from analysts can be generated if the management can demonstrate that it is taking proactive steps, particularly if these are innovative or different solutions, to manage the pension situation. For example, Marks & Spencer recently received favourable attention for structuring a solution to its pension deficit around its property assets. Many other companies have also received similar commentary for introducing changes to their pension arrangements that were seen to be good solutions by the equity analysts.

Therefore being seen to be in control and on top of your pension scheme issues is vital before floating; otherwise analysts may perceive that the pension scheme is potentially an issue that could spiral out of control in the future.

Another feature of the increasing attention of analysts on pension issues is that accounting disclosures of listed companies in respect of pensions tend to be significantly more extensive and detailed than those of private companies. More explanation and commentary are typically provided than the minimum requirements of the accounting standards.

Further, the assumptions used for accounting calculations are subject to more scrutiny than those of private companies where only the auditors need to be satisfied. A public company will find its assumptions questioned by analysts if they are considered to be significantly out of line or where significant assumptions, such as the mortality tables used, are not part of the pension disclosure. Any assumptions that are out of line with the averages in the public market, even if they are entirely appropriate for the circumstances of the company and its scheme, will be picked up on by the numerous accounting surveys and highlighted by analysts and other market participants. Owing to this higher level of scrutiny that will be applied to the pension disclosures, auditors of public companies tend to spend longer determining that the assumptions are appropriate.

Accounting for pension costs is therefore likely to become a much more involved and detailed annual exercise when a company moves on to the public equity market.

This higher level of scrutiny of the accounting disclosures draws out the final area where equity analysts are increasingly focusing their attention and that is any uncertainties as regards pension matters. The stock market in general is wary of any matters that have a high degree of uncertainty, and thus if there is a particular significant area where the company has not or cannot provide clarity this can cause problems.

Actions before a float

Taking the above into account, it is not usually necessary to have dealt with a pension deficit before a float and indeed funding a deficit up to the full accounting value may reduce the value achieved. However, management should ensure that market participants have sufficient comfort that the pension problem is being managed and if possible is being dealt with in a creative way.

The likely actions that a company should consider before floating include:

■ Closing any defined benefit scheme to future accrual (or alternatively taking steps to reduce the value of defined benefits such as raising retirement ages or increasing member contributions), as this will be perceived as having taken decisive action to prevent matters worsening.

■ Clarifying any areas of uncertainty, particularly with regard to short-term cash contributions. In the event of a triennial valuation coming up shortly after float this should be brought forward and resolved before float so that potential investors can be given clear guidance as to the agreed contributions over the next few years.

■ Bringing the pension disclosure note in the statutory accounts, along with any other documentation provided to potential investors such as the prospectus, up to the standard that is deemed appropriate for the public markets.

■ Reviewing the investment strategy in conjunction with the trustees to ensure that a modern approach is taken with a clear rationale for the approach agreed from a corporate perspective. Often there is a benefit from an accounting and cash perspective of a more aggressive investment strategy, but the reality is that whatever investment strategy is undertaken the company should have a clear rationale as to the merits of its approach.

Many other steps will be appropriate in different circumstances but the key is to start the planning for the float early, as pension changes often proceed at glacial speed. At least a year is required before float to achieve the optimal positioning of the pension issues in our experience.

Summary

DC arrangements do not presently give rise to any issues on raising capital, but DB arrangements can present both pricing issues and risk issues, which different market participants treat very differently.

Public equity markets take a long-term view of pension deficits and therefore there is usually little value from clearing them in full in advance of a float. However, other capital providers will take a harsher view and thus if debt financing is important then paying down a deficit can be more attractive.

Equity market analysts are becoming increasingly sophisticated in their understanding of pension matters and increasingly focused on this area. The key to pleasing equity market analysts is for management to be seen to be on top of pension matters and proactively managing the situation.

There are actions that management should take before float to maximize the pension position, but advance planning is vital owing to the long lead time that surrounds most pension matters.

28

Opportunities on AIM for non-UK companies

Geoffrey Gouriet, Lawrence Graham LLP

Introduction

There are a number of reasons why an overseas company might seek a listing on an international market. The most common of these are to raise capital, to enable or increase trade in the company's shares, to facilitate expansion by acquisition and to increase the company's profile. There are various international markets where this objective may be achieved, such as NASDAQ and Euronext, but the market that seems to appear on every high-growth company's list at the moment is AIM (formerly known as the Alternative Investment Market).

Why choose AIM?

The statistics

AIM's expansion, particularly in the last few years, has been a huge success for the London Stock Exchange, with 355 new admissions in 2004, 519 new admissions in 2005 and 462 new admissions in 2006. As at the end of 2006, there were in total 1,634 companies admitted to AIM, with an aggregate market capitalization of £94,364 million (compared with an aggregate market capitalization of £31,753 million at the end of 2004).

This high growth has been matched by the increasingly international character of the market. In 2004, there were 61 new admissions of international companies, in

2005 the figure was 120 and by 2006 this figure had grown to 124. At the end of 2006, 304 international companies were admitted to AIM. However, this figure underestimates the actual level of internationalization of AIM, as it does not include groups whose assets and operations are primarily located overseas but that have a UK holding company – for instance, there are no Chinese entities quoted on AIM but there are in excess of 40 substantially Chinese groups on the market. Figures vary according to the measures used but most commentators accept that over 450 companies quoted on AIM could be described as being 'international'.

'Light' regulation?

The recent success of AIM as an international market is beyond dispute. The reasons for this success are less easy to establish but it is clear that AIM offers a number of significant advantages over many of its rival markets, including:

- There is no requirement for a minimum number of shares to be owned by the public (although, in practice, a 'free float' of less than 20–30 per cent is often problematic owing to the need to create sufficient liquidity in the stock).
- There is no set requirement on AIM regarding the size of the company or its trading record.
- There is no requirement for an AIM company to be profitable.
- The market is much more flexible with regard to ongoing compliance than many of its rivals, and particularly so when compared to senior markets such as the UKLA's Official List.

However, the flexibility and relatively light touch of regulation on AIM should not be confused with a lack of rules. The market is 'policed' on a day-to-day basis by the nominated adviser or 'nomad', who performs a dual role as corporate finance adviser to the AIM company and, effectively, a nominee for the regulator. This dual role often leads overseas companies to raise questions about an apparent conflict of interest but, in practice, it has worked well. The consequences of a nomad losing its nomad status and facing public censure are sufficient to ensure that nomads take their regulatory duties very seriously. These duties have been brought into sharp focus by the introduction in February 2007 of new AIM Rules for Nominated Advisers, which have articulated the duties of nomads to a greater extent than existed previously.

Practical considerations for the float

The procedure for floating an overseas company on AIM is essentially the same as that for a UK company and it is beyond the scope of this chapter to examine the process in detail. However, there are a number of additional complications and factors that should be considered when floating an overseas company on AIM, some of which are set out below.

Legal due diligence

Legal due diligence performs the function of identifying any legal problems with the company and ensuring that they are either fixed before the float or properly disclosed to the market in the admission document or prospectus. It is sometimes argued that these matters can be addressed as part of the verification exercise, but this misunderstands the process – no amount of verification will identify an undisclosed liability.

The AIM Rules for Nominated Advisers provide that the nomad should oversee the due diligence process with the aim of 'satisfying itself that it is appropriate to the applicant and to the transaction and that any material issues arising from it are dealt with or otherwise do not affect the appropriateness of the applicant on AIM'. The AIM Rules for Nominated Advisers also provide that the nomad must agree the scope of the due diligence reports and be satisfied that appropriate professional firms are used in their preparation. In the case of an overseas company, it is therefore vital that the company's UK lawyers are involved in the project management of the legal due diligence reporting. Different jurisdictions have different expectations of the level of reporting required, but it is important to note that the final legal due diligence report will be addressed to the nomad as well as the company and so needs to be in a form and to a level of detail that satisfy the nomad's regulatory requirements. Failing to manage this process at an early stage can lead to lengthy delays.

Financial and commercial due diligence

Financial and commercial due diligence essentially follows a similar pattern to that for the flotation of a UK company. A short-form report and a long-form report are prepared by the reporting accountants together with a working capital report to sit behind the company's working capital statement. However, Rule 19 of the AIM Rules for Companies provides that an AIM company incorporated in an EEA country must prepare its accounts in accordance with International Accounting Standards and that an AIM company incorporated in a non-EEA country must prepare its accounts to one of the following: International Accounting Standards, US Generally Accepted Accounting Principles, Canadian Generally Accepted Accounting Principles, Australian International Financial Reporting Standards or Japanese Generally Accepted Accounting Principles. Whilst this rule applies once a company has been admitted, in practice overseas companies will often choose one of the acceptable accounting standards for their admission document in order to avoid later confusion. This may require a restatement of pre-existing accounts, which can extend the timescale for the transaction as a whole.

Structure

Applicants wishing to list an overseas entity on AIM (as opposed to a UK holding company) need to ensure that the entity in question is suitable for the market. The nomad and broker are likely to have views on the jurisdiction in question from a commercial perspective, and there are a number of additional technical factors to be considered, including:

■ Rule 32 of the AIM Rules for Companies, which requires that the company's shares must be freely transferable (except in any jurisdiction where restrictions are placed by statute or regulation on such transferability);

■ Rule 36 of the AIM Rules for Companies, which requires that the company must ensure that appropriate settlement arrangements are in place so that, save where the London Stock Exchange otherwise agrees, the company's AIM securities must be eligible for electronic settlement (CREST is the usual form of electronic settlement in the UK but, in broad terms, only UK securities can be admitted to CREST so, in the case of companies incorporated in overseas jurisdictions, an indirect mechanism is used involving depositary interests); and

■ the overall tax structuring for the group as a whole, which will be determined by a variety of factors including where operations are carried out and the tax domicile of major shareholders.

In practice, these issues often mean that a UK incorporated parent company will be utilized and a pre-float group reorganization will be carried out. Offshore jurisdictions such as the Channel Islands, Cayman Islands and Bermuda are also often favoured for the parent company, as well as other common law jurisdictions such as Australia and Canada. The constitutional documents of companies incorporated in civil law jurisdictions, such as the Netherlands, must be adapted as far as possible to mirror relevant English Companies Act provisions and to replicate some of the provisions of the City Code on Takeovers and Mergers (albeit with disenfranchisement of shareholders and non-payment of dividends as the major sanctions for breach).

Admission document/prospectus

Although often referred to as an initial public offering or 'IPO', an AIM float is rarely a 'public offer' in practice. This is because AIM is operated as an exchange regulated market rather than an EU 'regulated market'. This means that, in broad terms, provided there is no public offer of securities over 2,500,000 (cumulatively in any one year) or the offer is made to fewer than 100 persons in each member state of the EU, an AIM company will not have to produce a full prospectus complying with the Prospectus Rules. Rule 3 of the AIM Rules for Companies provides that an applicant to AIM must produce an 'admission document', which must contain some of the information required by the Prospectus Rules, but certain of the more onerous requirements are carved out. The publication of an admission document also avoids the need for the UK Listing Authority to 'sign off' on the document. In short, the process is streamlined compared with that involving a prospectus, whilst the AIM Rules for Companies ensure that the admission document contains a sensible level of disclosure. Directors of the AIM company are still liable for the accuracy of the contents of the admission document and therefore it must be verified to the same standard as a prospectus.

Lock-in arrangements

Another important practical consideration is the impact of Rule 7 of the AIM Rules for Companies. This provides that, where an AIM applicant's main activity is a business that has not been trading for at least two years, the company must ensure that all related parties and applicable employees as at the date of admission agree not to dispose of any interest in its shares for a period one year after the date of admission, subject to certain caveats. The term 'related party' is defined widely to include, amongst other things, any person with a direct or indirect interest in 10 per cent or more of the voting rights of the AIM company and all directors and their associates.

In practice, even if the AIM company is not required by Rule 7 to lock in its substantial shareholders and applicable employees, a nomad and broker will typically insist on some form of lock-in arrangement – either a so-called 'hard' lock-in, which broadly mirrors Rule 7, or alternatively a so-called 'soft' lock-in, which might require a selling shareholder to use the company's broker so that the sale process can be managed in order to minimize any adverse impact on the share price that might be caused by the sudden sale of a thinly traded stock. Practically, this means that existing substantial shareholders may have the opportunity to sell some of their shares to institutional investors at the time of the float but should then expect to hold their shares for some time post-IPO.

Fast track

Rule 3 of the AIM Rules for Companies provides that a quoted applicant that has had its securities traded on an AIM designated market for at least 18 months prior to applying to have its securities issued on AIM is not required to produce an admission document. This does not circumvent the requirement for a prospectus if such a document is required under the Prospectus Rules. As at 22 April 2007, the AIM designated markets were the Australian Stock Exchange, Deutsche Börse, Euronext, Johannesburg Stock Exchange, NASDAQ, New York Stock Exchange, Stockholmsbörsen, Swiss Exchange, Toronto Stock Exchange and the UKLA Official List. East Asian readers will note the absence of the Hong Kong Stock Exchange from this list.

Applicants wishing and eligible to use this so-called 'fast-track' route are required to inform the Exchange 20 days prior to admission of all the usual information required of an AIM applicant plus additional details relating to, amongst other things, historical company and financial matters.

Although this process is potentially faster, it is important to note that the AIM Rules for Nominated Advisers provide, amongst other things, that a nomad must confirm, to the best of its knowledge and belief, that, having made due and careful enquiries and considered all relevant matters under both sets of AIM Rules, all applicable requirements of the AIM Rules for Companies and the AIM Rules for Nominated Advisers have been complied with and the applicant company and its securities are appropriate to be admitted to AIM. This means that the nomad will still need to carry out an appropriate level of legal and financial due diligence in advance of the application and will need to ensure that the working capital statement is sufficiently supported by financial review.

Similarly, in practice, a company wishing to raise money when seeking an AIM admission will, provided it is not required to produce a prospectus, still be likely to be required to produce a detailed presentation and/or information memorandum in addition to the requirements under the fast-track route. For this reason, the fast-track route is most attractive in circumstances where the applicant does not seek to raise new funds and simply wishes to be admitted to trading on AIM.

Continuing obligations

Detailed consideration of the continuing obligations imposed by the rules of AIM is beyond the scope of this chapter, but they are relevant to an overseas company considering a flotation. In particular:

■ An AIM company must announce a 'substantial transaction', which, in broad terms, is any transaction or transactions in a 12-month period that represent more than 10 per cent of the gross assets, profits, turnover, market capitalization or gross capital of the AIM company.
■ An AIM company must obtain shareholder approval for a reverse takeover, which, in broad terms, is a transaction or transactions in a 12-month period that represent more than 100 per cent of the gross assets, profits, turnover, market capitalization or gross capital of the AIM company.
■ Shareholders must approve any disposal resulting in a fundamental change in the business, which is deemed to be any disposal or disposals in a 12-month period that exceed 75 per cent of the gross assets, profits, turnover, market capitalization or gross capital of the AIM company.
■ AIM companies must publish annual audited accounts prepared in accordance with International Accounting Standards or, if applicable, US Generally Accepted Accounting Principles, Canadian Generally Accepted Accounting Principles, Australian International Financial Reporting Standards or Japanese Generally Accepted Accounting Principles.
■ An AIM company must produce and announce half-yearly results.

There are also extensive ongoing disclosure obligations imposed upon an AIM company, including the requirement to announce without delay:

■ any dealings by its directors in its securities;
■ any relevant changes to significant shareholders;
■ the resignation, dismissal or appointment of a director;
■ any material change between its actual trading performance and any publicly disclosed profit forecast, estimate or projection;
■ any decision to declare dividends; and
■ the reasons for dismissal or appointment of its nomad or broker.

In addition to these requirements, directors and employees must not deal in the company's shares during close periods (which are two months preceding the publication of the AIM company's annual results, two months preceding publication of any interim results, any other period when the AIM company has unpublished price-sensitive information or any time when it is probable that such information is required to be announced). An AIM company must also maintain a broker and nomad at all times. In short, overseas applicants must have regard to a significant level of public disclosure and accountability to shareholders after the float has been completed.

Conclusion

In the past two or three years, AIM has transformed itself from a market primarily focusing on UK companies to a genuinely international market eager to welcome high-growth companies from around the world. Notwithstanding the recent changes to the rules governing AIM, it remains a flexible and relatively lightly regulated market for international companies. There are great opportunities for those wishing to take advantage of the capital and profile of AIM, and careful consideration of the pros and cons at the planning stage, together with a properly managed process, should enable most applicants with an attractive commercial proposition to look forward to a successful IPO.

29

Taking your company private

Simon Boadle and Helen M Jeffery,
PricewaterhouseCoopers LLP

What is a public to private (PTP)?

A public to private transaction is one in which a private equity-backed company makes an offer for a quoted company (a plc with shares quoted on the London Stock Exchange Main Market or AIM). The private equity-backed company (the 'offeror') will typically be funded by a combination of 1) senior bank debt, 2) private equity-funded debt in the form of loan notes and 3) ordinary equity (approximately 80–90 per cent subscribed by the private equity house). Management of the plc will typically subscribe for the balance of the equity in the offeror and take senior positions in the offeror company.

The offer is made by the offeror in accordance with the Takeover Code and may constitute a 'financial promotion' under the Financial Services and Markets Act 2000. It is required to be 'sponsored' by an adviser authorized by the Financial Services Authority (eg investment bank, broking firm or accountancy practice). Once sufficient acceptances have been received from the plc's shareholders (typically over 75 per cent) the offer is declared wholly unconditional. The plc becomes a subsidiary of the offeror, and the offeror applies for the plc's shares to be removed from AIM or the Main Market of the London Stock Exchange. An EGM resolution is then passed to change the plc to a private limited company.

Why management would want to do a PTP

Small-cap companies outside the FTSE 350 (typically less than £500 million market capitalization) with limited growth prospects or that have 'fallen from grace', perhaps after a series of profit warnings, can suffer from low valuation and limited liquidity of their listed shares. They can also be neglected by financial advisers, institutional funds and brokers, who focus on larger, more liquid public companies.

The added pressure on management time and costs borne by listed companies by increased reporting and corporate governance regulations, and the need to maintain disclosure with a dispersed set of institutional investors, can also make delisting by way of a PTP an attractive option.

Management options or incentives through long-term incentive plans may also offer little financial incentive to management to grow shareholder value aggressively.

In the late 1990s a combination of these factors led to many small-cap companies opting to go private.

The history of public to privates in the UK

There has been an active market in PTPs in the UK since 1998. The number of deals peaked at 49 in 2000. In comparison there were 25 deals in 2006.[1] Market focus has moved towards larger deal sizes, with an average market capitalization of £240 million in 2006. This has been driven in large part by the availability of credit (senior debt and mezzanine debt) for leveraged buy-outs.

Although there have been a number of high-profile PTPs in the UK in recent months (eg Alliance Boots), the vast majority of PTPs remain in the sub-FTSE 350 size bracket.

Successful completion of public to private deals is also in decline, with levels falling to the lowest in three years. Investors (increasingly including hedge funds) are becoming resistant to accepting takeover offers from management that can be perceived as undervaluing the target plc. The growing incidence of failed PTPs is demonstrated by the bid by 3i for Countrywide plc, in December 2006, where shareholders rejected the offer on the basis that it did not offer them sufficient value. Further resistance has been seen by the investors of J Sainsbury plc, where the board rejected the 560p bid proposed by the CVC consortium (CVC Capital Partners, Blackstone and Texas Pacific Group) in April 2007, which eventually led to a withdrawal of their offer.

The public to private market in 2006

Transactions in the UK

The decline of the UK PTP market, from £7.2 billion in 2005 to £6 billion in 2006, is in sharp contrast to the movement of the US PTP market, where activity in 2006 has exceeded that of 2003, 2004 and 2005 combined.

In 2006 there was a 25 per cent increase in the number of UK transactions over the previous year, taking the total to 25. However, value fell 17 per cent over the same period to £6 billion. PTP bid premiums have stayed level, with an average of 25 per cent. Table 29.1 shows the top 10 deals by value in 2006.

Table 29.1   Top 10 PTP buy-outs in 2006

Deal name	Value (£m)	Type	Month
McCarthy & Stone (Mother Bidco)	1,105	IBO	October
John Laing	887	IBO	December
Matalan (Missouri Bidco)	817	Buy-out	December
Gondola (Paternoster Acquisitions)	559	IBO	December
Peacock Group (Henson No.1)	404	Buy-out	January
DX Services (Mail Acquisitions)	349	IBO	August
Wyevale Garden Centres	311	IBO	June
Center Parcs (UK) (Forest Bidco)	205	IBO	May
Incisive Media (Apax Summer)	199	IBO	December
Richmonds Foods	182	Buy-out	June

Source: CMBOR/Barclays Private Equity/Deloitte

The PTP of McCarthy & Stone, a retirement homes house builder, was the largest in 2006, valued at £1.1 billion. In 2007 the largest private equity deal in the UK to date has been completed: the take-private of Alliance Boots plc for approximately £12 billion.

Transactions overseas

PTPs in Continental Europe have risen dramatically from 3.8 billion in 2003 to 25.7 billion in 2006. PTP volume has remained low, with 16 transactions in 2006, but deal value has risen sharply. There has been an increasing trend for PTP transactions exceeding 1 billion.

Is my company suitable to be taken private?

The key factors that determine whether a listed company is suitable to be taken private include the following.

Management

A strong and willing management team who support the transaction should be in place within the plc. Absence of this will make the company unattractive to private equity buyers, who prefer to keep senior management employed to drive the business forward. Management should have a strong desire to enhance their personal financial rewards through holding a greater stake in their business following delisting.

For managers of listed companies, the increasing burdens of the listed company arena contrast with the financial rewards available once a company is taken private. The opportunity to take a significant equity stake for a small investment in a tax-efficient manner is a large attraction for the more entrepreneurially minded manager.

The non-executive directors of the plc ('independent directors') play a critical role. Their consent and cooperation are necessary for access to be granted to the funders of the offer (private equity house or banks) to perform proper due diligence, and they must recommend the offer to shareholders. The independent directors will be responsible for appointing advisers to the plc, negotiating the offer price and deciding whether to run an auction for the company or let the private equity-/management-backed bid proceed with exclusivity.

Earnings/cash flow

Acquirers will examine the financial history and projections of the company with specific attention to the cash flows, to ensure that the company can support reasonable debt leverage.

Rate of return

Private equity would expect an anticipated blended internal rate of return (IRR) of approximately 20–25 per cent from their investment in loan notes and ordinary shares of the offeror. This IRR is dependent upon the entry multiple, anticipated exit multiple and timing of exit, growth in operating profit and cash flow between entry and exit, and value created by disposals of non-core businesses and bolt-on acquisitions.

Shareholders

The ability to secure acceptances from major shareholders prior to an offer reduces the risks for the bidder. Shareholders with, in aggregate, greater than 25 per cent have the ability to block the offer.

To reduce this risk it is normal practice for the offeror to obtain 'hard' or 'soft' irrevocables from shareholders. 'Hard' irrevocables are most likely to be obtained from independent directors recommending the offer, and management who are accepting a stake in the business going forward. These commitments are unconditional and will not lapse in the presence of a higher offer. In comparison, institutional shareholders are more likely to give a 'soft' irrevocable that commits to accept, subject only to a higher offer not being made. Our research shows that irrevocables are typically received from 45 per cent of shareholders.

Banking and due diligence

The availability of bank finance is largely dependent upon the projected cash flow performance of the company and the credibility of the projections. Financial, legal, commercial and property due diligence will be carried out by the offeror on behalf of the bank, and any findings will have implications on the offer price and the capital structure of the offeror. The result will be that the indicative offer is reconfirmed, renegotiated or withdrawn.

Why private equity houses target listed companies

Managers of pension funds and insurance company investment portfolios, and investment and commercial banks have been allocating a higher proportion of their investment portfolios to private equity, attracted by the relatively high long-term returns generated in the 1990s and early 2000s from private equity investment compared to other asset classes. As of November 2006, commentators estimate that £132 billion of funds globally have been committed to private equity groups but remain uninvested.[2] Larger fund sizes allow private equity groups to target larger (often listed) companies.

In addition, the availability of debt to fund leveraged buy-outs is currently high. Banks have enjoyed a good credit history lending to private equity-backed companies in the past 5 to 10 years. High levels of leveraged bank debt allow private equity funds to compete aggressively on price when bidding for quoted companies.

Private equity houses see the small to mid-size listed company market as a source of potential deals and as a possible way of avoiding the auction process they go through when buying private companies. They use their expertise gained from evaluating and investing in private companies to access PTP opportunities. They also use their understanding of the risks associated with high levels of debt to maximize leverage. For instance, a typical buy-out vehicle might be 60–70 per cent debt and 30–40 per cent equity-funded, whereas small to mid-sized listed companies are on average funded 20–25 per cent debt and 75–80 per cent equity. It is partly these high levels of debt funding that allow private equity houses to generate the internal rates of return they require on their investment, typically 20–25 per cent per annum.

The advantages and disadvantages of private equity (PE) ownership are displayed in Table 29.2.

Table 29.2 Advantages and disadvantages of private equity ownership through a PTP

Advantages	Disadvantages
Provides a clean cash exit for shareholders at a premium to the prevailing share price, often in respect of an investment in a company with poor liquidity.	Costs of executing a PTP can be high, typically adding 5–10 per cent to total funding costs, given the complex nature of the transaction and the number of advisers involved.
Private equity owners can make quick decisions (control the board) and provide additional finance to back the strategy of the management.	Leverage – increased chance of company failure.
Management participate in the equity of the company, such that they should get a significant financial reward when the private equity house exits, if the firm has reached its targets.	Private equity ownership is very different from plc status, and management may struggle to accept the new corporate structure and demands on financial results.
Independent directors are no longer required, simplifying the board structure and decision making.	If the company does not perform, management may be dismissed at the discretion of the private equity house.
There are reduced financial reporting regulations and costs associated with being a plc.	Management will be tied in until the 'exit event' (sale of the company) (typically three–four years after acquisition).

How to select a financial adviser

Both the plc and the private equity-funded offeror will appoint financial advisers to manage the transaction process. There are a vast number of advisers to choose from and it is important to select an adviser with significant PTP experience to advise on what is a complex transaction. The top 10 UK advisers in 1997 are listed in Table 29.3.

Table 29.3 Top 10 UK PTP advisers since 1997

Rank	Adviser	No. of deals	Value ($m)
1	PricewaterhouseCoopers LLP	57	14,870.2
2	NM Rothschild	51	40,864.7
3	KPMG LLP	48	5,957.5
4	UBS AG	33	25,759.4
5	Hawkpoint Partners Limited	31	8,597.8
6=	Deutsche Bank AG	30	43,721.2
6=	Close Brothers Ltd	30	14,703.5
6=	Dresdner Kleinwort Limited	30	25,501.6
9	Citigroup Inc	28	38,748.0
10	Deloitte & Touche LLP	25	3,322.3

Source: Thomson Financial, 5 April 2007

The public to private process

The public to private process usually starts with the management team being given approval by the company's independent directors, typically the non-executive directors of the company who are not involved in the buy-out, to test the feasibility of a PTP. The receptiveness of the company's independent directors and financial advisers to the possibility of a PTP is therefore key.

This is usually followed by the appointment of financial advisers to the offeror to assist in the development of management's business plan and to find private equity and debt support for a PTP. Once this is in place an indicative offer letter setting out the proposed offer price or price range can be sent to the independent directors of the company. The offer proposal would at this stage be subject to detailed due diligence, as private equity and debt providers will only commit to finance a PTP after they have had access to company information and been able to carry out due diligence in support of management's business plan. Due diligence can be expected to take a minimum of four to six weeks to complete.

The private equity house may at this stage be granted 'exclusivity' and an 'inducement fee'. This will take the form of an agreement by the company and its financial advisers not to solicit other offers for a specified period and for the company to pay the private equity house an inducement fee, up to a maximum as set by the Takeover Panel, of 1 per cent of the value of the offer, in the event of its offer lapsing owing to a higher competing bid or in other specific circumstances.

While due diligence is being undertaken, the legal and offer documentation will be finalized and the buy-out vehicle formed. Assuming due diligence supports the offer price, or a revised offer price can be agreed, then the PTP can proceed, with an offer document being sent to the company's shareholders. The PTP offer will include the standard 90 per cent offer acceptance condition. At this level of acceptances of the offer, the buy-out vehicle can compulsorily acquire the minority non-assenting shareholders and take the company private, so ensuring that the debt provider will obtain security over the underlying assets of the company. Although debt providers increasingly show flexibility in waiving the 90 per cent offer acceptance condition once offer acceptances reach 75 per cent, there remains a transaction risk that shareholders with stakes of 10 per cent or more can potentially block a PTP.

A typical timetable for the PTP process is shown graphically in Table 29.4.

Table 29.4 Typical timetable for the PTP process

Week:	1	2	3	4	5	6	7	8	9	10	11	12	13	14	15	16	17	18	19	20	21	22	23	24	25
Step 1 – Consent granted to management to approach private equity providers	▓																								
Step 2 – Business plan prepared and finance raised			▓	▓	▓	▓																			
Step 3 – Indicative offer tabled							▓	▓																	
Step 4 – Confirmatory due diligence carried out										▓	▓	▓	▓												
Step 5 – Legal and structural preparation carried out											▓	▓	▓												
Step 6 – Offer executed																									
– announce offer														▓											
– post-offer document														▓											
– first closing date																	▓								
– offer unconditional in all respects																	▓								
– compulsory acquisition completed																							▓		
– Company delisted, taken private and financial assistance given																								▓	▓

Case study: Matalan

Matalan is the pioneer of value retailing in the UK. Selling clothing and home-wares, it is one of the UK's largest such retailers, with nearly 200 stores and a turnover of £1 billion. Matalan was founded by John Hargreaves in 1985 and floated in 1998 to realize value for the founder and raise capital for expansion. In its early years, Matalan was a stock market favourite and grew very rapidly, but in recent years new competitors eroded Matalan's dominant position in the value retail sector and the company suffered a downturn in trading.

John Hargreaves, Chairman, controlled over 53 per cent of the company's shares and believed that private ownership would allow him to simplify the business and effect the changes necessary to restore the original values and ethos that enabled the company to grow.

Certain features of Matalan made a buy-out a distinct possibility:

■ The Hargreaves family controlled 53 per cent of the share capital.
■ Matalan had very low borrowings and was cash generative, allowing John Hargreaves to purchase the remaining 47 per cent of the share capital funded only by debt and mezzanine finance (provided by Kaupthing).
■ The board recognized that the changes that the business needed were best effected as a private company.
■ No competing offer was possible given the Hargreaves family's controlling position.

John Hargreaves's £817 million bid (a premium of 20.8 per cent to the share price immediately before bid talks were announced) was successful, and the company was delisted from the Main Market of the London Stock Exchange on 22 December 2006.

Conclusion

Being a listed company offers certain advantages to both companies and management but in certain circumstances both would benefit from private equity ownership, for example where a small-cap company has 'fallen from grace' or where the market is systematically undervaluing the company relative to its prospects. Such companies should think about whether they can attract private equity interest by considering a range of factors, including the strength and ability of the management, the attitude of the independent directors, the company's financial history and projections, and the internal rate of return that could be achieved by an investor. It is important for the offeror to select suitable advisers, since a PTP is a risky transaction with increased failure rates in recent years. However, if it is successfully executed it presents an opportunity for management to benefit from a more focused ownership and board structure, and financial incentives that offer significant personal rewards for creating shareholder value.

Notes

1. *CMBOR Quarterly Review*, Winter 2006/2007.
2. *Financial Times*, 27 November 2006.

Appendix:
Contributors'
contact list

Bevan Brittan
Fleet Place House
2 Fleet Place
Holborn Viaduct
London EC4M 7RF
Tel: +44 (0) 870 194 5012
Fax: +44 (0) 870 194 1000
Contact: Sarah Cartwright
Direct line: +44 (0) 870 194 5012
e-mail: Sarah.Cartwright@bevanbrittan.com
www.bevanbrittan.com

Charles Stanley Securities
25 Luke Street
London EC2A 4AR
Tel: +44 (0) 20 7149 6412
Contact: Tim Davis
e-mail: tim.davis@csysecurities.com
www.csysecurities.com

CMS Cameron McKenna LLP
Mitre House
160 Aldersgate Street
London EC1A 4DD
Tel: +44 (0) 20 7367 2816
Contact: Peter Smith
e-mail: Peter.Smith@cms-cmck.com
www.cms-cmck.com

Corfin Communications
Floor 11
78 Cannon Street
London EC4N 6HH
Tel: +44 (0) 20 7929 8998
Fax: +44 (0) 20 7929 4869
Contact: William Cullum
e-mail: wcullum@corfinpr.com
www.corfinpr.com

Ernst & Young
1 More Place
London SE1 2AF
Tel: +44 (0) 20 7951 2335
Fax: +44 (0) 20 7951 1345
Contact: David Wilkinson
e-mail: dwilkinson@uk.ey.com
www.ey.com/uk/fast_growth

Freeth Cartwright LLP
Cardinal Square
2nd Floor, West Point
10 Nottingham Road
Derby DE1 3QT
Tel: +44 (0) 1332 361000
Fax: +44(0) 1332 348929
Contact: Mike Copestake
Direct line: +44 (0) 1332 546101
e-mail: Mike.Copestake@freethcartwright.co.uk
www.freethcartwright.co.uk

Grant Thornton Corporate Finance
Grant Thornton House
22 Melton Street
Euston Square
London NW1 2EP
Contact: Colin Aaronson
Tel: +44 (0) 870 991 2942
e-mail: colin.p.aaronson@gtuk.com

Hazlewoods LLP
Windsor House
Barnett Way
Gloucester GL4 3RT
Tel: +44 (0) 1452 634800
Fax: +44 (0) 1452 371900
Contact: David Main
e-mail: dgm@hazlewoods.co.uk
www.hazlewoods.co.uk

Hoare Govett Limited
250 Bishopsgate
London EC2M 4AA
Tel: +44 (0) 20 7678 8000
Fax: +44 (0) 20 7678 1587
Contact: Justin Jones
Direct line: +44 (0) 20 7678 7303
e-mail: justin.jones@uk.abnamro.com

H W Fisher & Company
Acre House
11–15 William Road
London NW1 3ER
Tel: +44 (0) 20 7388 7000
Fax: +44 (0) 20 7380 4900
Contact: Gary Miller
Direct line: +44 (0) 20 7398 4938
e-mail: gmiller@hwfisher.co.uk
www.hwfisher.co.uk

The Irish Enterprise Exchange
28 Anglesea Street
Dublin 2
Ireland
Tel: + 353 1 6174229
Fax: + 353 1 6174289
Contact: Daryl Byrne
e-mail: daryl.byrne@ise.ie
www.ise.ie

KBC Peel Hunt
111 Old Broad Street
London EC2N 1PH
Tel: +44 (0) 20 7418 8900
Contact: David Davies
e-mail: info@kbcpeelhunt.com
www.kbcpeelhunt.com

Lawrence Graham LLP
4 More London Riverside
London SE1 2AU
Tel: +44 (0) 20 7379 0000
Fax: +44 (0) 20 7379 6854
Contact: Geoffrey Gouriet
e-mail: geoffrey.gouriet@lg-legal.com
www.lg-legal.com

The London Stock Exchange
10 Paternoster Square
London EC4M 7LS
Tel: +44 (0) 20 7797 1726
Fax: +44 (0) 20 7959 9703
Contact: Virginia Perez-Foy
e-mail: vperezfoy@londonstockexchange.com
www.londonstockexchange.com

Pinsent Masons
Contact: Martin Shaw
Tel: +44 (0) 113 244 5000
e-mail: martin.shaw@pinsentmasons.com

London:
City Point
One Ropemaker Street
London EC2Y 9AH
Tel: +44 (0) 20 7418 7000
Fax: +44 (0) 20 7418 7050

30 Aylesbury Street
London EC1R 0ER
Tel: +44 (0) 20 7490 4000
Fax: +44 (0) 20 7490 2545

Birmingham:
3 Colmore Circus
Birmingham B4 6BH
Tel: +44 (0) 121 200 1050
Fax: +44 (0) 121 626 1040

Bristol:
33–35 Queen Square
Bristol BS1 4LU
Tel: +44 (0) 117 924 5678
Fax: +44 (0) 117 924 6699

Edinburgh:
18–22 Melville Street
Edinburgh EH3 7NS
Tel: +44 (0) 131 225 0000
Fax: +44 (0) 131 225 0099

Glasgow:
123 St Vincent Street
Glasgow G2 5EA
Tel: +44 (0) 141 248 4858
Fax: +44 (0) 141 248 6655

Manchester:
100 Barbirolli Square
Manchester M2 3SS
Tel: +44 (0) 161 234 8234
Fax: +44 (0) 161 234 8235

Leeds:
1 Park Row
Leeds LS1 5AB
Tel: +44 (0) 113 244 5000
Fax: +44 (0) 113 244 8000

PLUS Markets Group plc
Standon House
21 Mansell Street
London E1 8AA
Tel: +44 (0) 20 7553 2000
Fax: +44 (0) 20 7553 2004
Contact: Deborah Medley Foye
e-mail: deborah.medleyfoye@plusmarketsgroup.com
www.plusmarketsgroup.com

PricewaterhouseCoopers LLP
1 Embankment Place
London WC2N 6RH
Tel: +44 (0) 20 7213 8247
Contact: David Snell
e-mail: david.a.snell@uk.pwc.com
www.pwc.com/uk

Punter Southall Transaction Services
126 Jermyn Street
London SW1Y 4UJ
Tel: +44 (0) 20 7839 8600
Fax: +44 (0) 20 7533 6978
Contact: Richard Jones
Direct line: +44 (0) 20 7533 6967
e-mail: Richard.Jones@Pstransactions.co.uk
www.pstransactions.co.uk

ShareMark
Oxford House
Oxford Road
Aylesbury
Bucks HP21 8SZ
Contact: Emma Vigus
e-mail: emma.vigus@share.co.uk
www.share.co.uk

Index

Index of advertisers